# *Incredible Commitments*

Why do warring parties turn to United Nations peacekeeping and peace-making even when they think it will fail? Dayal asks why UN peacekeeping survived its early catastrophes in Somalia, Rwanda, and the Balkans, and how this survival should make us reconsider how peacekeeping works. She makes two key arguments: First, she argues the UN's central role in peacemaking and peacekeeping worldwide means UN interventions have structural consequences: what the UN does in one conflict can shift the strategies, outcomes, and options available to negotiating parties in other conflicts. Second, drawing on interviews, archival research, and process-traced peace negotiations in Rwanda and Guatemala, Dayal argues warring parties turn to the UN even when they have little faith in peacekeepers' ability to uphold peace agreements – and even little actual interest in peace – because its involvement in negotiation processes provides unique tactical, symbolic, and post-conflict reconstruction benefits only the UN can offer.

ANJALI KAUSHLESH DAYAL is an assistant professor of international politics at Fordham University.

T0371541

# Incredible Commitments

How UN Peacekeeping Failures Shape
Peace Processes

ANJALI KAUSHLESH DAYAL
*Fordham University*

# CAMBRIDGE
## UNIVERSITY PRESS

Shaftesbury Road, Cambridge CB2 8EA, United Kingdom

One Liberty Plaza, 20th Floor, New York, NY 10006, USA

477 Williamstown Road, Port Melbourne, VIC 3207, Australia

314–321, 3rd Floor, Plot 3, Splendor Forum, Jasola District Centre, New Delhi – 110025, India

103 Penang Road, #05–06/07, Visioncrest Commercial, Singapore 238467

Cambridge University Press is part of Cambridge University Press & Assessment, a department of the University of Cambridge.

We share the University's mission to contribute to society through the pursuit of education, learning and research at the highest international levels of excellence.

www.cambridge.org
Information on this title: www.cambridge.org/9781108824095

DOI: 10.1017/9781108915151

© Anjali Kaushlesh Dayal 2021

First published 2021
First paperback edition 2023

A catalogue record for this publication is available from the British Library

ISBN   978-1-108-84322-5   Hardback
ISBN   978-1-108-82409-5   Paperback

# Contents

# Tables

# Acknowledgments

This is a book about failure, but if it succeeds on any front, it will be because so many people helped me. This project began as an uneasy sense that a body of literature I read in David Edelstein's exceptional International Security seminar could not possibly be right. Accordingly, I am first grateful for the assistance, advice, and insight of my dissertation committee – Lise Morjé Howard, Erik Voeten, David Edelstein, and Andy Bennett. Their constant, constructive, and kind engagement with my work was indispensable. I particularly appreciate their willingness to challenge my ideas and preconceptions from multiple epistemological, methodological, and theoretical perspectives, which has made me a far better scholar, thinker, and writer. Although there are many reasons to give them all thanks, I am grateful to Lise for generously inducting me into a community of peacekeeping scholars while also guiding me through the conduct of new, exciting research alongside her; to Erik, for patiently encouraging me to think about international organizations in new, creative, and disciplined ways, and for supporting my research in both practical and intellectual ways; to David, for constantly pushing me to think harder about how to make my arguments and its alternatives sharper, clearer, and better, and for giving me a solid base in international security from which to make these arguments; and to Andy, for enabling me to refine my qualitative methodological skills, and for giving me the opportunity to conduct research on mass atrocity that was ultimately instrumental to my case studies.

The Department of Government at Georgetown University has supported me long after my departure. I am grateful for the continuing mentorship and collegiality of so many other senior scholars whom I met there, including Matthew Carnes, Charles King, Kate McNamara, James Raymond Vreeland, and Clyde Wilcox.

Jennifer Raymond Dresden, Megan McConaughey, and Michael Weintraub have all been invaluable at each step of this project.

I would not have finished this book without their exceptional support, generosity, and friendship.

Administrative staff at Georgetown and Fordham Universities were essential to all my work. I am especially thankful to Joan Hewan, Anne Musica, and Annmarie O'Connor, without whom no work would ever have been possible.

I am very grateful at Fordham University for support from Ida Bastiaens, Susan Berger, Nicole Fermon, Christina Greer, Robert Hume, and Zein Murib.

The staff and scholars at the Georgetown Institute for Women, Peace and Security at Georgetown University – Rebecca Turkington, Sarah Rutherford, Luis Mancilla, Jen Parsons, Agathe Christien, Jeni Klugman, and Ambassador Melanne Verveer – were vital and thoughtful interlocutors during a critical year of this project. I am especially grateful to Melanne for helping me understand the social dimensions of diplomacy.

I am deeply appreciative of the institutional awards I received from the Harry S. Truman Good Neighbor Award Foundation, the Georgetown University – Graduate School of Arts and Sciences, the Georgetown University's Department of Government, and the Academic Council on the United Nations System. Maria Snyder, Gerry Mara, and Marc Howard provided assistance on critical grant applications, for which I am also thankful. I am also grateful for the financial support of a faculty research grant from Fordham University that supported the completion of this manuscript. At Fordham University, Melissa Labonte, Robert Hume, Jonathan Crystal, George Hong, and John Harrington helped me seek out vital institutional opportunities for research and professional growth.

For providing helpful comments on various parts of the manuscript, I am very thankful to David Buckley, Susanna Campbell, Rebecca Davis Gibbons, Matthew Eckel, Paula Ganga, Desha Girod, Marina Henke, Ivan Ivanovic, Andrew Imbrie, Michelle Jurkovich, Rebecca Friedman Lissner, Timothy Longman, Giovanni Mantilla, Luis Felipe Mantilla, Elizabeth Mercurio, Krzyzstof Pelc, Jack Santucci, Hesham Sallam, Tom Scherer, Holger Schmidt, Jake Shapiro, Megan Stewart, and David Tingle. Maddie Schramm, Dani Nedal, Alex Stark, Nik Kalyanpur, Jennifer Erickson, Marika Landau-Wells, Sungmin Cho, and Layla Hashemi all provided indispensable advice at a critical end stage of the project.

An astounding number of people throughout the United States, Europe, and Africa assisted me in my field research, often unexpectedly, often based on remote personal connections, and with absolutely nothing to gain by helping me. My interviews and archival work would not have been possible without the help of Letitia Anderson, Séverine Autesserre, Elizabeth Barad, Michael Barnett, Carla Bellota at the UN Library and Archive in Geneva, Günther von Billerbeck, Yolande Bouka, Ruth Carlitz, Mary Curry of the National Security Archive, Rick Ehrenreich, Willa Friedman, Oliver Jütersonke, Brian Kritz, Samantha Lakin, Cecelia Lynch, Kimberly Marten, Heather Messera, Enzo Nussio, Alissa Orlando, Melina Platas Izama, Matthew Rudolph, Scott Straus, Gretchen and Brian Steidle, Scott Taylor, Marko Tomicic, and Lawrence Woocher.

Although I have elected not to single out by name the many Rwandans who helped me with everything from basic logistics to securing interviews to understanding the very nature of the peace there, I do not want this necessary omission to marginalize their importance: I am grateful beyond measure for their help and generosity. The analysis of the Rwandan peace process and contemporary Rwanda I present here reflects *solely my own opinions*, and should not in any way be interpreted as representing the viewpoint of anyone who lent me assistance.

The chapter on the Arusha Peace Process is indebted from start to finish to the generosity of the late Lee Ann Fujii, who – in a sequence that will be recognizable to many who crossed her path – responded to a cold email by helping me plan a trip, introducing me to a half dozen people without whom I could not have learned what I needed to learn, taking me to dinner, and keeping in touch for years afterward. I cannot thank her for the mark she left on the text; I can only hope to offer others some of the same kindness.

At Cambridge University Press, Robert Dreesen and John Haslam each shepherded the book through critical parts of the publication process. I am grateful for their assistance, and to the three anonymous reviewers whose incisive critiques sharpened and strengthened the text.

Many people have helped me navigate the thorny writing and research processes that came with this project. For these various feats of valor, friendship, argument, care, and, in one case, bedevilment, I am grateful to Jacob Bathanti, Laura Burgess, Zainab Chaudary, Devin Coats, Kate Cronin-Furman, Nick Danforth, Geraldine Davies

Lenoble, Soha El-Achi, Devin Finn, Laura Gaensley Cordeiro, Patricia Gomez Gonzalez, Isabelle Levy, Rachael Levy, Yu-Ming Liou, Manuel Mera, Adam Mount, Paul Musgrave, Rachel Neugarten, Daniel Neep, Daniel Ortega Nieto, Lindsay Pettingill, Fouad Pervez, Kerstin Perez, Peter Rožič, Angélica Zamora, and Tian Zhang.

Above all, I am immeasurably thankful for my extraordinary family. Words cannot express my gratitude to my exceptional grandparents and parents, Kalika Srivastava, Rama Rani Srivastava, Shashikar Dayal, and Jyoti Srivastava; to my stepfather Robert Castracane; and to Lina Srivastava, Pinki and Sunjay Verma, Bhuneshwari Sinha, Dinkar and Deepa, Madhukar and Sheelu, and Daisy Mae. Their love, care, and affection serve as daily examples of success in kindness and wild generosity of heart; whatever strength, joy, and compassion I have in life, I owe to them. This book is for them.

# 1 | *Introduction*

Failure should have consequences. When it does not, we should ask why. The United Nations' (UN) peacekeeping and peacemaking failures in Somalia, Rwanda, West Africa, and the Balkans provoked introspection at the UN, but they did not doom the UN's peacekeeping or peacemaking enterprises: Demand for UN intervention increased in the aftermath of these failures, with parties to civil wars worldwide seeking UN assistance to end their conflicts and rebuild their states. Why does UN peacekeeping remain a desirable part of peace processes despite its reputation as an ineffective measure of protection for civilian populations and warring parties alike? Why do combatants in civil wars engage in UN-led negotiations even when they believe the UN is a failed, flawed contributor to the peace process?

This book attempts to provide some of these answers. I investigate why peacekeeping survived its early catastrophes and how this survival should lead us to reconsider how peacekeeping works. There are two key contentions in this book: First, drawing on evidence from the United Nations Security Council (UNSC) and extensive scholarship about the UN, I argue that the UN's central role in peacemaking and peacekeeping worldwide means peace operations have structural consequences: What the UN does in one place can shift the strategies, outcomes, and options available to parties to conflict in other places. Second, drawing on interviews, archival work, and process traced peace negotiations in Rwanda and Guatemala, I argue that even when they have little faith in peacekeepers' ability to uphold peace agreements, or little interest in the UN's ability to guarantee peace and security, warring parties turn to the UN because its presence in negotiation processes enables unique tactical, symbolic, and post-conflict reconstruction outcomes that have little to do with the end of fighting. Governments and rebels who negotiate with the UN's assistance after peacekeeping failures may do so because negotiation affords them benefits even when they are neither invested in peace nor convinced the UN can help them achieve it.

I investigate four potential benefits to negotiation. The first is peace: Some parties to negotiation will primarily want to end bloodshed and suffering. Negotiation with international assistance may also, however, bring tactical, material, or symbolic benefits to the conflict termination process: It might offer combatants time away from the battlefield to regroup, rearm, and launch unexpected attacks; it might bring economic benefits in the form of aid, state building, or post-conflict reconstruction; or it might be a process through which rebels secure recognition from the international community as legitimate political actors. Only peace requires effective peacekeepers – each other benefit is equally available from the UN even when it cannot keep the peace.

Scholars have good answers about both the UN's ability to learn across cases and its tendency to replicate solutions across dissimilar contexts. What we do not have yet are good answers about how the behavior of peacekeepers in one case influences other cases – and what combatants seek from peacekeepers if they think the UN cannot actually keep the peace. Influential theories of peacekeeping posit that UN peacekeeping works by providing combatants with a credible, neutral force to forestall the backsliding into war that can plague the implementation of negotiated settlements to conflict. In this vision of peacekeeping, which implicitly assumes security dilemmas drive negotiation behavior, mistrust is the critical problem that belligerents must surmount if their peace processes are to succeed. Accordingly, peacekeepers work to alleviate the credible commitment problem: Combatants negotiate with international assistance, and they demobilize and disarm to a force of international peacekeepers, who also provide each side with information about the intentions of the other and prevent accidents or misunderstandings from reigniting war.

But if peacekeeping works this way – if this is actually why most combatants seek out international involvement in their peace processes and settlements – then peacekeepers have to both be effective *and* be known to be effective, or combatants have to be desperate for *any* intervention to secure a peace. Yet UN peacekeeping is often perceived as futile or ineffective, despite substantial scholarly work to the contrary, and many negotiating combatants seem minimally invested in actually forging a peace.

My work suggests that this credible commitment theory of war termination is insufficient: By focusing on whether peacekeepers can forestall recidivism with information, technical support, and credible force, scholars have neglected the corollary question of what demonstrably *incredible*, failing peacekeepers might provide to combatants. In doing so, our understanding of peace operations has overstated the credibility concerns that drive combatants to seek international intervention and understated the ways in which distributional and status concerns lead warring parties to seek out international assistance. This book therefore offers both a new account of the negotiation dynamics that drive the desire for intervention, and joins other work that interrogates influential bargaining models of war. In arguing that international innovations to manage conflict in fact shift combatant incentives in unexpected ways, sometimes producing perverse outcomes, my work also affirms recent scholarship examining international law's unexpected effects on conflict.[1]

In the chapters that follow, I develop this argument with evidence from the UNSC; evidence evaluating the relationship between peacekeeping failures and negotiated settlements globally; and process traced analyses of peace negotiations in Rwanda from 1990 to 1994 and Guatemala in the 1980s and 1990s. I draw on archival documents; on interviews with combatants and negotiators where possible; and on oral histories and contemporaneous journalistic accounts to offer a new set of arguments about the relationship between parties to civil wars and peacekeepers, placing individual interventions within the evolving global apparatus of UN conflict management.

Chapter 2 lays out the book's theory, presenting the two hypotheses that guide the rest of the analysis: a distributional theory, where combatants are motivated by many different goals to seek out UN involvement in peacemaking and peacekeeping; and a credible commitment theory, where combatants are primarily motivated by security concerns. I begin by articulating the structural nature of peace operations, demonstrate how we can observe the social connection between peace operations by examining the high politics of the UNSC, which authorizes the missions, and then argue that scholars in multiple intellectual traditions anticipate this social connection. Followed to

---

[1] See, for example, Tanisha Fazal, *Wars of Law: Unintended Consequences in the Regulation of Armed Conflict* (Ithaca: Cornell University Press, 2018).

their logical conclusions, rationalist, social constructivist, and cognitive psychological arguments all converge on the idea that combatants in one case should not just pay attention to the UN's behavior in other places, but should also reframe their behavior according to what they observe. Proceeding from this point, if we believe that parties to conflict might watch the UN and conclude peacekeepers might not be able to guarantee their security, then our theory of what peace operations are doing in post-conflict places has to account for the varying goals that combatants might bring to the negotiating table. Accordingly, I argue that parties to conflict seek the UN's involvement in negotiation and settlement because they are interested in the distributive and symbolic benefits of intervention – not just international actors' abilities to manage mistrust between warring parties and resolve the credible commitment problem that scholars often associate with war termination, but what intervention can give them, and what international actors can bring to the post-conflict state.

If combatants are interested in the distributional contribution that international actors can make to the negotiation process, then peacekeepers are valuable not just for the peace they can help secure, but for other contributions they may make to the post-conflict space. I investigate four potential benefits to negotiation. The first is peace. Some parties to negotiation will want little more than to strike a deal, end bloodshed and suffering, and mitigate the costs of war. But critically, all parties to a conflict are not necessarily invested in real peace, and many combatants sit down at bargaining tables even when they are not desperate to end war at any cost. For these combatants, negotiation instead of fighting may also bring *tactical, material,* or *symbolic benefits.* Meeting with mediators and negotiators may afford combatants periods away from the battlefield to regroup, rearm, and launch unexpected attacks: International actors and meetings buy belligerents time.[2] Negotiation may also offer tactical benefits by

---

[2] Scott Wolford, Dan Reiter, and Clifford J. Carrubba make a similar point in "Information, Commitment, and War": "Thus, the kinds of power shifts most consistent with our analysis are advantages that accrue to states after agreeing to peace settlements and taking advantage of a pause in fighting, such as the opportunity to regroup or rearm, to launch a surprise attack or even to receive third-party assistance" (Scott Wolford, Dan Reiter, and Clifford J. Carrubba, "Information, Commitment, and War," *Journal of Conflict Resolution* 55, no. 4 [August 2011]: 556–579, 561).

empowering factional leaders, who represent their parties at the negotiation table,[3] or by granting domestic political parties a way to "launder" domestic political reforms that they would otherwise be unable to
enact.[4] Negotiations may also have straight material benefits. In this
way, international involvement in negotiations can be a way of securing future rents, either because intervention will reconstitute the
local economy in a way that benefits elites,[5] or because international
intervention into conflict-torn states can evolve into state building.
Combatants interested primarily in post-conflict or state-building
assistance, either because they are seeking to convert foreign aid into
rent or because they cannot reconstruct the state on their own, will
seek a negotiated settlement overseen by an intervener that they know
can assist them in this reconstruction, irrespective of whether this
intervener has a good track record of upholding negotiated settlements. Finally, negotiation may also have symbolic benefits for parties
to a conflict. There may be important discursive aspects to negotiating
whose value resides in the process and not the outcome.[6] These
include: recognition from the international community as valid partners and legitimate political actors in the peace process[7]; the discursive
value of airing grievances; and presenting the domestic population
with an opportunity to view the parties to the conflict as actors who

---

[3] Christopher Clapham, "Being Peacekept," in *Peacekeeping in Africa*, ed. Oliver
Furley and Roy May (Aldershot: Ashgate, 1998), 303–319.
[4] Kenneth W. Abbott and Duncan Snidal, "Why States Act through Formal
International Organizations," *Journal of Conflict Resolution* 42, no. 1 (February
1998): 3–32.
[5] Clapham 1998, 307.
[6] This is similar but not identical to the argument that Fortna makes about the
UN's moral authority as a deterrent to reigniting hostilities (Virginia Page Fortna,
*Does Peacekeeping Work? Shaping Belligerents' Choices after Civil War*
[Princeton: Princeton University Press, 2008], 89). She and other scholars argue
that peacekeeping "provides a moral barrier to hostile action" (Paul Diehl,
*International Peacekeeping* [Baltimore: Johns Hopkins University Press, 1993],
10; see also Michael W. Doyle and Nicholas Sambanis, *Making War and
Building Peace: United Nations Peace Operations* [Princeton: Princeton
University Press, 2006], 15, 56). Here, I argue instead that the UN is actually
legitimating combatants as political actors through the negotiation process.
[7] Klaus Schlicte and Ulrich Schneckener, "Armed Groups and the Politics of
Legitimacy," *Civil Wars* 17, no. 4 (2015): 409–424; Lee J. M. Seymour,
"Legitimacy and the Politics of Recognition in Kosovo," *Small Wars &
Insurgencies* 28, no. 4–5 (2017): 817–838; Reyko Huang, "Rebel Diplomacy,"
*International Security* 40, no. 4 (Spring 2016): 89–126.

favor the consultative process of mediation and bargaining over the battlefield.

Combatants who come to the bargaining table to rearm or regroup, to secure aid and economic infusions from third parties, or to cultivate their images and identities as appropriate, equal parties in conflict resolution and international recognition may have goals other than the successful implementation of their peace agreements. Peacekeeping after a negotiated settlement has usually been understood as the solution to a security problem, but we may be better poised to understand why parties to a conflict seek out the UN's assistance if we reframe it as a potential solution to a range of security, tactical, material, and symbolic problems. The chapter concludes with observable implications for both hypotheses – what we would expect to see in the world if these processes were at work.

Chapter 3 lays out the methods and the logic of case selection that underpin the book. This book is both a theory-building and theory-probing undertaking: I build a theory of how the alternative benefits of bargaining lead combatants to seek out UN peacekeepers while probing how the credible commitment theory of war termination drives the desire for peace operations. Process tracing using a most-similar cases approach is one way to accomplish both undertakings. In this chapter, I outline first the method by which I selected cases, building a catalog of the UN's peacekeeping successes and failures in order to do so, and then discuss the evidence and tools I use to process trace the Rwandan and Guatemalan peace processes. Readers who are interested primarily in the substance of the text and not in methodological discussion can proceed to the subsequent three chapters without reading Chapter 3.

Chapter 4 examines the conflict resolution processes surrounding the 1990–1994 civil war in Rwanda. The Rwandan genocide is emblazoned in popular consciousness and in the UN's institutional memory as the paradigmatic peacekeeping failure. It is an intrinsically important case for scholars interested in peacekeeping by dint of both the introspection it provoked at the UN and by the sheer, catastrophic scale of the violence that tore through Rwanda while Blue Helmets looked on. From a policy perspective, Rwanda's role in ordering and informing many subsequent interventions makes it a necessary case for assessing the long-term and across-case effects of intervention. But what are the effects of other peacekeeping failures in Rwanda? Was a negotiated settlement surprising in Rwanda, and how did the UN's failures elsewhere affect the course of the civil war? We know failure in Somalia made UNSC members unwilling to commit resources to the United Nations Assistance Mission for Rwanda (UNAMIR), and we know that failure in Rwanda prompted policymakers to reconsider the traditional prohibition on UN peacekeepers using force. This chapter investigates the negotiations that preceded the Rwandan genocide and examines what effect the UN's past performance had on the Rwandan peace process; how the peacekeeping failures in Somalia and Burundi may have conditioned the course of the conflict in the crucial months between the Arusha Accords and the genocide; and what led the Rwandan Patriotic Front (RPF) to invite a second UN peace operation into Rwanda following the cataclysmic failure of the first mission.

Drawing on multiple archival sources; interviews I conducted with key RPF figures; and observers' accounts of the Arusha peace process, UNAMIR, and the UN's decision-making on Rwanda, I argue that the negotiating table at Arusha was populated by actors with diverse motives: desperate negotiators who had to settle because they could no longer fight; hardliners who used the negotiation process to pursue tactical, distributional, and symbolic goals other than peace; and spoilers who ultimately strove to break the peace. In this context, the international community's unique abilities to assist in demobilization and refugee resettlement, as well as their ability to confer legitimacy upon political groups, were important dimensions of the negotiations. I also argue that the parties to the conflict had a mixed picture of the UN's efficacy as a guarantor at the start of the negotiations, but often held onto earlier unfavorable impressions from the decolonization period, as well; and that they were concerned with peacekeeping failure in Somalia, but that they interpreted this failure in accordance with their own strategic situations, either assuming that they were different than the warring parties in Somalia or calibrating their strategies to upend the peace process according to the UN's observed vulnerabilities. Finally, I find that, despite the UN's massive failures during the genocide, the RPF returned again to seek the UN's help after the genocide both because they were desperate and because they required its assistance rebuilding the state and resettling the displaced – and that they were particularly interested in the UN's legitimacy-conferring capabilities. In the extremely turbulent period after the genocide, amid massive population transfers and the RPF's consolidation of power, the RPF's desire to be viewed as legitimately pursuing post-conflict peace, rather than exacting retribution on political opponents, was a key reason to seek out a UN mission to Rwanda.

Chapter 5 evaluates the UN's engagement in Guatemalan negotiations from 1989 to 1996. It asks how the Government of Guatemala (GoG) and the Unidad Revolucionaria Nacional Guatemalteca (URNG), the coalition of rebel groups fighting and negotiating with the GoG, assessed the UN's performance as the guarantor of agreements elsewhere, especially the concurrent peacekeeping success in neighboring El Salvador and the temporally simultaneous failure in the Balkans, and how these assessments influenced the course of negotiations and the final agreement that emerged from their peace process. The chapter draws on archival material from the UN; the National Security Archive (which, given the destruction of parallel documents in Guatemala, is a primary source of documentation on this period even for Guatemalan authorities currently prosecuting the era's genocides); oral histories of the primary actors involved on all sides of the conflict; and the extensive scholarly literature on the Guatemalan Civil War and peace process.

I find that participants looked nearly exclusively at El Salvador to assess the contours and possibilities of UN intervention, but that they perceived the Salvadoran example as a negative one: Both sides believed their Salvadoran counterparts had given too much away during their negotiations. Thus, despite lobbying for multiple forms of UN assistance during the course of negotiations, the GoG and URNG worked to guard against the same distributional losses and gains they saw the UN as having pushed into the Salvadoran agreement. Both sides actively pursued UN intervention for the symbolic, material, and tactical benefits it brought to the negotiation process, even as the Guatemalan government actively sought to minimize the UN's role as security guarantor to the peace process. This is surprising; credible commitment theories of peacekeeping would anticipate that the UN's success in El Salvador would enhance the Guatemalan parties' confidence in the UN as guarantor, and most accounts of UN peacekeeping in Guatemala frame the mission as a success. Instead, the UN's banner success in El Salvador first prolonged the war in Guatemala and then produced a weaker agreement, a degraded capacity to enforce the peace, and inferior human rights outcomes for the Guatemalan domestic public.

Indeed, although the formal peace has held, it is bitter for many in Guatemala: The peace accords quickly deteriorated in the implementation period, constitutional reforms proposed by the negotiated agreement were rejected by popular referendum, and judicial impunity, drug trafficking, and organized crime have conspired to make Guatemala one of the most dangerous places in the world in the years since the war. These realities are, in part, dark fruit borne from belligerents' work at the negotiating table nearly twenty years ago, when governments and rebels alike sought to continue their work by actively curtailing the UN's activities in Guatemala.

The conclusion examines my argument's implications for both scholarship and policy. For scholars, the evidence I offer here challenges the strict geographic and chronological separation between time periods and peacekeeping missions that some studies take as given. For policymakers, the arguments and evidence I advance contribute to ongoing debates about the future of peace operations. Peacekeeping today is turning increasingly toward a more military posture – but key among my argument's implications is the idea that if the reconstruction, investment, and refugee resettlement services the international community can provide are more important than security protection to some combatants, then tying negotiation, peacekeeping, and intervention more tightly to the UN's aid and humanitarian agencies may represent another, better direction for the UN.

This book's insights should be relevant to students and scholars of peacekeeping, peace processes, and the UN. Important foundational works on peacekeeping focus on peacekeeper actions and learning with the UN system,[8] while influential new books on peacekeeping have focused on the local level as an important site for innovation, conflict resolution, and consultative peacebuilding[9]; this book knits the two together to posit a dynamic theory of how international peacekeepers' actions systematically shape domestic negotiating decisions.

---

[8] Doyle and Sambanis 2006; Lise Morjé Howard, *UN Peacekeeping in Civil Wars* (New York: Cambridge University Press, 2008); Fortna 2008.

[9] Séverine Autesserre, *The Trouble with the Congo: Local Violence and the Failure of International Peacebuilding* (Cambridge: Cambridge University Press, 2010); Sarah B. K. von Billerbeck, *Whose Peace? Local Ownership and United Nations Peacekeeping* (Oxford: Oxford University Press, 2017); Susanna Campbell, *Global Governance and Local Peace: Accountability and Performance in International Peacebuilding* (Cambridge: Cambridge University Press, 2018).

Its integrative arguments should speak to scholars and students of both the UN and state-level conflict processes.

Empirically, the two peace processes I examine remain intrinsically important for scholars and analysts of peacemaking, peacekeeping, post-conflict reconstruction, and transitional justice: The dynamics of negotiation I examine in Rwanda and Guatemala shed light on current debates about restitution, prosecution, and reconstruction, and help illuminate ongoing regional problems of violence, migration, and displacement alongside the book's central implications about peacekeeping and peace processes.

The Rwandan case sits at the epicenter of debates on genocide, intervention, and the appropriate role for peacekeepers in the world, and this book offers a new account of the negotiation processes that preceded the genocide. For understandable reasons, few scholarly works focus on the negotiation process that preceded the genocide;[10] the Arusha Accords were never formally implemented and provided only months of respite from conflict. Accordingly, this book draws on interviews with RPF actors involved in negotiating the Accord and archival documents to reconstruct the peace process, and in doing so presents a new analysis of a widely researched case that for decades has structured policy debates on genocide, the Responsibility to Protect, and the use of force in peace operations.

The Guatemalan case is less frequently discussed in the peacekeeping literature, in part because the UN's mission there was substantially more limited than other missions at the time. This in and of itself constitutes a puzzle worth explaining, given that the mission to neighboring El Salvador was initially one of the UN's only unambiguous successes; the case should accordingly be interesting to both scholars who work on peacekeeping and peacemaking, and to scholars who are interested in how the nature of international intervention contributed to post-conflict Guatemala's violence. Although war in Guatemala ended more than two decades ago, the consequences of incomplete demobilization and disarmament, impunity for human rights violations, and never-implemented land reform – all on the table during

---

[10]  Only one full-length book, Bruce Jones, *Peacemaking in Rwanda: The Dynamics of Failure* (Boulder: Lynne Rienner, 2001) deals with the Arusha peace process; chapters of Howard Adelman and Astri Suhrke's in *The Path of a Genocide: The Rwanda Crisis from Uganda to Zaire* (New York: Routledge, 2000) discuss the negotiations as well.

negotiations – continue to reverberate across the Americas, with displacement affecting US domestic political debates, as well. The case remains, unfortunately, timely for conflict and violence scholars.

The next chapter lays the groundwork for these case studies, examining evidence from the high politics of the Security Council and Secretariat to offer a theory of how the UN's actions in one civil war case can shift incentives in other negotiation processes, and how what happens at the negotiating table can reflect actions the UN has taken elsewhere.

# 2 | The Social Context of International Peacekeeping and the Alternative Benefits of Bargaining

Why do combatants negotiate after peacekeeping failures? Scholars and policymakers have focused on international actors' abilities to alleviate the credible commitment problem that scholars often associate with war termination, and on peacekeepers' abilities to provide security guarantees. But what if combatants think security is unlikely, or what if peace is only a secondary goal? What drives them to seek the assistance of the UN's peacekeepers and peacemakers even after these parties have proved themselves ill-equipped to credibly guarantee agreements? Why do they return to the negotiating table with the UN as their guarantor again and again, despite contravening evidence that suggests they could be better off pursuing alternative strategies – perhaps returning to the battlefield to seek an armed solution to their grievances, or perhaps attempting internally brokered negotiated settlements that dispense with outside guarantees? Put another way, why does UN peacekeeping remain a desirable part of peace processes if combatants do not believe it will effectively protect civilian populations and warring parties, or if they do not want this protection?

These questions hinge on a simple but consequential claim: that the UN's multiple simultaneous peace operations have structural properties, and that combatants considering negotiation with international assistance have a universe of other interventions in which they can observe the UN's behavior. Accordingly, this book makes two interlinked arguments: First, in this chapter, I argue that peace operations have systemic properties that place civil war peace processes in a shared social context. Second, I argue here and in the rest of the book that, given this shared social context, parties to negotiation can and do seek out the UN's services in an effort to secure a wide range of services beyond a security guarantee, and a wide range of benefits that are not peace – and in fact are sometimes at odds with peace.

If each peace operation is part of a *system* of peace operations, and if combatants pay attention to the world around them, not just to their

12

own immediate relationship with the UN, then combatants who participate in peace processes are unlikely to be all motivated by a similar
desire for peace and security. Instead, if combatants learn vicariously –
if they observe the *system* of UN peace operations and have as rich a
sense of what the UN does in the world as any observer could – then
their motives for requesting international involvement in their peace
processes will vary.

A standard way of thinking about peacekeeping is therefore incomplete – and completing it offers us a fuller, and a strikingly different,
picture of peacekeeping's role in peacemaking. If peace operations are
a social endeavor, then combatants' reasons for seeking out the UN's
assistance will reflect a varied universe of wins and losses, and needs
and desires, not some common, shared, steadfast map for reaching a
safe and secure world. I argue that combatants negotiate UN involvement in their peace processes even after UN peacekeeping failures
because negotiation has material, tactical, and symbolic benefits that
are *only* available through the presence of international actors, and
that are distinct from the benefits of either war or peace. In this
context, parties to conflict draw on the UN's past performance as they
assess their strategic situations and what they want out of their peace
process, and negotiating with international assistance *itself* has a value
that is separate from the value of ending war.[1] Each leg of my argument – first, that disparate peace operations share a common social
context, and second, that peace and security are not necessarily primary goals for many parties to peace talks – is a departure from much
of the current scholarship and policy on peacekeeping and peace
processes, but can be deduced from multiple epistemological perspectives. Together, both parts of the argument help us see the many ways
peacekeeping works to support the political goals and aspirations of
parties to conflict *even* when peace seems distant, or even when peace is
beside the point for many combatants.

In this chapter, I begin by outlining the structural dimensions of
peace operations, which are apparent when we look around the world
yet rarely addressed in scholarship and policy about peace operations'
effects. I first demonstrate that we can *see* the social connection

---

[1] This is similar to the game-theoretic concept of continuation values – cf. Nolan
McCarty and Adam Meirowitz, *Political Game Theory: An Introduction*
(Cambridge: Cambridge University Press, 2007).

between peace operations by examining the high politics of the UNSC, which authorizes the missions, and then I argue that we can theoretically demonstrate the social connection between peace operations from multiple intellectual perspectives. Rationalist, social constructivist, and cognitive psychological arguments should all lead us to believe that combatants in one case should not just pay attention to other cases, but also reframe their behavior according to what they observe. If we proceed from this point, and we believe that parties to conflict are not always certain the UN can provide them with a security guarantee, then our theory of what combatants want from peace operations has to account for the varying goals that combatants bring to the negotiating table.

Accordingly, I then argue that parties to conflict seek the UN's services in their negotiation and settlement processes because they are interested in the distributive and symbolic benefits of intervention – what intervention will give them, and what international actors can bring to the post-conflict state – not just international actors' abilities to alleviate the credible commitment problem that scholars often associate with war termination. The next section of the chapter investigates these credible commitment theories of peace operations, specifically taking up their expectation that combatants are *primarily* motivated by the desire to address security concerns. This leaves us with two theories that guide the rest of this book: a *distributional* theory, where combatants are motivated to seek out the UN's involvement by many different goals at the negotiating table; and a credible commitment theory, where combatants are motivated *primarily* by the desire to address security concerns. The last section of this chapter lays out these theories and outlines their observable implications.

## The Social Context of International Peacekeeping

This book's central argument depends upon an intuitive but often overlooked point: Because the UN is the focal point for contemporary conflict resolution, parties to a conflict are attentive to the UN's performance in other conflict cases. Accordingly, international peacekeepers' conduct can shape civil wars globally.[2] International peacekeeping is

---

[2] Put another way, it is the agreed-upon venue to which states take their security problems for collective resolution; see Thomas C. Schelling, *The Strategy of Conflict* (Cambridge, MA: Harvard University Press, 1960).

therefore a social enterprise in the simplest sense – both individual cases of UN involvement and the collective set of UN peacekeeping cases interact meaningfully.

While this idea is inherent in social constructivist, world polity, and sociological approaches to international politics, norm diffusion, and peacebuilding,[3] many studies of civil war privilege a bounded, discrete understanding of conflicts, often for analytical clarity.[4] For methodological reasons, these works often assume that civil wars are unaffected by one another – but we know conflicts do not confine themselves within states: They bleed across borders, trigger regional crises, and provoke transnational refugee flows.[5] Work on diffusion effects across conflicts frequently addresses conflict contagion or refugee flows, but this strand of scholarship does not usually examine how the systemic properties of international peacekeeping and peacemaking might link these cases.[6] As Beck, Gleditsch, and Beardsley note, however, space is

---

[3] See, for example, John W. Meyer, John Boli, George M. Thomas, and Francisco O. Ramirez, "World Society and the Nation-State," *American Journal of Sociology* 103, no. 1 (July 1997): 144–181; Alexander E. Kentikelenis and Leonard Seabrooke, "The Politics of World Polity: Script-Writing in International Organizations," *American Sociological Review* 82, no. 5 (October 2017): 1065–1092; Susan Park, "Theorizing Norm Diffusion within International Organizations," *International Politics* 43 (2006): 342–361; Martha Finnemore and Kathryn Sikkink, "International Norm Dynamics and Political Change," *International Organization* 52, no. 4 (1998): 887–917; Séverine Autesserre, *Peaceland: Conflict Resolution and the Everyday Politics of International Intervention* (Cambridge: Cambridge University Press, 2014); Susanna P. Campbell, *Global Governance and Local Peace: Accountability and Performance in International Peacebuilding* (Cambridge: Cambridge University Press, 2018).

[4] Cf. Halvard Buhaug, Lars-Erik Cederman, and Kristian Skrede Gleditsch, "Square Pegs in Round Holes: Inequalities, Grievances, and Civil War," *International Studies Quarterly* 58, no. 2 (June 2014): 418–431; James D. Fearon and David Laitin, "Ethnicity, Insurgency, and Civil War," *American Political Science Review* 97, no. 1 (February 2003): 75–90; Michael W. Doyle and Nicholas Sambanis, "International Peacebuilding: A Theoretical and Quantitative Analysis," *American Political Science Review* 94, no. 4 (December 2000): 779–801; Paul Collier and Anke Hoeffler, "Greed and Grievance in Civil War," *Oxford Economic Papers* 56 (2004): 563–595.

[5] Kristian Skrede Gleditsch, "Transnational Dimensions of Civil War," *Journal of Peace Research* 44, no. 3 (May 2007): 293–309; Idean Salehyan, *Rebels without Borders: Transnational Insurgencies and World Politics* (Ithaca: Cornell University Press, 2009).

[6] Peter Collier and Nicholas Sambanis, "Understanding Civil War: A New Agenda," *Journal of Conflict Resolution* 46, no. 1 (2002): 3–12; Idean Salehyan and Kristian Skrede Gleditsch, "Refugee Flows and the Spread of Civil War,"

more than just geography, and we should "expect the connectivity of units to be a function of political and social, as well as geographic, variables."[7]

In fact, there are good reasons to believe that contemporary conflict resolution mechanisms create meaningful social interaction between civil wars. Scholarship on global governance and international organizations frames the UN system as the forum and focal point for contemporary conflict resolution – a global clearinghouse for managing complex security and humanitarian crises.[8] Recent work on mediation argues "conflict-resolution norms spread not only over the course of one crisis, but – owing to learning and emulation – also across different disputes if these are closely linked to each other."[9] Accordingly, international peacekeepers may dynamically link civil wars – peacekeepers' performance in one place could affect the information set or incentive structures for combatants in other places.[10] Thus, for example, at minimum, the 1993 peacekeeping failure in Somalia may plausibly have changed wartime calculations in Rwanda and Burundi later that year; at maximum, the "Somalia syndrome"[11] and other peacekeeping failures might color combatants' decisions in cases unfolding decades later. Indeed, scholars have already asserted that peacekeeping failures in the Somalia case affected the

*International Organization* 60, no. 2 (2006): 335–366; Kyle Beardsley, "Peacekeeping and the Contagion of Armed Conflict," *The Journal of Politics* 73, no. 4 (October 2011): 1051–1064.

[7] Nathaniel Beck, Kristian Skrede Gleditsch, and Kyle Beardsley, "Space Is More Than Geography: Using Spatial Econometrics in the Study of Political Economy," *International Studies Quarterly* 50 (2006): 27–44, 42. Beck, Gleditsch, and Beardsley also write that "We do not think of nations as isolates, and there is no reason that our models should treat nations in isolation either, or study interactions in a non-systematic manner" (42).

[8] Michael Barnett and Martha Finnemore, *Rules for the World: International Organizations in Global Politics* (Ithaca: Cornell University Press, 2004); Erik Voeten, "The Political Origins of the UN Security Council's Ability to Legitimize the Use of Force," *International Organization* 59, no. 3 (2005): 527–557; Ian Hurd, *After Anarchy: Legitimacy and Power in the United Nations Security Council* (Princeton: Princeton University Press, 2008).

[9] Tobias Böhmelt, "The Spatial Contagion of International Mediation," *Conflict Management and Peace Science* 32, no. 1 (2015): 108–127, 121.

[10] Frank Dobbin, Beth Simmons, and Geoffrey Garrett, "The Global Diffusion of Public Policies: Social Construction, Coercion, Competition, or Learning," *Annual Review of Sociology* 33 (2007): 449–472.

[11] Letitia Lawson, "US Africa Policy since the Cold War," *Strategic Insights* VI, no. 1 (January 2007), https://core.ac.uk/download/pdf/36704615.pdf.

international community's willingness to *send* peacekeepers to other countries, even framing it as a nearly exogenous shock to the supply of peace operations, troop contributions, and financial contributions to peacekeeping.[12]

First-blush evidence of this claim abounds for even casual observers of UN politics. The high politics of the UN Security Council, for example, offer ample evidence that the UN's central role in peacemaking and peacekeeping informs both the rhetoric and strategies of actors addressing the UNSC. Letters and petitions lodged before the UNSC and General Assembly (UNGA); the records of UNSC and UNGA meetings on peacekeeping cases; and interviews with key actors all establish that representatives of war-torn states are attentive to how effectively the UN implements and upholds peace agreements globally, how effective it is at civilian protection, and how it apportions resources across conflict cases. In some cases, the linkages are clear and predictable – UNSC meetings about the Balkans crises or wars in Liberia and Sierra Leone, for example, repeatedly relate interventions in these enmeshed conflicts to one another. In the early years of the Balkans crises, for example, Croatia's representative repeatedly tied the UN's success in Croatia to its future actions in Bosnia. Speaking at the Council in November 1992, the Croatian representative argued,

If the United Nations peace plan in Croatia is not implemented, that will decrease chances for the success of the even more complex peace plan in Bosnia. Furthermore, failure of the peace-keeping plan in the Republic of Croatia would open the door for recognition of the fruits of aggression launched against Bosnia and Herzegovina ... the weakness of UNPROFOR and its lack of determination are providing fruitful soil for the rise of an aggressive Serbian policy.[13]

---

[12] Michael Tiernay, "Which Comes First? Unpacking the Relationship between Peace Agreements and Peacekeeping Missions," *Conflict Management and Peace Science* 32, no. 2 (April 2015): 135–152, doi: 10.1177/0738894213520396; James Traub, *The Best Intentions: Kofi Annan and the UN in the Era of American World Power* (New York: Farrar, Straus and Giroux, 2006); Adekeye Adebajo, *UN Peacekeeping in Africa* (Boulder: Lynne Rienner, 2012). Journalists' accounts framed the incident similarly. See, for example, Tom Ashbrook, "UN Effects Everywhere Turn to Dust: Downed Helicopter in Somalia Doomed a 'New World Order'," *Boston Globe*, April 30, 1995.

[13] S/PV.3137: 38–39. See a similar discussion on Liberia and Sierra Leone in S/PV.3138: 56. The Security Council documents cited in this chapter were uncovered as part of a systematic survey of archival UN documents to determine

Beyond regional conflicts, members of the Secretariat report that the public in conflict zones are sometimes themselves well-informed about the UN's multiple and simultaneous intervention theaters. In 1999 testimony before the UNSC on the situation in Sierra Leone, for example, Olara Otunnu, Special Representative of the Secretary-General for Children and Armed Conflict, testified before the Council that he had "discovered that Sierra Leoneans at all levels are remarkably well-informed about Kosovo. Everywhere I went, I was challenged to explain perceived discrepancies in the attitude of response of the international community in regard to the needs in the two situations."[14]

Connections between peace operations are also clear when peacekeepers are attacked, or when actors on the ground attempt to blackmail the UN into their preferred course of action. When peacekeepers are under

---

how frequently parties appearing at the UNSC invoke other cases of UN action. To select from among the UNSC's astounding number of yearly meetings, I assembled a portfolio of documents by reading the *Repertoire of the Practice of the Security Council* for all years from 1989 to 2009 and gathering all available letters, petitions, and provisional meeting records for conflict cases that the *Repertoire* itself cites, totaling approximately 510 documents in addition to the 28 Chapter VI and Chapter VII sections of the *Repertoire*. The *Repertoire* is a survey mandated by the UN General Assembly (S/RES/686) that provides comprehensive coverage of the Security Council's interpretation of and action concerning the UN Charter and its Rules of Procedure. Details are available at www.un.org/en/sc/repertoire/actions.shtml. This selection mechanism produces a sample biased in favor of the cases UN bureaucrats thought were most important, but it enables me to identify communication between the UNSC and other states negotiating UN intervention without making assumptions about which cases *should* be important. Although this selection mechanism likely overrepresents cases in which the Department of Political Affairs (DPA) was involved, the biases that this selection introduces into the evidence are unlikely to bias results in favor of my theory unless we have some reason to expect that DPA bureaucrats are also interested in the way the simultaneity of peace operations affects peace processes. Subsequently, I examined these documents primarily for statements made by the actors whose conflict cases were under consideration during that UNSC session, evaluating two competing hypotheses: whether these actors explicitly leverage information about other cases in the service of their own goals, or whether actors lobbying before the UNSC meaningfully reference only their own situations or P5 interests. This sample includes both international and civil wars because it is difficult to distinguish between them in several notable cases. The protracted conflicts in the Balkans and in the African Great Lakes region, for instance, can be read as successive national conflicts or longer international conflicts. Although only a few documents are cited in this chapter, there were vivid, direct, and explicit references to other cases in 62 out of 510 documents evaluated.

[14] S/PV.4054: 4.

attack, UNSC discussions are rarely confined to single cases; attacks against UN forces are condemned in general terms, and with explicit attention to repercussions for other cases.[15] Members of the UN Secretariat, troop-contributing countries, and combatants all draw connections between these cases.

United Nations Secretaries-General Boutros Boutros-Ghali and Kofi Annan both explicitly connected attacks on individual peacekeepers to the larger social context of peace operations. In his memoir, for example, Boutros-Ghali recalls chiding the UNSC on the dangerous precedent it had set by granting concessions to hostage-takers during the Balkans crises:

At my monthly Friday lunch with the Security Council, on May 26, 1995, I was bluntly confrontational. "Unfortunately, I was correct in my forecasts," I said. "We now have three unmistakable precedents. Each air strike brings a new wave of hostage taking and takes us a month of negotiations with the Serbs to get the UN personnel released."[16]

Similarly, the precedent of American withdrawal from Somalia after the October 1993 Black Hawk Down incident reverberates across peacekeeping cases. Scholars and diplomats alike have stressed the UN's unwillingness to sustain further failures in Somalia's immediate aftermath for fear that another peacekeeping crisis would forever doom the enterprise.[17] Indeed, armed actors worldwide seemed to zero in on that fear. Days after the Black Hawk Down incident, an American Embassy car carrying the UN-Organization of American States (OAS) envoy to Haiti was attacked while en route to meet the USS *Harlan County*, which was bringing US and Canadian soldiers to join the UN mission in Haiti. On arrival at the dock, they found "more thugs [who] shouted and gesticulated, declaring that Haiti would become 'another Somalia' for the United States, and protestors held up a sigh saying, 'Welcome to Mogadishu.' Within a few hours the *Harlan County* weighed anchor and steamed away, apparently ordered by the White House to return to Norfolk,

---

[15] See, e.g., Cape Verde and Brazil in S/PV.3229, and Djibouti in S/PV.3277.

[16] Boutros Boutros-Ghali, *Unvanquished: A US-UN Saga* (New York: Random House, 1999), 235.

[17] Ibid.; Michael Barnett, *Eyewitness to a Genocide: The United Nations and Rwanda* (Ithaca and London: Cornell University Press, 2003); Kofi Annan and Nader Mousavizadeh, *Interventions: A Life in War and Peace* (New York: The Penguin Press, 2012).

Virginia. The dockside demonstration had succeeded."[18] Although the United States later denied the connection between Somalia and the *Harlan County's* retreat,[19] the explicit references to Mogadishu and Somalia certainly indicate that some Haitians were attentive to the US and the UN's failures elsewhere, and that this awareness shaped their strategy vis-à-vis the UN.

The Black Hawk Down incident also inspired Rwandan government officials to target Belgian peacekeepers during the Rwandan genocide's first days in 1994. A government official later explained that the decision to kill peacekeepers was specifically inspired by the Mogadishu ambush and calibrated to force UNAMIR's withdrawal: "We watch CNN too, you know," he said.[20] Kofi Annan reports the same claim in his memoirs while mourning the tactic's success: "[The Government of Rwanda official] was referring to the lesson that they had garnered from Somalia the year before: that the death of just a few foreign peacekeepers would be enough to end the appetite for intervention and allow them to get on with their murderous plans. They were right."[21]

Even less violent modes of blackmail reveal how the UN's centrality to contemporary conflict resolution shapes the strategies of disparate parties to conflict. In post-conflict 1994 Mozambique, the Resistência Nacional Moçambicana (RENAMO) guerilla leader Afonso Dhlakama announced he would withdraw his party from UN-overseen elections on the first day of voting, forcing concessions from the UN while specifically referencing its recent failure in Angola. Dhlakama knew

the UN could not allow itself to have elections with only FRELIMO and a few scattered small parties. Four months earlier, on a visit to the United Nations Secretariat in New York, [Dhlakama] had declared publicly, "Regarding the Secretary General, Mozambique could well be his only success during his term as head of the UN; if he misses that opportunity, he could also lose his second term."[22]

---

[18] Boutros-Ghali 1999, 109.      [19] Ibid.

[20] Barbara F. Walter, *Committing to Peace: The Successful Settlement of Civil Wars* (Princeton: Princeton University, 2002), 155; Bruce D. Jones, *The Best Laid Plans . . . Peace-Making in Rwanda and the Implications of Failure* (New York: Sage, 2001), 80.

[21] Annan and Mousavizadeh 2012, 57.

[22] Béatrice Pouligny, *Peace Operations Seen from Below: UN Missions and Local People* (Bloomfield: Kumarian Press, 2006), 233–234, citing a June 19, 1994 *Le*

Here, a key actor involved in peace negotiation and post-conflict processes strategically examined the full universe of UN interventions alongside internal UN politics. Dhlakama used the UN's efficacy in other cases as a strategic lever against the UN Secretariat itself, holding out to get better treatment from the UN; in exchange, he offered the success they could not secure elsewhere during the dark years of disaster in Rwanda, Somalia, and the Balkans.[23] The tactic was successful, and the elections were in fact postponed.[24]

As these examples illustrate, international peacekeeping and peace-making are *social* endeavors. What the UN does in one case has implications for other cases – and accordingly, we should expect that the UN's failures anywhere could affect its efforts to secure peace everywhere. This idea that the UN's central role in contemporary conflict resolution must affect the way civil wars end globally is to some extent intuitive – but few studies of either peace processes or peacekeeping posit meaningful or consequential social interaction between civil war cases. Accordingly, the clearly social nature of conflict cases in an era of centralized multilateral conflict resolution requires that we reconsider key theories of conflict termination and what combatants want from international actors when they sit down to negotiate the ends of their conflicts. As I argue in the next section of this chapter, however, it does not require us to fundamentally reject any of the core tenets of these theories. We can approach credible commitment theories of war termination on their own terms and find they are congruent with social constructivist and social psychological theories of learning, cognition, and decision-making that *would* anticipate peace operations are socially responsive to one another.

## Social Endeavors through Any Lens

Peacekeeping studies have flourished in the last two decades. Recent scholarship undertakes rigorous empirical testing, and a growing body

---

*Monde* article. See also Marion Georges in *Le Monde* on June 10, 1994, October 29, 1994, and October 30, 1994.

[23] Pouligny notes similarities between this case and the negotiation and implementation of the Dayton Accords during the US national election (Pouligny 2006, 233–234); see also Jon Western, "Sources of Humanitarian Intervention," *International Security* 26, no. 4 (Spring 2002): 112–142.

[24] Georges 1994.

of work has emphasized the importance of both supply- and demand-side explanations for peacekeeping.[25] Assessments of peacekeeping's efficacy reveal that, *ceteris paribus*, peacekeeping is effective at upholding the terms of negotiated settlements,[26] and is more successful after an agreement has been signed than it is when peacekeepers are deployed during active conflict.[27] Having an agreement in place matters – but *why* having an agreement in place matters is not always clear, as both successful peace operations and long-lasting agreements may ultimately be endogenous to combatants' commitments to ending war.[28] Recent research has also revealed that peacekeeping is even more successful when we evaluate multiple pathways through which it might operate, including peace enforcement and civilian protection.[29] This research has also examined how peacekeeping

---

[25] Virginia Page Fortna, *Does Peacekeeping Work? Shaping Belligerents' Choices after Civil War* (Princeton: Princeton University Press, 2008); Virginia Page Fortna and Lise Morjé Howard, "Pitfalls and Prospects in the Peacekeeping Literature," *Annual Review of Political Science* 11 (2008): 283–301; Michael J. Gilligan and Ernest J. Sergenti, "Do UN Interventions Cause Peace? Using Matching to Improve Causal Inference," *Quarterly Journal of Political Science* 3, no. 2 (2008): 89–122; V. Page Fortna and Lisa L. Martin, "Peacekeepers as Signals: The Demand for International Peacekeeping in Civil Wars," in *Power, Interdependence, and Nonstate Actors in World Politics*, ed. Helen V. Milner and Andrew Moravcsik (Princeton: Princeton University Press, 2009), 87–107; Khusrav Gaibulloev, Todd Sandler, and Hirofumi Shimizu, "Demands for UN and Non-UN Peacekeeping: Nonvoluntary versus Voluntary Contributions to a Public Good," *Journal of Conflict Resolution* 53, no. 6 (December 2009): 827–853; Lisa Hultman, Jacob Kathman, and Megan Shannon, "United Nations Peacekeeping and Civilian Protection in Civil War," *American Journal of Political Science* 57, no. 4 (October 2013): 875–891; Andrea Ruggeri, Han Dorussen, and Theodora-Ismene Gizelis, "Winning the Peace Locally: UN Peacekeeping and Local Conflict," *International Organization* 71, no. 1 (Winter 2017): 163–185; Lisa Hultman, Jacob D. Kathman, and Megan Shannon, "United Nations Peacekeeping Dynamics and the Duration of Post-civil Conflict Peace," *Conflict Management and Peace Science* 33, no. 3 (2016): 231–249; Michelle Benson and Jacob Kathman, "United Nations Bias and Force Commitments in Civil Conflicts," *The Journal of Politics* 76, no. 2 (April 2014): 350–363.

[26] Fortna 2008; Michael Doyle and Nicholas Sambanis, *Making War and Building Peace: United Nations Peace Operations* (Princeton: Princeton University Press, 2006).

[27] Gilligan and Sergenti 2008.

[28] Suzanne Werner and Amy Yuen, "Making and Keeping Peace," *International Organization* 59, no. 2 (Spring 2005): 261–292.

[29] Håvard Hegre, Lisa Hultman, and Håvard Mokleiv Nygård, "Evaluating the Conflict-Reducing Effect of UN Peacekeeping Operations," *The Journal of*

can shape belligerents' decisions about whether to maintain peace or resume fighting,[30] how the narratives that peacekeepers themselves carry across cases affect domestic outcomes,[31] how the UN's embrace of local ownership can systematically put international and local peacebuilding goals at cross-purposes,[32] and how the neutrality and identity of different kinds of interveners affect the duration of conflict.[33] We also have good answers about the UN's ability to learn across cases and its tendency to replicate solutions across dissimilar contexts.[34] But what we do not have yet are good answers about how the behavior of peacekeepers in *one* case influences domestic actors in *other* cases.

Influential arguments about peacekeeping in the rationalist tradition posit that third-party guarantors make peace agreements more likely to succeed by helping parties to conflict overcome the credible commitment problem of war termination. We can derive a sense of the social and structural nature of peace operations even from these rationalist accounts, taking them on their own terms, because there are a finite number of third-party guarantors from whom combatants can anticipate intervention and assistance, and the UN intervenes simultaneously

*Politics* 81, no. 1 (published online November 2018): 215–232; Hanne Fjelde, Lisa Hultman, and Desirée Nilsson, "Protection through Presence: UN Peacekeeping and the Costs of Targeting Civilians," *International Organization* 73, no. 1 (Winter 2019); Hultman, Kathman, and Shannon 2013.

[30] Fortna 2008; Pouligny 2006; Séverine Autesserre, *The Trouble with the Congo: Local Violence and the Failure of International Peacebuilding* (Cambridge: Cambridge University Press, 2010).

[31] Séverine Autesserre, "Dangerous Tales: Dominant Narratives on the Congo and Their Unintended Consequences," *African Affairs*, February 2012: Advanced Access; Autesserre 2014; Christopher Clapham, "Being Peacekept," in *Peacekeeping in Africa*, ed. Oliver Furley and Roy May (Aldershot: Ashgate, 1998), 303–319.

[32] Sarah B. K. von Billerbeck, *Whose Peace? Local Ownership and United Nations Peacekeeping* (Oxford: Oxford University Press, 2017).

[33] Patrick M. Regan, "Third-Party Intervention and the Duration of Interstate Conflicts," *Journal of Conflict Resolution* 46, no. 1 (February 2002): 55–73; Aysegul Aydin and Patrick M. Regan, "Networks of Third-Party Interveners and Civil War Duration," *European Journal of International Relations* 18, no. 3 (September 2012): 573–597.

[34] Lise Morjé Howard, *UN Peacekeeping in Civil Wars* (New York: Cambridge University Press, 2008); Lise Morjé Howard and Anjali Kaushlesh Dayal, "The Use of Force in UN Peacekeeping," *International Organization* 72, no. 1 (Winter 2018): 71–103.

in multiple peace processes.[35] Where the pool of potential interveners is comparatively well-defined and finite, repeated interaction between combatants and guarantors creates the possibility of reputation-building, learning, and adjustment on both sides.[36] Combatants can consequently draw *ex ante* conclusions about guarantors' capability and willingness to help uphold their peace agreements – and these conclusions could structure the course of negotiation and war by changing combatants' willingness to reach a negotiated settlement in the first place, by altering their incentives for assistance, or by influencing their tactics and strategy.[37] Parties to conflict preparing to negotiate could look around the world and find instances in which the UN successfully helped combatants navigate the tricky demobilization and disarmament phases following a peace process – but they could also look around the world and observe cases where the UN manifestly failed to provide that security guarantee.

Much of the scholarship on third-party interventions, however, has largely envisioned interaction between combatants and guarantors as a single-shot game, thus ignoring the fact that combatants could gain vital information about guarantors based on the guarantor's behavior in previous cases, and that combatants might be actively distinguishing between the good and bad peacekeeping they observe – but there are a limited number of potentially credible third-party guarantors in the world. In most parts of the world, these guarantors are likely to be UN peacekeepers, but other potential interveners include great powers, such as the United States; regional hegemons, such as Brazil or India; or other multilateral forces, such as the African Union (AU) or North Atlantic Treaty Organization (NATO). Each of these actors may have intervened in past cases from which combatants could draw information. In this way, guarantors may build reputations across cases, and combatants can consequently draw conclusions about how

[35] Finnemore, drawing on Ruggie, identifies Western powers as the most likely interveners; the growth of UN and regional peacekeeping has changed this pool, but not to the point of unpredictability (Martha Finnemore, *The Purposes of Intervention* [Ithaca: Cornell University Press, 2003], 84).

[36] James E. Alt, Randall L. Calvert, and Brian D. Humes, "Reputation and Hegemonic Stability: A Game-Theoretic Analysis," *The American Political Science Review* 82, no. 1 (June 1988): 445–466.

[37] Beth Simmons and Zachary Elkins, "The Globalization of Liberalization: Policy Diffusion in the International Political Economy," *American Political Science Review* 98, no. 1 (February 2004).

effectively the guarantor might uphold the agreement. Guarantors may be playing an iterated game, and combatants may actually have strong preconceived ideas about what type of guarantor they are getting, and may choose their own strategies accordingly.

These two factors might reverberate across every stage of war termination. Indeed, in Barbara Walter's touchstone work on third-party security guarantees in civil wars, she notes that one of the key shortcomings in her coding of third-party security guarantees is that it "Ignores the effect an offer of assistance might have in getting combatants to sign a settlement (even if they do not then implement the terms) ... the fact that the UN [fails] to follow through does not mean that the offer [plays] no role in the final outcome of the peace process."[38] Put another way, Walter's work suggests that even those actions that the UN does *not* take might send negotiating actors meaningful signals about the credibility of their guarantee.

We are left with an empirical observation that reveals a theoretical problem with credible commitment theories of peace operations. United Nations peacekeepers are present in more conflict cases than any other military force, and most civil wars today receive peace operations at the request of at least one of the parties to the conflict.[39] If peacekeepers resolve the credible commitment problem that plagues war termination, then *any* peacekeeping failure should make wars less likely to end in peace agreements. Given trends in war termination that point toward greater negotiation over time, however, we know this is not the case.[40]

---

[38] Walter 2002, 66–67. Scholars like Isak Svensson ("Who Brings Which Peace: Biased versus Neutral Mediation and Institutional Peace Arrangements in Civil Wars," *Journal of Conflict Resolution* 53, no. 3 [2009]: 446–469) have built on her idea of guarantor credibility, but without expanding her game across multiple rounds or cases.

[39] Howard and Dayal 2018.

[40] United Nations, "A More Secure World: Our Shared Responsibility," Report of the High-Level Panel on Threats, Challenges and Change (New York, 2004); Virginia Page Fortna, "Where Have all the Victories Gone? Peacekeeping and War Outcomes," paper presented at the Annual Meeting of the American Political Science Association, September 2009; Peter Wallensteen, *Understanding Conflict Resolution*, 3rd ed. (London: Sage, 2012); Lise Morjé Howard and Alexandra Stark, "How Civil Wars End: The International System, Norms, and the Role of External Actors," *International Security* 42, no. 3 (Winter 2017/18): 127–171.

The empirical reality of the contemporary international system makes addressing this question imperative: Peacekeeping has become increasingly common in the post-Cold War world, and UN peacekeepers constituted the largest military presence deployed in conflict zones across the world as of 2020.[41] The UNSC legally authorizes all international force, leaving the organization's imprimatur on all missions alongside its staff, personnel, and infrastructure. A predictable group of actors – great powers, former colonial powers, NATO, or AU forces – usually helm even non-UN missions. Instructive examples need not be historical, as UN interventions are often simultaneous – in 2020, for example, UN Blue Helmets were deployed to thirteen separate missions worldwide.[42] Negotiating parties thus are constantly exposed to different information about how effective the UN will be as a third-party guarantor during the course of negotiation through both their own experiences and other ongoing UN interventions.

Thus, if we proceed along the rationalist and game-theoretic terms that anchor credible commitment theories, then combatants can evaluate the potential credibility of a guarantee in light of a historical record. Reputations are expectations about future behavior based on previous patterns of behavior,[43] and possible guarantors can acquire reputations for, among other things, being poor or strong enforcers of peace agreements, or weak or strong defenders of civilians in conflict, or for providing certain kinds of post-conflict reconstruction goods. Following a rationalist logic, combatants' negotiation strategies should be based at least in part on their observations of a guarantor's previous behavior, and on information they receive about other cases where the guarantor has kept the peace.[44] Barbara Walter's work on reputation and separatist movements indicates that reputation-building dynamics

---

[41] Anjali Dayal and Lise Morjé Howard, "Peace Operations," in *Oxford Handbook of International Organizations*, ed. Jacob Cogan, Ian Hurd, and Ian Johnstone (Oxford: Oxford University Press, 2016), chapter 9, 191–210; "Global Peacekeeping Data," UN Department of Peacekeeping Operations, https://peacekeeping.un.org/en/data.

[42] https://peacekeeping.un.org/en/where-we-operate.

[43] Avner Greif, "Reputations and Coalitions in Medieval Trade: Evidence on the Maghribi Traders," *Journal of Economic History* 49, no. 4 (December 1989): 857–882; Daryl G. Press, "The Credibility of Power: Assessing Threats During the Appeasement Crises of the 1930s," *International Security* 29, no. 3 (2004): 136–169.

[44] I draw loosely on Walter's game-theoretic models here. She deals with the idea that combatants do not necessarily know what kind of guarantor they are

can emerge even in comparatively short games, and that these dynamics influence both governments and their challengers.[45] If combatants are even minimally rational, strategic actors, then our baseline expectation should be that they respond to new information about peacekeepers with shifts in strategy whenever possible. If, further, we imagine – as many scholars do – that civil war negotiations are games of incomplete information, then combatants should make their choices of strategy based at least in part on their observations of a guarantor's previous behavior. The strategic interaction between potential combatants and potential guarantors is likely to be an iterated game of asymmetric incomplete information in which combatants develop beliefs about the type of guarantor they can anticipate.[46]

Acquiring a reputation in this model requires *information flows*, either between combatant groups or from world media to combatant groups,[47] which enable learning processes.[48] An explanation that takes learning into account does not dismiss the role of material or political factors, but rather argues that changing perceptions about these factors may have a powerful mediating influence on the direction, magnitude, and timing of policy changes or strategic decisions.[49] Learning can be a rational process of Bayesian updating; a learning process based on cognitive inference in which actors do not systematically look for relevant facts, but rather use available information that may be more vivid and psychologically striking than relevant or representative; or a

dealing with by specifying *uncertainty*, but she does not actually build any games by specifying types of potential guarantors (Walter 2002).

[45] Barbara F. Walter, *Reputation and Civil War: Why Separatist Conflicts Are So Violent* (Cambridge: Cambridge University Press, 2009).

[46] The game is asymmetric because we cannot reverse the strategies assigned to the players without changing the payoffs, as well.

[47] Greif 1989, 879.

[48] Learning is a change in cognitive structure as the result of experience or study, where cognitive structures may either be (1) specific historical analogies, which help narrow focus on a problem; (2) schemata or operating codes (generalized principles about life; a set of ideas about political life); and (3) ideological codes (Andrew Bennett, *Condemned to Repetition? The Rise, Fall, and Reprise of Soviet-Russian Military Interventionism 1973–1996* [Cambridge: MIT Press, 1999]), and there are several different models of learning, all of which encompass an enhanced understanding of the cause-and-effect relationships of factors in light of experience (even if this understanding is incorrect) (Covadonga Meseguer, *Learning, Policy Making, and Market Reforms* [Cambridge: Cambridge University Press, 2009]).

[49] Bennett 1999, 11.

cognitive process that takes place in a social context in which individuals observe both behavior and the consequences of behavior.[50] Most theories of international relations expect states will learn from each other's experiences, while many empirical studies focus on direct learning by foreign policymakers. Vicarious learning theories, as Benjamin Goldsmith argues, help bridge this divide by demonstrating how states can learn from vicarious successes – can imitate other state behaviors – and that this imitation helps shape beliefs following major failures.[51] Where there are multiple interventions into a conflict, combatants will also draw lessons from their own experiences. Where conflict has recurred in these cases, combatants are likely to interpret this as a history in which peacekeepers have failed to keep the peace.

The presence of the same peacekeepers across multiple civil wars can therefore change the social context in which combatants make their decisions, or, put another way, can change the information set on

---

[50] Weyland articulates four different types of learning, two of which are coercive, one of which is rational choice updating, and the last of which rests on cognitive psychology mechanisms like vividness (Kurt Weyland, "The Diffusion of Revolution: '1848' in Europe and Latin America," *International Organization* 63, no. 3 [2009]: 391–423). On cognitive inference, see, for example, Rose McDermott, *Risk-Taking in International Politics* (Ann Arbor: University of Michigan Press, 2001); for a full discussion of psychological theories in political science, see James Goldgeier and Philip Tetlock, "Psychology and International Relations Theory," *Annual Review of Political Science* 4, no. 1 (2001): 67–92. These two kinds of learning lend themselves to different hypotheses and observable implications: If combatants process previous guarantor behavior and rhetoric in a rational process of Bayesian updating, then they will draw lessons from the cases that are most similar to their own. If they process previous guarantor behavior and rhetoric using cognitive shortcuts, then they will draw lessons from the most vivid, recent, proximate, or well-reported cases. Given that my key concern here is not the manner in which previous behavior is processed, but rather the ways in which this previous behavior is consequential, social learning theory's idea of vicarious reinforcement is perhaps most relevant; I anticipate that belligerents will draw lessons from *both* the cases that are most similar to their own *and* from the most recent, vivid, and dramatic cases. While social learning theory is not without its own problems, it provides an intellectual framework for imagining how this kind of learning and cognition is a social process (see Albert Bandura, *Social Learning Theory* [Oxford: Prentice-Hall, 1977]).

[51] Martha Finnemore, *National Interests in International Society* (Ithaca: Cornell University Press, 1996); Jeffrey T. Checkel, "Why Comply? Social Learning and European Identity Change," *International Organization* 55, no. 3 (2001): 553–588; Benjamin Goldsmith, "Imitation in International Relations: Analogies, Vicarious Learning, and Foreign Policy," *International Interactions* 29, no. 3 (2013): 237–267.

which combatants base their decisions. If we begin with even the thinnest conception of social interaction possible, then peacekeepers' records of success and failure inform combatants through reputational mechanisms: Guarantors acquire reputations, and belligerents in civil wars weigh these reputations alongside other calculations as they decide whether to strike a bargain or continue waging war. Greif defines reputational mechanisms as "Establishing ex ante a linkage between past conduct and a future utility stream ... [so] an agent could acquire a reputation as honest, that is, he could credibly commit himself ex ante not to break a contract ex post."[52] In this vein of argument, reputations are expectations about behavior colored by evaluation or opinion.[53] In negotiations, for instance, guarantors or fellow combatants may acquire reputations as trustworthy (they will reciprocate cooperation or reward those that do) or untrustworthy (they will exploit cooperation or fail to sanction those that do)[54]; they could also simply acquire reputations as being good or bad at upholding the terms of an agreement.

Existing scholarship on reputation bridges both the game-theoretic perspectives that descend from Schelling and social psychological perspectives that posit reputation as a relational property between actors.

---

[52] Greif 1989, 858–859.

[53] Press distinguishes between "reputation" and "credibility." Credibility is the perceived likelihood that an actor will carry out its threats and promises, whereas reputation is the perception others hold of the state's pattern of past behavior (Press 2004, 3). For simplicity's sake, I incorporate both the perceived likelihood of future action and the perception of past behavior in my definition of reputation. One could certainly build a theory that *ex ante* classifies guarantor reputations according to strength, weakness, bias, or neutrality. I do not attempt to do so, however, because I believe these designations will vary according to belligerents' preferences. An actor that insurgents perceive as biased could equally well be perceived as strong by the state. As such, the conception of reputation that I begin with is to some extent open-ended, but is still consequential. The idea that guarantors generate "empty" reputations that might subsequently pattern behavior is very similar to North's conception of institutions – any kind of institution can pattern behavior, and one need not assign any kind of valence to an institution to make it causally consequential (Douglass North, *Structure and Change in Economic History* [New York: Norton, 1981]).

[54] Andrew Kydd, *Trust and Mistrust in International Relations* (Princeton: Princeton University Press, 2005); Robert Axelrod, *The Evolution of Cooperation* (New York: Basic Books, 1984); Elinor Ostrom, "Collective Action and the Evolution of Social Norms," *Journal of Economic Perspective* 14, no. 33 (Summer 2000): 137–158.

Social psychological approaches argue that we can only sensibly speak of reputations as situational, given the difficulties of interpreting actions: Reputations exist bounded between actors. Game-theoretic approaches, on the other hand, posit that in some situations and iterated games, actors can signal their types and intentions as conditional strategies in ways that are not simply relational between pairs of actors. This divide is fluid, and many scholars whose work is game-theoretic are wary of broad claims about reputation or diffuse reciprocity.[55]

In both strands of scholarship, however, the valence that actors attach to particular behaviors – the way they read the history of any case – is inextricably linked to what actors already believe and want. Accordingly, reputation does not inhere in guarantors. As Jonathan Mercer notes, no one keeps their reputation in their pocket, to be presented to interlocutors like a calling card – your reputation is what someone else thinks about you.[56] As Tomz defines it, an actor's reputation is the impression others hold about the actor's preferences and abilities. Put another way, reputations are beliefs about types.[57] In this sense, both game-theoretic and social psychological approaches converge around the importance of expectations, regardless of whether these expectations are analogous to game-theoretic types or information sets, or whether they represent webs of shared meaning in which actors are embedded.

Accordingly, whether reputation is a belief about a type or whether it is relational and perceptual, a shared international context allows combatants to learn something about guarantor behavior across cases, and combatants *must* learn from beyond the closed circuit of their own interaction with the UN. The UN's role in international peace and security need not be all-powerful to be consequential; instead, its institutions need only be recognizably authoritative[58] – if you expect the UN might become involved in your conflict or your peace process, then

---

[55] See, for example, George W. Downs and Michael A. Jones, "Reputation, Compliance, and International Law," *Journal of Legal Studies* 31, no. S1 (January 2002): S95–S114.

[56] Jonathan Mercer, *Reputation and International Politics* (Ithaca: Cornell Studies in International Affairs, 1996).

[57] Michael Tomz, *Reputation and International Cooperation: Sovereign Debt across Three Centuries* (Princeton: Princeton University Press, 2007), 17.

[58] Hurd 2008, 3.

what the UN has done elsewhere will become relevant to your considerations. And from any epistemological perspective, the central position that the UN occupies in contemporary conflict resolution must mean that the UN's behavior anywhere could inform combatants' decisions everywhere: A rationalist theory of the world supports this idea through game-theoretic ideas about reputation; social learning theories propose vicarious reinforcement mechanisms that argue people learn through observing the world around them, not merely through first-hand experience; and social constructivist theories of the world depend on shared webs of meaning that shape belief and action – indicating that in the post-Cold War world, civil war negotiations occur in a social context shaped by the UN's focal conflict resolution institutions.

## Preference, Strategy, and Desire

We need, then, a theory of what international actors can bring to post-conflict places that accounts for this social dimension of peace operations. Given that parties to conflict can look around the world and observe the UN in action, I argue that they are not solely driven by the desire for security guarantees or their efforts to address the credible commitment problem of war termination. Instead, I argue that belligerents seek the services of UN peacekeepers and peacemakers during civil war peace processes to secure a set of material, tactical, and symbolic benefits that are distinct from UN peacekeepers' role as guarantor to the peace agreement.

Scholars have focused their attention on how well peacekeepers uphold negotiated settlements and keep the peace, with success understood across time frames that span short-term to long-term, and in ways that range from learning within the UN, to strong enforcement of treaty terms, protection of civilians, and reduction of violent conflict.[59]

[59] See, for example, Gilligan and Sergenti 2008; Doyle and Sambanis 2000, 2006; Victoria K. Holt and Tobias C. Berkman, *The Impossible Mandate? Military Preparedness, The Responsibility to Protect, and Modern Peace Operations* (Washington, DC: The Henry L. Stimson Center, 2006); Lisa Hultman, "UN Peace Operations and Protection of Civilians: Cheap Talk or Norm Implementation?" *Journal of Peace Research* 50, no. 1 (2013): 59–73; Lisa Hultman, Jacob Kathman, and Megan Shannon, "Beyond Keeping Peace: United Nations Effectiveness in the Midst of Fighting," *American Political Science Review* 108, no. 4 (2014): 737–753; Paul F. Diehl, *Peace Operations*

Evaluating the success or failure of missions is vital, but missions have many other potentially consequential dimensions, and what combatants take away from any past event hinges on *interpretation*. Again, we can make this argument from multiple epistemological perspectives. Social constructivist, critical, and psychological theories are clear on this front: People understand similar experiences differently, and understand their own relationship to events differently than others do. So, for instance, while the United States might technically have won its 1991 war with Iraq, US policymakers could still have convinced themselves they lost; so, too, for instance, could shared experiences recast even such a stark enmity as the American Civil War into a bond of shared suffering for the population.[60] And if we take rationalist arguments on their own terms, as a practical consideration for combatants, mission success and failure may mean less than net loss and gain. Whether the mission will be beneficial for the parties to the agreement once it is on the ground may be independent of whether it keeps the peace, and in focusing on whether peacekeepers can forestall recidivism with information, technical support, and credible force, scholars have neglected the corollary question of what benefits demonstrably *in*credible, failing peacekeepers provide to combatants.

I argue negotiation may follow failure when there are good domestic reasons for negotiation that are not peace. If combatants are interested in the distributional contribution that international actors can make to the negotiation process, then peacekeepers are valuable not just for the peace they can help secure, but for other contributions they may make to the post-conflict space. I build on three separate traditions of peacekeeping scholarship here: Page Fortna's rationalist theory of peacekeeping; Lise Morjé Howard and Séverine Autesserre's constructivist

(London: Polity, 2008); Paul F. Diehl, Daniel Druckman, and James Wall, "International Peacekeeping and Conflict Resolution: A Taxonomic Analysis with Implications," *Journal of Conflict Resolution* 42, no. 1 (1998): 35–55.
[60] Goldgeier and Tetlock 2001; Wesley W. Widmaier, Mark Blyth, and Leonard Seabrooke, "Exogenous Shocks or Endogenous Constructions? The Meanings of Wars and Crises," *International Studies Quarterly* 51, no. 4 (December 2007): 747–759; Jack L. Amoureux and Brent J. Steele, eds., *Reflexivity and International Relations: Positionality, Critique, and Practice* (London: Routledge, 2015); Joshua Rovner, "Delusion of Defeat: The United States and Iraq, 1990–1998," *Journal of Strategic Studies*, 37, no. 4 (2014): 482–507; Drew Gilpin Faust, *This Republic of Suffering: Death and the American Civil War* (New York: Vintage, 2009).

work on how the UN's learning and organizational adaptions shape outcomes on the ground; and Sarah von Billerbeck's work on the local dimensions of peace operations. Fortna notes that "Peacekeepers can change incentives through carrots as well as sticks,"[61] and argues that even when missions do not have enforcement capability "to the extent that international aid and legitimacy are tied to cooperation, the presence of peacekeepers monitoring behavior can change the costs and benefits of war and peace. The impact of a peacekeeping mission on the economy of a war-torn country, or more direct payoffs to the peacekept, may also alter their incentives, making peace preferable to war."[62] Howard notes that peacekeepers very rarely exercise *coercive* force in defense of mandates, usually instead relying on other mechanisms of power; she writes "Nowhere – not in these cases nor anywhere else – have peacekeepers provided military-based security guarantees as the main cause of their effectiveness in keeping the peace. Actual militaries may legitimately and effectively employ compellence, but not peacekeepers. Peacekeepers effectively and legitimately use other types of power."[63] Finally, Sarah B. K. von Billerbeck, in her book on local ownership in peace operations, argues that "National and international actors understand ownership very differently and therefore have different expectations of their respective roles in peacekeeping."[64] She calls for "building theories of the interaction of international and national actors in a variety of contexts, while also contributing to the refinement of existing theories about various models of peacekeeping and the behavior of international organizations."[65]

These insights all apply to peace operations once they are on the ground. Extending them backward to earlier phases of conflict resolution, I investigate why combatants who may have no expectation of being held to the terms of their peace agreements would still seek the UN's assistance. I find the material and symbolic benefits the international community can bring to conflict-stricken places are key to understanding why combatants might choose to seek out the services of a failed security guarantor: Their beliefs and desires drive them to seek out the services of international actors even when peace is either unwanted or unlikely.

---

[61] Fortna 2008, 89.    [62] Ibid., 92–93    [63] Howard 2019, 186.
[64] von Billerbeck 2017, 13.    [65] Ibid., 154.

## Material, Tactical, and Symbolic Benefits

In his work on the benefits of stalemate in protracted wars, Charles King writes that "There is a political economy to warfare that produces positive externalities for its perpetrators. Seemingly perpetual violence in Sierra Leone, Myanmar, Liberia, and elsewhere has less to do with anarchy – of either the social or the institutional kind – than with the rational calculations of elites about the use of violence as a tool for extracting and redistributing resources."[66] In this model of warfare, settlement is less preferable than the drawn out process of war, or than a "frozen conflict" in which stalemate has economic and logistical benefits.[67] King focuses on the wars of Soviet succession, and writes, "In each of these conflicts, international involvement has been frequent if not frequently successful,"[68] and has come with otherwise unattainable infusions of international capital, humanitarian aid, and interest from humanitarian relief agencies.[69]

In a similar vein, Christopher Clapham argues peacekeepers and the peacekept view peacekeeping very differently:

> Peacekeepers necessarily view themselves as bringing *solutions* to the conflicts which they are concerned to resolve: that is why they are there ... they differ from participants, for whom peacekeepers are perceived as contributing *resources*, which may be captured and used by one or more of the internal parties to the conflict, in order to improve their own position within the conflict itself.[70]

In this sense, peacekeepers generate a post-conflict war economy through their presence and activities.[71] In the same vein, Naazneen Barma examines post-conflict peacebuilding, and argues that "peacebuilding outcomes are best understood as the result of a dynamic contest between two alternative

---

[66] Charles King, "The Benefits of Ethnic War: Understanding Eurasia's Unrecognized States," *World Politics* 53, no. 4 (July 2001): 524–552, 528.

[67] This vision of conflict is one that Fearon seems to exclude from the rationalist model. He writes, "Unless states enjoy the activity of fighting for its own sake, as a consumption good, then war is inefficient *ex post*" (383). There is good reason to believe, however, that war is a consumption good for at least some actors in all cases (James D. Fearon, "Rationalist Explanations for War," *International Organization* 49, no. 3 [Summer 1995]: 379–414).

[68] King 2001, 548.      [69] Ibid., 549.      [70] Clapham 1998, 306.

[71] Fortna 2008, 91–92; Pouligny 2006, 206; Peter Andreas, *Blue Helmets and Black Markets: The Business of Survival in the Siege of Sarajevo* (Ithaca: Cornell University Press, 2008).

visions of post-conflict political order—that of the international community and that of domestic elites."[72] While international actors, she writes, "viewed peace deals in the Democratic Republic of the Congo, Liberia, and Sudan as binding commitments among belligerents, the parties to conflict saw these settlements in more instrumental terms, such that they continually adapted their actions to the evolving context in ways that served their own conceptions of political order."[73]

My argument builds from these works: Negotiation can have positive externalities that are distinct from the settlement of conflict. International involvement in civil war settlements "has been frequent if not frequently successful,"[74] and governments and rebels who negotiate after peacekeeping failures may do so because negotiation affords them multiple benefits from the international community, some of which may have nothing to do with actual settlement of the conflict.

I investigate four potential benefits to negotiation. The first is peace. Some parties to negotiation will want little more than to strike a deal, end bloodshed and suffering, and mitigate the costs of war. Negotiation instead of fighting may also bring *tactical, material,* or *symbolic benefits.*

First, meeting with mediators and negotiators may afford combatants stints away from the battlefield to regroup, rearm, and launch unexpected attacks, buying belligerents time.[75] Negotiation may also offer tactical benefits by empowering factional leaders who represent their parties at the negotiation table,[76] or by granting domestic political parties a way to "launder" domestic political reforms that they would otherwise be unable to enact.[77]

---

[72] Naazneen H. Barma, *The Peacebuilding Puzzle: Political Order in Post-Conflict States* (Cambridge: Cambridge University Press, 2017) 3.

[73] Barma 2017, 103–104.     [74] King 2001, 548.

[75] Scott Wolford, Dan Reiter, and Clifford J. Carrubba make a similar point in "Information, Commitment, and War": "We assume shifts in power occur only in the event that the belligerents do not fight for some time. Thus, the kinds of power shifts most consistent with our analysis are advantages that accrue to states after agreeing to peace settlements and taking advantage of a pause in fighting, such as the opportunity to regroup or rearm, to launch a surprise attack or even to receive third-party assistance" (Scott Wolford, Dan Reiter, and Clifford J. Carrubba, "Information, Commitment, and War," *Journal of Conflict Resolution* 55, no. 4 [August 2011]: 556–579, 561).

[76] Clapham 1998.

[77] Kenneth W. Abbott and Duncan Snidal, "Why States Act through Formal International Organizations," *Journal of Conflict Resolution* 42, no. 1 (February 1998): 3–32.

Second, negotiations may also have straightforward material benefits. In this way, international involvement in negotiations can be a way of securing future rents, either because intervention will reconstitute the local economy in a way that benefits elites – Clapham, for instance, notes how peacekeepers in part fueled conflict in Somalia by reinvigorating the devastated local economy with their presence[78] – or because international intervention into conflict-torn states can evolve into state building. Post-conflict reconstruction, or "capacity building," is the redesign or construction of economic and social state institutions after civil war.[79] Combatants interested primarily in post-conflict or state-building assistance, either because they are seeking to convert foreign aid into rent or because they cannot reconstruct the state on their own, will seek a negotiated settlement overseen by a intervener that they know can assist them in this reconstruction, irrespective of whether this intervener has a good track record of upholding negotiated settlements.

Finally, negotiation may also have symbolic benefits for parties to a conflict. There may be important discursive aspects to negotiating whose value resides in the process and not the outcome.[80] These include: recognition from the international community as valid

---

[78] Clapham 1998, 307.

[79] Desha M. Girod, "Effective Foreign Aid Following Civil War: The Nonstrategic-Desperation Hypothesis," *American Journal of Political Science* 56, no. 1 (January 2012): 188–201; Charles T. Call and Elizabeth M. Cousens, "Ending Wars and Building Peace: International Responses to War-Torn Societies," *International Studies Perspectives* 9, no. 1 (February 2008); Bruce Jones and Rahul Chandran, *From Fragility to Resilience: Concepts and Dilemmas of State Building in Fragile Situations* (Organization for Economic Co-operation and Development, 2008); Francis Fukuyama, *State-Building: Governance and World Order in the Twenty-first Century* (Ithaca: Cornell University Press, 2004). On the perceived necessity of state-building among the prospective recipients of intervention, see David M. Edelstein, "Occupational Hazards: Why Military Occupations Succeed or Fail," *International Security* 29, no. 1 (Summer 2004): 49–91.

[80] This is similar but not identical to the argument that Fortna makes about the UN's moral authority as a deterrent to reigniting hostilities (Fortna 2008, 89). She and other scholars argue that peacekeeping "provides a moral barrier to hostile action" (Paul F. Diehl, *International Peacekeeping* [Baltimore: Johns Hopkins Press, 1994], 10; see also Doyle and Sambanis, 2006). Here, I argue instead that the UN is actually legitimating combatants as political actors through the negotiation process.

partners and legitimate political actors in the peace process[81]; the discursive value of airing grievances; and presenting the domestic population with an opportunity to view the parties to the conflict as actors who favor the consultative process of mediation and bargaining over the battlefield – put another way, they may simply believe it is politically important, and that it offers them legitimacy.

All of these benefits, with the exception of peace, may be available from guarantors with poor or excellent records securing negotiated settlements. Combatants who come to the bargaining table to rearm or regroup, to secure aid and economic infusions from third parties, or to cultivate their images and identities as appropriate, equal parties in conflict resolution and international recognition may have goals other than the successful implementation of their peace agreements. Peacekeeping after a negotiated settlement is usually understood as the solution to a security problem, but reframing it as a potential solution to a range of security, tactical, material, and symbolic problems may better position us to understand why and when parties welcome UN assistance.

Because both expectations about future behavior and desired outcomes from particular situations hinge on interpreting past action,[82] we need to develop a sense of the relationship between what combatants want and what they think about peacekeeping success and failure. Again, in order to compare my distributional hypothesis directly to credible commitment theories of war termination, I take these credible commitment theories on their own terms, and consider negotiations as processes in which participants have strategic situations and bargaining ranges. Failure can arise from many sources, and the basic contention here is that combatants will draw different lessons from potentially different cases or examples contingent on the strategic situation in which they find themselves. Here, I present a stylized account of three kinds of combatants. I classify their strategic situations according to their options aside from negotiation and how wide

[81] Klaus Schlicte and Ulrich Schneckener, "Armed Groups and the Politics of Legitimacy," *Civil Wars* 17 (2015): 409–424; Lee J. M. Seymour, "Legitimacy and the Politics of Recognition in Kosovo," *Small Wars & Insurgencies* 28, no. 4–5 (2017): 817–838; Reyko Huang, "Rebel Diplomacy," *International Security* 40, no. 4 (Spring 2016): 89–126.

[82] Robert Jervis, *The Logic of Images in International Relations* (Princeton: Princeton University Press, 1970); Mercer 1996.

their bargaining range is at the negotiating table, and argue that actors will assess peacekeeping failures contingent on their own strategic situations.

I argue there will be three broad factions in many negotiations: (1) desperate negotiators, or actors whose only options aside from negotiation are weak, who accordingly value negotiated outcomes over battlefield outcomes, and who have a wide range of acceptable bargaining outcomes as a result; (2) hardliners, or actors who have a limited bargaining range and who are willing and able to pursue actions other than negotiations; and (3) spoilers, who have strong outside options aside from negotiation. These three factions will crosscut the actual parties involved in the conflict: all parties, rebels and government alike, may include desperate negotiators, for whom negotiating *any* peace trumps a return to the battlefield; hardliners, who privilege securing material, tactical, and symbolic goals over striking a bargain; and spoilers, who ultimately have no interest in actually reaching a bargain, but who may negotiate nonetheless because doing so serves their immediate tactical goals.[83]

Combatants may believe peacekeeping failures stem from a wide variety of causes, and these beliefs may affect the way in which they interpret past peacekeeping failures. Observers will likely assume failure is precipitated by two groups of actors: The UN actors who supply peacekeeping and the combatants who request or are subject to peacekeeping. When observers locate failure within the UN, they may fault either mandate weakness or mandate implementation. When peacekeeping missions seemingly collapse because of combatants, observers may fault either spoilers or mistrust. These causes are not mutually exclusive; several may operate in each of the cases, and it is likely that observers will always blame the UN for failures it did not necessarily precipitate with its organizational shortcomings.

Mandate weakness stems from the UNSC and associated actors drafting a mandate inadequate to the scope or specifics of conflict on the ground. Missions may fail because they are inadequately equipped to succeed from their onset, and they may fail irrespective of combatant

---

[83] On spoilers, see Stephen John Stedman, "Spoiler Problems in Peace Processes," in *International Conflict Resolution after the Cold War*, ed. Paul C. Stern and Daniel Druckman (Washington, DC: National Academies Press, 2000). I draw on his conception of "inside" spoilers; outside spoilers will not negotiate at all, preferring instead to upset agreements from the outside.

commitment: Combatants may approach the drafting and implementation of peace agreements in good faith *or* bad faith and find the mission they receive is structurally unable to meet the difficulty of their situation with credible force, equipment, or legal authorization to do what combatants expect.

Failed mandate implementation occurs at the operational level. Peacekeepers may receive a mandate that is adequate to the situation on the ground, but they may subsequently fail to adequately execute the terms of their mandate and uphold the agreement. Missions may fail because actors on the ground cannot actively manage the conflict. Combatant commitment might precipitate failure here; active spoilers may make a peace agreement unenforceable in ways that appear identical to failures of mandate implementation, and weak mandate implementation and spoiler problems might be at first blush hard to distinguish from each other empirically. They could certainly be difficult to distinguish for combatants observing other cases.

Failure might also appear to be precipitated by combatants, either because of mistrust – the classical bargaining failure that drives credible commitment models of war termination – or because of spoiler problems. Distinguishing between these failures hinges on interpreting combatants' intentions: Spoilers never make a good-faith effort to abide by agreements and deliberately seek to upset them. Thus, spoilers may force mission failure irrespective of the UN's strength, whereas mistrust may befall any kind of combatant and may be alleviated by careful work on the UN's part.

In the shared social context of international peacekeeping, I expect that different kinds of combatants will draw different kinds of lessons from past peacekeeping failures, and that these lessons will reflect the multiple possible purposes negotiation can serve. If distributional concerns animate combatants' requests for peace operations, then we should see different rhetoric and behavior from combatants who are interested in negotiation for different reasons; we should see these combatants invoking different kinds of historical analogies to guide or justify their behavior; and we should see combatants expressing preferences for particular kinds of guarantors contingent upon their strategic situations and goals.

I test this hypothesis against the credible commitment theory of war termination's predictions for peacekeeping, which would anticipate that the desire for a security guarantee should dominate conversations and debate about the potential consequences of intervention – and which would anticipate that combatants would be most concerned about problems of mistrust, and peacekeeping failures driven by mistrust – at the bargaining table.

## Credible Commitment Theories

The credible commitment theory of war termination implicitly animates influential accounts of whether and how peacekeeping works.[84] Following Walter (2002) and Fearon (1995), this scholarship frames negotiation as a preferable alternative to war if combatants can surmount potential bargaining failures.[85] Peacekeeping, these scholars note, alleviates the credible commitment problem that prevents a negotiated settlement from supplanting a war that neither side is likely to win quickly or inexpensively.[86] Walter argues that we can understand civil war termination as a commitment problem, where the dangerous demobilization and disarmament phases of negotiated settlements explain why actors cannot strike a bargain *ex ante*. Her credible commitment theory of civil war resolution argues that successful negotiations and credible promises to abide by the original terms of the peace agreement rest, first, on whether a third party is willing to

---

[84] Fortna 2008; Gillian and Sergenti 2008; Walter 2002; Hultman, Kathman, and Shannon 2016.

[85] Fearon 1995, 379–414; Barbara Walter, "The Critical Barrier to Civil War Settlement," *International Organization* 51, no. 3 (1997): 335–364; Walter 2002.

[86] It is worth noting that peace operations are increasingly deployed even when there is no formally negotiated settlement, and that the UN's model of peacekeeping has moved beyond early "interpositional" peace operations to missions that are more like traditional military operations in their posture. These newer missions have been less effective but nonetheless continue to be authorized (Gilligan and Sergenti 2008; Hultman 2013; Howard and Dayal 2018) and the UN has increasingly become not just the overseer of agreements, but also the arbiter of situations in which civilians are falling victim to civil war, genocide, state failure, and state predation (Council on Foreign Relations, "More than Humanitarianism," Task Force Report No. 56 (Washington, DC, January 2006); Lisa Hultman, "UN Peace Operations and Protection of Civilians: Cheap Talk or Norm Implementation?," *Journal of Peace Research* 50, no. 1 (2013): 59–73. James Fearon and David Laitin, "Neotrusteeship and the Problem of Weak States," *International Security* 28, no. 4 (2004): 5–43. I return to this point in the conclusion.

enforce or verify demobilization and, second, on whether combatants are willing to extend power-sharing guarantees to one another.[87] Only under these two conditions will negotiation processes lead to civil war resolution.[88] Other literature in this vein notes that strong negotiated settlements ameliorate the security dilemma inherent in the first phases of peace.[89]

Important scholarship on peacekeeping has taken this insight as an implicit starting point in theorizing how intervention into civil wars works.[90] Hultman, Kathman, and Shannon, for example, tie peace-keepers' success in reducing battlefield hostilities to credible commitment dynamics: "When UN forces are deployed to a civil conflict," they write, "they function to resolve the security dilemma that exists between the belligerents. By providing security guarantees, UN missions assist the combatants in overcoming commitment problems that would otherwise make peaceful forms of resolution difficult to pursue. Security guarantees allow the belligerents to pull back from battlefield hostilities as a means of resolving the dispute."[91] "Having a credible security guarantee from UN peacekeepers in the form of troops on the ground," they continue, "allows belligerents to refrain from continued battlefield violence and initiate the process of demobilization. By signaling to the combatants that the UN mission has the capacity to protect the parties against attacks from their adversary, peacekeepers can reduce tensions and battlefield hostilities."[92]

Similarly, in their 2017 piece on UN peacekeeping and local conflict, Ruggeri, Dorussen, and Gizelis posit subnational mechanisms by which peacekeeping works: "Local peacekeeping," they write, "is expected to matter because it reassures local actors, deters resumption of armed hostilities, coerces parties to halt fighting, and makes

---

[87] Although I focus here on the "demand side" of the peacekeeping equation, agreements also materialize or fail because of supply-side issues such as political will or self-interest (see, for instance, Stephen John Stedman, Donald Rothchild, and Elizabeth M. Cousens, *Ending Civil Wars: The Implementation of Peace Agreements* [Boulder: Lynne Rienner, 2002]; Howard 2008).

[88] Walter 2002, 5–6.

[89] Matthew Hoddie and Caroline Hartzell, "Civil War Settlements and the Implementation of Military Power-Sharing Arrangements," *Journal of Peace Research* 40, no. 3 (May 2003): 303–332.

[90] On this point, see Fortna 2008; Fortna and Howard 2008.

[91] Hultman, Kathman, and Shannon 2014, 737.     [92] Ibid., 740–741.

commitment to agreements credible."[93] "Effective peacekeeping," in their model, "halts the escalation and spread of conflict, it maintains trust in the peace process, and avoids zones of lawlessness ... peacekeepers deter the onset of local conflict when their presence and actions discourage parties to use force."[94] In Hegre, Hultman, and Nygård's omnibus 2018 piece evaluating peacekeeping efficacy, "Evaluating the Conflict-Reducing Effect of UN Peacekeeping Operations," credible commitments also undergird the first of three pathways – preventing conflict from breaking out or recurring – through which peacekeeping works.[95]

These arguments represent a strand of scholarship on peacekeeping that draws on Walter's influential account of third-party involvement in civil war termination; Walter's argument, in turn, derives its explanations of credibility problems in contemporary civil wars from the classic Waltzian and defensive realist conceptions of the security dilemma.[96] Accordingly, these arguments frame *mistrust* as the central problem that international actors must solve to help combatants end civil war. Following this logic, credible commitment accounts of the way peacekeeping works would assume that all parties to a conflict are similarly motivated at the negotiating table, and that they should seek the services of a guarantor who can guarantee their security: International actors are desirable because they mitigate mistrust by ensuring the credibility of a negotiated settlement. This understanding of international involvement in peace processes therefore implies that good peacekeeping and bad peacekeeping should have different effects on combatants' willingness to strike a bargain: Combatants who expect to receive bad peacekeepers should not expect these peacekeepers to alleviate the credible commitment problem that plagues civil war termination.

By the internal logic of credible commitment theories of war termination, if parties to a conflict do not trust one another, and if they have no reason to have faith in the UN's capabilities, they may continue

---

[93] Ruggeri, Dorussen, and Gizelis 2017, 163.       [94] Ibid., 164–166.
[95] Hegre, Hultman, and Nygård, 2018.
[96] Kenneth Waltz, *Theory of International Politics* (New York: McGraw-Hill, 1979); Robert Jervis, "Cooperation under the Security Dilemma," *World Politics* 30, no. 2 (January 1978): 167–214; Jeffrey W. Taliaferro, "Security Seeking under Anarchy: Defensive Realism Revisited," *International Security* 25, no. 3 (Winter 2000/01): 128–161.

fighting, or they may attempt to make other arrangements to ensure the credibility of their bargain – but they should not repeatedly turn to the UN for assistance overseeing their settlement without giving observers any indication that the UN's track record as guarantor concerns them.[97]

Credible commitment theories of peacekeeping are anchored in rationalist approaches to war. As Fearon writes, the central puzzle in the rationalist approach is: What prevents states from reaching an *ex ante* agreement that avoids the costs of battle they know will be paid *ex post* if they go to war?[98] In this approach, most wars are the result of bargaining failures: States would prefer to achieve their goals via negotiation instead of the expensive, bloody process of war. Instead, they continue fighting because they cannot cleanly, clearly divide what they seek; because a lack of information obscures the path to a negotiated agreement; and because they cannot trust the other side to uphold their end of the deal – the classic bargaining failures of indivisible stakes, private information, and credible commitment problems.

In their subsequent contributions to the literature on crisis bargaining and rationalist explanations for international war, Gartzke, Kirchner, Slantchev, and Reiter all critique this framing of war.[99] They produce powerful qualifications on the indeterminacy of rationalist theories, the degree to which leaders are risk-averse, the indivisibility of certain kinds of issues, and the extent to which private information generates a risk for war. Two features to this body of scholarship are relevant here. First, international structure is a key dimension of these arguments: The anarchic nature of international politics itself produces commitment problems between states at war.

---

[97] The conflicts under consideration here are distinct from the rational, wanted wars that Fearon discusses. These occur when no negotiated settlements exist that both sides prefer to gambling on military conflict, and where both sides have a positive expected utility for fighting that is greater than the expected utility of remaining at peace (383–386). By Fearon's logic, these cases are not candidates for negotiation.

[98] Fearon 1995, 384.

[99] Erik Gartzke, "War Is in the Error Term," *International Organization* 53, no. 3 (Summer 1999): 567–587; Dan Reiter, "Exploring the Bargaining Model of War," *Perspectives on Politics* 1, no. 1 (March 2003): 27–43, Branislav L. Slantchev, "The Principle of Convergence in Wartime Negotiations," *American Political Science Review* 97, no. 4 (November 2003): 621–632.

Second, asymmetric information and commitment problems constitute central issues in "the most prominent rationalist accounts of war,"[100] often at the expense of the distributional concerns that may have animated conflict to begin with.

First, the absence of a centralized authority between states is key to rationalist accounts of international war – where no authority sits above the sovereign state, no authority can easily, credibly enforce war-ending bargains between states. Commitment problems are therefore likely to derail negotiated settlements to end wars. The literature on third-party guarantors in civil war, however, including some of Fearon's own work on intrastate conflict, proceeds from the idea that commitment problems *can* be meaningfully attenuated in civil wars.[101]

In recent years, at the subnational level, as Reiter writes, "The international community continues to experiment with a variety of conflict resolution and prevention tools, such as ethnic partition in civil conflicts, war crimes tribunals, and the varied uses of international peacekeeping and peace-enforcing troops; awareness of the outcomes of these experiments can only improve and facilitate the development and test of the bargaining model."[102] Although Reiter does not make this argument, the international community's deliberate testing of these tools across conflict, and its work to refine them across cases, indicates that conflict resolution is a social process for combatants in civil wars – conflicts may be meaningfully responsive to one another. Accordingly, for actors in these conflict cases, international relations have a meaningful hierarchy: They may be patterned around the UN's conflict resolution mechanisms.

Investigating the role of third-party guarantors in civil wars also brings us to the second relevant feature of this scholarship: The extent to which rationalist accounts sideline distributional concerns at the expense of informational and commitment concerns, and thus how these models treat both war and negotiation as commitment and informational problems *instead of* distributional processes.

---

[100] Wolford, Reiter, and Carrubba 2011, 574.
[101] See, for example, Walter 2002 and 1997; James Fearon, "Why Do Some Civil Wars Last So Much Longer than Others?" *Journal of Peace Research* 41, no. 3 (2004): 275–301; and Virginia Page Fortna, "Does Peacekeeping Keep Peace? International Intervention and the Duration of Peace after Civil War," *International Studies Quarterly* 48, no. 2 (2004): 269–292.
[102] Reiter 37.

Distributional concerns initially animate rationalist explanations for war: Actors are fighting over *something*. Given the costs of war, self-interested people ought to prefer acquiring that *something* in nonviolent ways. Distributional concerns thus lie at the rationalist model's heart, but most rationalist explanations for war quickly turn to commitment problems and information scarcity as the true engines of ongoing conflict. Dan Reiter's book *How Wars End* and Robert Powell's "War as a Commitment Problem" both exemplify this move[103] – but as Ron Hassner argues, the shift underlies all rationalist models that treat issue indivisibility as a simple framing problem.[104] These models seem to argue that distribution ceases to be a meaningful obstacle to negotiation if goods can be easily divided; if creative diplomats come up with novel ways to slice a throne, a city, a sacred space, a diamond mine, or a president's powers into discrete tranches to serve all sides of a conflict; and if governments can avoid developing reputations that encourage cascading claims to territory or power from future insurgent groups.[105]

Bargaining ranges that overlap in some way are all that is therefore required to end war, but many arguments in this vein envision the process of war itself as primarily a process of revealing information about state capabilities.[106] Thus, although these theories begin by

---

[103] Dan Reiter, *How Wars End* (Princeton: Princeton University Press, 2009); Robert Powell, "War as a Commitment Problem," *International Organization* 60, no. 1 (Winter 2006): 169–203.

[104] Ron Hassner offers an alternative, interpretivist understanding of indivisibility, arguing that rationalist scholars fundamentally misunderstand why some kinds of goods cannot truly be divided (Ron E. Hassner, *War on Sacred Grounds* [Ithaca: Cornell University Press, 2009]).

[105] See, for example, Thomas Schelling, *Arms and Influence* (New Haven: Yale University Press, 1966); Monica Duffy Toft, *The Geography of Ethnic Violence: Identity, Interests, and the Indivisibility of Territory* (Princeton: Princeton University Press, 2005); Barbara F. Walter, "Building Reputation: Why Governments Fight Some Separatists but Not Others," *American Journal of Political Science* 50 (April 2006): 313–330; Walter 2009.

[106] Darren Filson and Suzanne Werner, "A Bargaining Model of War and Peace: Anticipating the Onset, Duration, and Outcome of War," *American Journal of Political Science* 46, no. 4 (2002): 819–838; Robert Powell, "Bargaining and Learning While Fighting," *American Journal of Political Science* 48, no. 20 (2004): 344–361; Alastair Smith and Allan C. Stam, "Bargaining and the Nature of War," *Journal of Conflict Resolution* 48, no. 6 (2004): 783–813; R. Harrison Wagner, "Bargaining and War," *American Journal of Political Science* 44, no. 3 (2000): 469–484; Slantchev 2003.

considering how goods can be divided, distributional concerns subsequently become secondary to the process of conflict termination. But if – as per Clausewitz – war and politics are simply strategic choices along the same spectrum, then distributional concerns should remain *casus belli* once war or negotiation begin, no matter whether parties to a conflict acquire more information about their adversaries or guarantors to make their commitments credible.

Agreement failure highlights the issue. As Suzanne Werner and Amy Yuen argue in their work on peace agreements, the recurrence of war is not just a commitment problem, but also a distributional problem: Both the terms and strength of the agreement are independently consequential for the likelihood of the peace holding *and* endogenous to combatants' commitment to holding the peace.[107] Flexible agreements can prevent recidivism when post-agreement material conditions change, but no agreement can withstand parties committed to returning to war: In some instances, "belligerents deliberately choose war because they believe that a new war will lead to a better settlement than previously realized."[108] If this is the case, then surely combatants might also look at third-party guarantors as a way to secure a better distributional outcome for themselves at the negotiating table.

We have, then, two sets of theories with comparable core assumptions that we can test against one another. United Nations interventions in civil wars provide combatants with information both about the credibility of the guarantee and about the behavior and intentions of the opposite side. In theory, then, UN peacekeepers alleviate the credible commitment problem, and they work to minimize the information problem. If combatants have good reason to believe that the UN cannot actually provide them with a strong, credible guarantee, however, then we need to ask what the UN *can* provide them. Even if negotiation with a failed guarantor is the best of bad options for parties brought to the brutal brink of war, even if the UN is the necessary port of last resort for parties seeking international assistance, and even if there is no way for warring parties to secure a better guarantor for their agreement, we should still see evidence that they consider the UN's past performance, that they try to assess the likelihood of failure

---

[107] Werner and Yuen 2005, 261–292.     [108] Ibid., 288.

in their own case, and that they try to mitigate the likelihood of failure in any way they can. Consequently, we must ask how placing distributional concerns back at the heart of bargaining models of war might shift our understanding of how third-party guarantees, peace processes, and intervention work. Page Fortna's influential casual theory of peace operations takes up this question – she argues that one of the pathways through which peacekeeping works is by shifting combatants' incentives to make peace more profitable than war.[109] The theory I have presented here builds on her work, arguing that, beyond providing security guarantees, the material, symbolic, and tactical benefits associated with UN intervention can also shape the processes of negotiating an end to war.

If civil wars take place in a shared international context and are bound together by international peacekeepers, then international involvement in negotiations after peacekeeping failures becomes puzzling. Credible commitment theories that frame mistrust between parties to conflict as the key barrier to peace fall short where parties to conflict actively mistrust international actors themselves. The distributional hypothesis helps us explain how peacekeeping works when warring parties have good reasons to believe the international community cannot remedy traditional bargaining failures – and how local and international actors may have consequentially different expectations about peace, peacekeeping, and interventions.[110]

## Observable Implications

Accordingly, we have two theories to test: a theory where combatants are motivated to seek out the UN's involvement by many different goals at the negotiating table, and a theory where they are motivated *primarily* by the desire to address security concerns.

---

[109] Fortna 2008 summarizes these arguments on pages 89 and 124–125.

[110] Here, my argument parallels and supports Sarah von Billerbeck's insights on local ownership in peace operations – particularly her argument that "national and international actors understand ownership very differently and therefore have different expectations of their respective roles in peacekeeping" (13), and her call for "building theories of the interaction of international and national actors in a variety of contexts, while also contributing to the refinement of existing theories about various models of peacekeeping and the behavior of international organizations" (154) (von Billerbeck 2017).

The bulk of this book's analysis hinges on process traced negotiations in Rwanda and Guatemala. Process tracing is a method that enables both theory development and plausibility probing,[111] and which draws on "diagnostic pieces of evidence that yield insight into causal connections and mechanisms, providing leverage for adjudicating among hypotheses."[112] Process tracing can enable scholars to test competing explanations against one another, ruling out some while confirming that others stand up to scrutiny,[113] and updating the likelihood that an explanation operates given a plurality of persuasive evidence.[114]

Cases were selected using a chronological analysis that I outline in the next chapter, which identifies three most-likely time periods for reputational effects before the early 2010s: (1) from 1992 to August of 1993, a period bookended by the peacekeeping successes in El Salvador and the conclusion of the Arusha Accords in Rwanda, with variation in the success of peace operations during that time; (2) from October 1993, when the Black Hawk Down incident in Somalia took place, to August 1994, when the Rwandan genocide concluded; and (3) between June 1995 and December 1996, eighteen months that were framed by failures in the Balkans and success in Guatemala. These are times in which the UN's performance is likely to be visible and clear to parties in ongoing peace processes. Although actors may of course draw lessons from cases at other times, if there is no evidence that they examine the UN's past performance in these periods, there is unlikely to be evidence of it at other times.

As I discuss at length in Chapter 3, examining the Rwandan and Guatemalan peace processes allows me to exploit variation in exposure to success and failure; regional variation; and variation in whether combatants experience within-case failure or not. While my case study

---

[111] Alexander L. George and Andrew Bennett, *Case Studies and Theory Development in the Social Sciences* (Cambridge, MA: MIT Press, 2005), 214.

[112] David Collier, Henry E. Brady, and Jason Seawright, "Outdated Views of Qualitative Methods: Time to Move On," *Political Analysis* 18, no. 4 (2010): 506–513, 506.

[113] David Collier and Henry E. Brady, *Rethinking Social Inquiry: Diverse Tools, Shared Standards* (Lanham: Rowman and Littlefield, 2004), 260.

[114] Andrew Bennett, "Disciplining Our Conjectures: Systematizing Process Tracing with Bayesian Analysis," in *Process Tracing: From Metaphor to Analytic Tool*, ed. Andrew Bennett and Jeffrey Checkel (Cambridge: Cambridge University Press, 2014).

method is process tracing, and not controlled case-comparisons, examining the Rwandan and Guatemalan peace processes together does allow me to account for some potentially confounding factors. The cases took place over roughly the same time period, allowing me to similarly account for the way the end of the Cold War reconstituted some peacekeeping practices. Both processes unfolded in small countries that experienced genocide during the course of internationalized civil wars with ethnic dimensions. Both cases included both P5 and regional organizations' involvement in negotiation processes alongside UN involvement, with the AU and the OAS figuring prominently in negotiation processes. Rwanda is a critical case, given its role in structuring contemporary peacekeeping and peacemaking policy, while Guatemala is a most-likely case for the credible commitment hypothesis: Given the UN's unambiguous success[115] next door in El Salvador, the parties to the Guatemalan Civil War were likely to have a very positive view of the UN's capability as a guarantor to the peace.

I examine the cases for causal process observations of both the credible commitment and distributional hypotheses. Within-case observable implications for the distributional hypothesis hinge on the strategic situation in which negotiating parties find themselves. Desperate negotiators who look at past failures and see their source in mandate weakness may be reluctant to begin bargaining without clear indications of interest from Security Council members; accordingly, they should advocate at the bargaining table for strong missions with robust mandates for civilian protection and ceasefire monitoring; they should be willing to buy the peace with concessions; and they should for the most part adhere to ceasefires, not using negotiating time primarily to regroup, rearm, or relaunch attacks. Desperate negotiators who find the sources of failure at the operational level or in mistrust may also advocate for a robust enforcement mission with a strong military force. This should reveal itself in both advocacy to the Security Council for a strong mandate and in strong preferences over who serves on the ground in the mission. In each instance, combatants should invoke past failures as cautionary tales, and should cull lessons from cases that went badly. If they believe that failure comes through spoilers, then we should see desperate negotiators looking backward to

---

[115] Howard 2008.

other cases of failures and underlining how they themselves are different, more committed, and more sincere.

Hardliners seek the material, tactical, and symbolic benefits of negotiation; they may be willing and able to continue fighting on the battlefield, but be primarily pursuing a narrow range of outcomes that are better procured through a peace process. They may be more interested in the rent, time, and status that negotiation can afford them than they are in peacekeepers' ability to keep the peace. As such, they are likely to sit down at the negotiating table after it becomes clear they are unlikely to win easily on the battlefield – and because peace at any cost is not necessarily their primary goal, they may be equally likely to sit down with either failed or successful guarantors. If they believe failure has its sources in mandate failure, they may lobby for a mandate that is strong in ways other than agreement enforcement, such as statebuilding, or refugee resettlement. If they believe failure has its sources in mandate implementation, they may advocate more strongly for other aspects of the mission than for forces on the ground, or they may advocate for participation from a weak and willing force if it comes with either recognition from the international community, time away from the battlefield, or an infusion of cash into the local economy. They are likely to be tough negotiators, attempting to maximize what they can secure from both their opponents and from the mediators representing the international community. They are unlikely to abide by ceasefires, and instead are likely to regroup and rearm during negotiation processes, either to strengthen their hand at the negotiation table or to relaunch war if concessions at the negotiating table are insufficient. If my theory is correct, then they will be comparatively uninterested in whether failure came from spoilers or mistrust, and they are likely to draw lessons from cases where combatants secured large dividends from the international community irrespective of the success of the agreement.

Finally, spoilers are not genuinely interested in the success of agreements. They may feel as though they must negotiate for the temporary sake of international legitimacy, or they may be compelled to do so by other members of their coalition, but they are more likely to see negotiation as a brief break from the battlefield in service of tactical ends. They may use time at the bargaining table to regroup and rearm; they may have an expressed presence for either previously failed or weak guarantors; and they may invoke past failures as positive lessons

Table 2.1 *Summary of observable implications*

*Observable Implications for Distributional Hypothesis: Combatants are
attentive to the UN's performance in other cases and seek the UN out after
peacekeeping failures because they seek the alternative benefits of
negotiation that are only available through international involvement.*

- Actors negotiating a peace agreement with international involvement should
  make direct and explicit reference to the UN's past performance and should
  invoke its record of success or failure elsewhere in their interactions with one
  another and with international actors.
- Within-case observable implications hinge on warring parties' strategic
  situations and how they perceive the UN's record of success and failure.
  Different kinds of actors should draw different lessons from different cases.
- Parties to negotiation may seek the UN's functions as a security guarantor,
  but they may also seek one of the alternative benefits of bargaining with
  international involvement: the material, tactical, and symbolic benefits that
  the international community can confer on the peace process. Alleviating the
  credible commitment problem may not be the most important benefit
  they seek.

*Observable Implications for Credible Commitment Hypothesis: Combatants
are primarily concerned with the UN's ability to serve as a security
guarantor.*

- Belligerents will be primarily concerned with the UN's capabilities as a
  security guarantor and with its ability to manage the credible commitment
  problem of war termination.
- Where we see negotiations after peacekeeping failures, we should expect
  negotiating coalitions that are largely dominated by desperate negotiators
  and by actors who attempt to offset the UN's weakness as a security
  guarantor with as many other alternative arrangements as possible.

among themselves. We should see little evidence that they are concerned with the intentions of other combatants whose agreements have
failed, except insofar as they may specifically look to and draw on
other cases where spoilers upset internationally brokered and overseen
settlements.

In each case where we see negotiation despite failure, there is likely
be some combination of desperate negotiators who need the peace
process to conclude swiftly, hardliners, and spoilers, and we should
see these actors drawing different lessons from different cases. In cases

where we see negotiation despite peacekeeping failures, we should see combatants either actively working to secure a better guarantee from the guarantor; to secure one of negotiation's alternative benefits; or actively discussing how their case, this time, is different from past peacekeeping failures. When negotiations follow peacekeeping successes, we should see these actors incorporating lessons from successful cases into their negotiating goals contingent on their own strategic situations and interests. If there is no evidence of these processes, and no evidence that negotiating parties are looking across peacekeeping cases to form their negotiation strategies, then my theory is wrong.

If the credible commitment hypothesis operates instead, then we should see belligerents who are primarily concerned with the UN's capabilities as a security guarantor. Where we see negotiations after peacekeeping failures, we should expect negotiating coalitions that are largely dominated by desperate negotiators and by actors who attempt to offset the UN's weakness as security guarantor with as many other alternative arrangements as possible. Where negotiations follow peacekeeping successes, we should see combatants turn to the UN for its ability to alleviate the credible commitment problem of war termination, and we should see these combatants attempt to maximize the UN's ability to help them manage mistrust between opposing factions in the functions they assign to peace operations at the bargaining table. Table 2.1 summarizes the observable implications of each hypothesis.

Where negotiations follow peacekeeping successes, we should see combatants turn to the UN for its ability to alleviate the credible commitment problem of war termination, and we should expect that these combatants attempt to maximize the UN's ability to help them manage mistrust between opposing factions in the functions they assign to peace operations at the bargaining table.

# 3 | *Methods and Case Selection*

The previous chapter argued that peace operations take place in the social context of other peace operations – and if we consider how they are socially bound to one another, then what parties to conflict hope to receive from peace operations must extend beyond a security guarantee to a full range of other tactical, material, and symbolic goals. The rest of this book is a theory-building and theory-probing endeavor: I put flesh on a theory of how the alternative benefits of bargaining lead combatants to seek out UN peacekeepers, and I probe how the credible commitment theory of war termination drives peace operations. In this chapter, I outline first the method by which I selected cases, and then the evidence and tools I use to process trace the Rwandan and Guatemalan peace processes. Chapters 4 and 5 examine these peace processes in detail. I end this chapter with a discussion of generalizability and how we should contextualize these cases.

Two case studies constitute the bulk of this book's empirical work. These cases were selected using the most-similar case selection strategy, with as many commonalities between them as possible, except for variation in the success of nearby peace operations. I do not undertake comparative case analysis, however, because I am not primarily or strictly interested in what a comparison between the two cases reveals about UN involvement in peace processes. Instead, I am interested in what *each case* reveals about the larger question. A most-similar case selection strategy allows me to focus on how perceptions of success and failure in nearby peace operations shape combatants' attitudes toward UN involvement. Subsequently, each case constitutes an individually process traced investigation, with fine-grained descriptive evidence from many sources laid out to link the theoretically posited cause (perceptions of the UN's success as a security guarantor) with empirically observed outcomes (seeking the UN's involvement in uphold-ing a peace agreement).[1]

Within each case, I weigh evidence for both my theory and the credible commitment theory of war termination. Both theories rest on explicit claims about causal processes, and process tracing is accordingly the best method to assess how well each theory explains the world.[2] Process tracing is particularly effective for assessing competing explanations, and represents an especially useful method when the specific mechanisms of a theory are less specified than the general theoretical relationship between independent and dependent variables.[3] It cannot tell us how *much* of some outcome a specific cause might explain – but it can help us see which theoretical mechanisms are best illuminated by a diverse, plural body of evidence.

## Case Selection

Selecting cases first requires clear definitions of peacekeeping successes and failures, then a sense of where these successes and failures are located, and finally a sense of the timing of peace processes relative to these successes and failures. Only by building out this body of evidence can we choose cases that vary in what kinds of nearby and recent successes and failures parties to conflict can observe while making their own negotiation decisions.

I begin by examining the frequency and incidence of success, failure, and negotiation between 1989 and 2004–2005, a period that encom-passes the end of the Cold War and peacekeeping's first set of post-Cold War transformations. Focusing on this time period allows me to take early works on peacekeeping efficacy on their own terms, testing my theory against the core cases that rationalist theories of peacekeeping build from, which is particularly vital given that the processes under consideration here involve learning over time. The charts I present in the next sections of the chapter are purely descriptive; choosing cases requires a sense of what combatants surveying the world would have

---

[1] Andrew Bennett, "Process Tracing and Causal Inference," in *Rethinking Social Inquiry: Diverse Tools, Shared Standards*, 2nd ed., ed. Henry E. Brady and David Collier (Lanham, MD: Rowman and Littlefield, 2010), 207–219.

[2] James Mahoney, "After KKV: The New Methodology of Qualitative Research," *World Politics* 62, no. 1 (2010): 120–147.

[3] Alexander L. George and Andrew Bennett, *Case Studies and Theory Development in the Social Sciences* (Cambridge, MA: MIT Press, 2005); John Gerring, "Is There a (Viable) Crucial-Case Method?" *Comparative Political Studies* 40, no. 3 (2007): 231–253.

seen, not a more scholarly evaluation of efficacy. If we want to know whether peacekeeping is an effective tool, we need the statistical analysis and deep case studies that so many important studies have undertaken. These assessments, however, cannot help us explain whether *combatants* think peacekeeping works. First, the cases I evaluate precede aggregate statistical scholarship on peacekeeping efficacy – parties to conflict in the early 1990s could not have known whether peacekeeping *was*, in the aggregate, an effective tool to end civil wars, because most studies making this assessment came later. Second, even *with* available studies, people are not necessarily instinctively statistical thinkers, and translating the probabilistic reasoning that undergirds statistical models to real-world outcomes can be a tricky, remote undertaking even in information-rich environments.[4] Accordingly, if we want to know how combatants themselves evaluate peacekeeping efficacy, we may need blunter tools – a catalog of success, failure, and negotiation that can help give us a rough sense of what combatants might have seen when they looked at peacekeepers around the world and considered their negotiation processes.

The catalog of success, failure, and negotiation I present in the rest of the chapter is a unified, additive list. It begins with Page Fortna's data – because I am building from her theory, I worked initially within the timeframe from which she builds her theory. It then adds incidents of success, failure, and negotiation by drawing on data from Doyle and Sambanis' 2000 and 2006 works; UCDP/PRIO's 2008 Peace Agreements dataset; Howard's 2008 book on UN peacekeeping in civil wars; and the UN's Department of Peacekeeping Operations, in that order.[5] I reference Monica Duffy Toft's 2010 book on peace agreements for some cases, as well. The final list adheres as closely to Fortna's original coding protocol as possible while striving to generate

---

[4] Nate Silver, "The Media Has a Probability Problem: The Media's Demand for Certainty – and Its Lack of Statistical Rigor – Is a Bad Match for Our Complex World," *FiveThirtyEight*, September 21, 2017, https://fivethirtyeight.com/features/the-media-has-a-probability-problem/.

[5] Virginia Page Fortna, *Does Peacekeeping Work? Shaping Belligerents' Choices after Civil War* (Princeton: Princeton University Press, 2008); Michael Doyle and Nicholas Sambanis, "International Peacebuilding: A Theoretical and Quantitative Analysis," *American Political Science Review* 94, no. 4 (December 2000): 779–801; Lotta Harbom, Stina Högbladh, and Peter Wallensteen, "Armed Conflicts and Peace Agreements," *Journal of Peace Research* 43, no. 5 (2006); Lise Morjé Howard, *UN Peacekeeping in Civil Wars* (New York: Cambridge University Press, 2008); Monica Duffy Toft, *Securing the Peace: The Durable Settlement of Civil Wars* (Princeton: Princeton University Press, 2010).

a cumulative list of mission performance and negotiated settlements from peacekeeping's immediate post-Cold War efflorescence.[6] Tables 3.1, 3.2, and 3.3 illustrate trends in peacekeeping and negotiation outcomes for civil wars since 1989.[7] I draw on them to select cases and to ascertain what kinds of peacekeeping success and failure parties approaching the negotiating table might observe.

Table 3.1 is a list of peacekeeping failures. "Failure" is the collapse of any peace agreement overseen by a guarantor, and it is drawn from Fortna's definition of mission failure. It includes the failure of truces and negotiated settlements.[8]

Between 1989 and 2004, the Security Council authorized fifty-three peace operations. Fourteen of these major missions failed, which makes for a failure rate of slightly more than one-fourth.[9] In contrast to the frequent public perception of peacekeeping as a failed enterprise,[10] these are comparatively favorable statistics – particularly when we consider that peacekeeping is often the Hail Mary solution to an extremely difficult problem. From the policymaker's perspective, and from the perspective of the peacekept in each of these cases, this is of course

---

[6] Fortna's data is survival data primarily dealing with the determinants and recurrence of conflict. As a result, many of the revisions I make to her data have no bearing on her analysis but are consequential to my question.

[7] Civil war is defined in accordance with Doyle and Sambanis (2000, 2006) as an armed conflict with the following attributes: a war that has caused more than one thousand battle deaths; which has presented a challenge to the sovereignty of an internationally recognized state; which took place within the recognized borders of that state; which involved the state as one of the principle warring parties; and in which rebels were able to both mount an organized military opposition to the state and to exact significant causalities from the state.

[8] I include the failure of truces alongside agreements on the grounds that combatants may not distinguish between the two. Negotiated settlements are coded according to the protocol that Fortna established in *Does Peacekeeping Work?* (2008). Fortna's dates are cross-referenced against Doyle and Sambanis' data (2006), UCDP/PRIO's 2008 data, and Toft's data (2010); where Fortna provides no treaty date, I use the date one of these sources provides.

[9] "Major failure" excludes the failure of ceasefires and truces for the most part and focuses on the failure of formally negotiated settlements, except where noted.

[10] Cf. Max Boot, "Paving the Road to Hell: The Failure of UN Peacekeeping," *Foreign Affairs* (March–April 2000): 143–148. Boot rather memorably writes that "The failures of the United Nations should not be blamed just on the great powers. They owe as much to the mindset of U.N. administrators, who think that no problem in the world is too intractable to be solved by negotiation. These mandarins fail to grasp that men with guns do not respect men with nothing but flapping gums" (144).

Table 3.1 *List of peacekeeping failures*[a]

| Case | Fail date | Guarantor |
|---|---|---|
| Djibouti[b] | 19-Jul-92 | France |
| Angola | 11-Oct-92 | UN |
| Liberia[c] | 15-Oct-92 | ECOMOG |
| Rwanda | 1-Jan-93 | UN |
| Yugoslavia-Croatia | 22-Jan-93 | UN |
| Somalia[d] | 3-Oct-93 | UN |
| Rwanda | 6-Apr-94 | UN |
| Bosnia | 1-May-95 | UN |
| Croatia | 15-May-95 | UN |
| Yugoslavia-Kosovo | 1-Dec-98 | UN |
| Angola | 4-Dec-98 | UN |
| Guinea-Bissau | 6-May-99 | ECOMOG |
| Liberia | 15-May-99 | ECOMOG/UN |
| Sierra Leone | 2-May-00 | ECOMOG/UN |

[a] Data from Fortna 2008; Howard 2008; Doyle and Sambanis 2006.

[b] The peacekeepers in Djibouti are French, not UN peacekeepers. I include them here on the grounds that Fortna includes them in her analysis.

[c] The peacekeepers here are ECOMOG peacekeepers (Virginia Page Fortna, *Peacekeeping and the Peacekept: Data on Peacekeeping in Civil Wars 1989–2004*, Data Notes, 2008, 32, www.columbia.edu/~vpf4/).

[d] UNOSOM II technically remained on the ground in Somalia until March of 1995. I code the failure in October of 1993, however, because there were a number of vivid, visually arresting indicators of the mission's failure between the summer and fall of 1993, included the killing of two dozen Pakistani UNOSOM troops in June 1993 and, most famously, the "Black Hawk Down" incident in which eighteen US rangers were taken hostage and killed by Mohamed Farah Aideen's men. One ranger was dragged through Mogadishu on live TV, and UNOSOM troops tried and failed to rescue the Rangers (William Durch, ed., *UN Peacekeeping, American Policy, and the Uncivil Wars of the 1990s* [London: Palgrave Macmillan, 1996]; Mark Bowden, *Black Hawk Down: A Story of a Modern War* [New York: New American Press, 2001]; Howard 2008). Because the UN and the US's failures in Somalia were literally broadcast to the world in 1993, I prefer that date over the eventual withdrawal of United States and European troops in March 1994, and over the UN's ultimate withdrawal of UNOSOM II in March 1995.

fourteen failures too many.[11] Combatants may consider failure not because it is common or likely, but because it is *vivid*, and because

[11] Anjali Kaushlesh Dayal and Paul Musgrave, "Teaching Counterfactuals from Hell," *Peace Review* 30, no. 1 (Spring 2018): 23–21.

negotiations are already so perilous that the added risk posed by a guarantor with a reputation for failure could concern combatants as they contemplate demobilization and disarmament.[12] This effect is heightened for within-case failure; repeated failed missions within a single country or conflict case should affect combatants' perception of peacekeepers' capabilities.

Peacekeeping failures are temporally concentrated in the 1990s and geographically concentrated in sub-Saharan Africa and the Balkans. Taken together, their human cost is staggering. Considering only casualties in Rwanda, Angola, and Bosnia-Herzegovina between 1992 and 1995, the list details incidents where, by conservative estimates, upward of 782,000 people died in cases with UN peacekeepers on the ground to keep the peace.[13] If, as the previous chapter argued,

---

[12] Cf. Rose McDermott, *Risk-Taking in International Politics* (Ann Arbor: University of Michigan Press, 2001); James Goldgeier and Philip Tetlock, "Psychology and International Relations Theory," *Annual Review of Political Science* 4 (2001): 67–92.

[13] Estimates drawn from M. J. Anstee, *Orphan of the Cold War: The Inside Story of the Collapse of the Angolan Peace Process, 1992–1993* (Basingstroke: Macmillan, 1996); Alison L. Des Forges, *Leave None to Tell the Story* (New York: Human Rights Watch, 1999); and Howard 2008. Des Forges estimates approximately 500,000 casualties during the Rwandan genocide, which is a conservative figure; the UN's estimations put the casualty total at 800,000. Des Forges also estimates between 25,000 and 60,000 Hutus were killed during the RPF advance, while Scott Straus estimates approximately 10,000 Hutus were killed for refusing to participate in the genocide (Scott Straus, *The Order of Genocide: Race, Power, and War in Rwanda* [Ithaca: Cornell University Press, 2006]).Drawing on Anstee's work, Howard reports the figures for Angola at 300,000 following Savimbi's electoral loss (Howard 2008, 37), and counts ethnic cleansing deaths during UNPROFOR's collapse as 47,000 (Howard 2008, 43). It is worth noting that neither UNAMIR in Rwanda nor the UNAVEM forces in Angola had Chapter VII mandates to protect civilians, while UNPROFOR's Chapter VII mandate authorized it to use force to protect convoys of released detainees if requested to do so by the International Committee of the Red Cross (S/RES/776 (1992)). "Failure" here does not mean a failure to execute a mandate to protect civilians, since these missions were (problematically) not authorized to do so. The failure is rather to keep the peace, since war recurred in each of these cases. Casualty numbers are offered here because they present the visceral, immediately observable indication and implication of reverting to war, and because they are the clearest signal to observers that peacekeepers have failed the local population (however ill-equipped these peacekeepers might have been to protect these populations in the first place). The majority of these casualties are civilian victims of mass atrocities. It is possible combatants care more about battle deaths than about civilian casualties, given that in many cases they themselves may be the executors of

combatants are attentive to the UN's behavior globally, then they should consider what these failures might mean for their own negotiation efforts.

This list does not include what were, by the early 2000s, three of the UN's longest running and most notable peacekeeping engagements: the Democratic Republic of the Congo (DRC), Sudan, and Haiti.[14] These missions were responsible for a great deal of the negative press UN peacekeeping received in this time period. In all three locations, moreover, the UN went on to compound intractable conflict with either scandal or highly visible inefficacy – for example, retreat when faced with M23 rebels in November 2012 in the DRC,[15] or peacekeepers precipitating Haiti's 2010 cholera epidemic,[16] or continued, high levels of fighting in Sudan amid the African Union-United Nations Hybrid Operation in Darfur (UNAMID) drawdowns.[17] In all three locations, if we were to choose an arbitrary date line and draw the mission to a close on that day, we would have had to call each mission a failure. In the time period I consider, they likely served the same function as failed missions, shadowing other ongoing missions with their setbacks and undercutting the credibility of peacekeeping's claims to stem conflict and protect civilians.

Today, the increasing and serious charges of sexual violence by peacekeepers may play a similar role, as well: As the Report of an Independent Review on Sexual Exploitation and Abuse by International Peacekeeping Forces in the Central African Republic argued, "In the absence of

mass attacks against civilians. By Lacina and Gleditsch's best estimates (2005), these three conflicts cost 85,806 combatant lives between 1992 and 1994. Their high and low estimates are 127,025 and 25,675 (Bethany Lacina and Nils Petter Gleditsch, "Monitoring Trends in Global Combat: A New Dataset of Battle Deaths," *European Journal of Population* 21, no. 2–3 [2005]: 145–166). Even if combatants care more about battle deaths than atrocities, the casualty toll from these years should still cast doubt onto the UN's ability to protect them even after they have reached a deal.

[14] The list is right-censored.
[15] Jessica Hatcher and Alex Perry, "Defining Peacekeeping Downward: The U.N. Debacle in Eastern Congo," *New Times (Rwanda)*, November 28, 2012.
[16] Jonathan Katz, "In the Time of Cholera: How the U.N Created an Epidemic – Then Covered It Up," *Foreign Policy*, January 10, 2013, www.foreignpolicy .com/articles/2013/01/10/in_the_time_of_cholera.
[17] Khalid Abdelaziz, "Heavy Fighting Rages in Sudan's Darfur Region," *Reuters*, January 9, 2013, http://news.yahoo.com/heavy-fighting-rages-sudans-darfur-region-220204026.html.

concrete action to address wrongdoing by the very persons sent to protect vulnerable populations, the credibility of the UN and the future of peacekeeping operations are in jeopardy."[18] In this sense, combatants are *always* being exposed to peacekeeping failures, and any understanding of general trends in peacekeeping must take into account the way ongoing and long-running cases and actions lurk behind more easily defined successes and failures.

The complexity of the "lesson" from past peacekeeping experiences – that combatants looking at similar events can draw very different conclusions, and that failure is not an unambiguous deterrent for all actors – requires that we evaluate not just failures, but also the effect of other, proximate missions: if failure has an effect, then so, too, may success. Table 3.2 is a list of successfully concluded peacekeeping missions from 1989 to 2014, where "success" is a measure based on Howard (2008): a highly complex mission that concluded with no relapse into war. The list of successes extends past the first decade of the 2000s because success takes a longer time to unfold than failure – but successful cases may shade perceptions of peace operations well before they formally conclude.[19]

This definition does not account for public security, the stability of the government, or the extent to which the state protects citizens' rights in the post-conflict polity, except insofar as they push the state back to war. These successfully concluded missions could also inform combatants' decisions as they assess whether they should strike a bargain or continue to fight, and accounting for both success *and* failure is important as we consider the diverse and often conflicting information that parties to a conflict may be attempting to synthesize into strategies for action.

---

[18] Marie Deschamps, Hassan B. Jallow, and Yasmin Sooka, "Taking Action on Sexual Exploitation and Abuse by Peacekeepers: Report of an Independent Review on Sexual Exploitation and Abuse by International Peacekeeping Forces in the Central African Republic," December 17, 2015, ii, www.un.org/News/dh/infocus/centafricrepub/Independent-Review-Report.pdf.

[19] The year of success is coded as the ending year of the mission, with the understanding that its ongoing success probably has some effect on combatants, because we cannot count a mission as successful until it has concluded. Not all missions that did not fail appear on this list, however; some missions were still ongoing as of 2014, and I do not include simple ceasefire monitoring missions in my definition of success. This undoubtedly means that my lists of success and failure are not exhaustive.

Table 3.2 *List of peacekeeping successes*[a]

| Mission | Concluded |
|---|---|
| Namibia (UNTAG) | Apr-90 |
| El Salvador (ONUSAL) | Apr-95 |
| Cambodia (UNTAC)* | Sep-93 |
| Mozambique (ONUMOZ) | Dec-94 |
| Eastern Slavonia | Jan-98 |
| Croatia (UNTAES) | Jan-98 |
| East Timor (UNTAET) | May-02 |
| Burundi (ONUB)* | Jun-06 |
| Central African Republic and Chad (MINURCAT)* | Dec-10 |
| Sudan (UNMIS)* | Jul-11 |
| United Nations Integrated Mission in Timor-Leste (UNMIT) | Dec-13 |

Asterisks indicate cases of partial or qualified success.[b]

[a] Data from Howard 2008 and UN Department of Peacekeeping Operations, www.un.org/en/peacekeeping/ (accessed August 2012).

[b] These cases would have been qualified successes as of 2014 because developments on the ground would have called into question the quality of the peace. Ongoing violence in Burundi then would not have risen to the level of civil war, but contributed to public insecurity. UNMIS concluded on a technicality with implementation of the Comprehensive Peace Process and the independence of South Sudan. The United Nations Mission in South Sudan (UNMISS) and the United Nations Interim Security Force for Abyei (UNIFSA) continued to operate within both states' territories, where there were media reports of abiding violence (cf. "Abyei Crisis: UN Confirms Sudan Troop Pullout," *BBC World News*, May 2012, www.bbc.co.uk/news/world-africa-18260082 [accessed July 2012]). It is unclear that MINURCAT fulfilled its mandate, although it was successful in the sense that no new war has broken out (www.amnestyusa.org/research/reports/annual-report-chad-2011). There are strong arguments to be made that El Salvador should also be qualified as a mixed success: While the negotiation of the Chapultepec Peace Agreement is regarded as one of the UN's more unambiguous successes (Howard 2008), there were some indications that post-civil war levels of violence became *higher* in cities like San Salvador after the civil war than they were during the civil war (see, for instance, International Human Rights Clinic, *No Place to Hide: Gang, State, and Clandestine Violence in El Salvador* [Cambridge, MA: Human Rights Program, Harvard Law School, 1997]).

Unlike failures, which are concentrated in sub-Saharan Africa and the Balkans between 1992 and 2000, successfully concluded missions occur in almost every theater of UN peace operations – Asia/Pacific, the Americas, sub-Saharan and North Africa – and range in time from 1990 to 2010. Failure, in addition to being vivid, is therefore a much more geographically and temporally bounded phenomenon than success.

Table 3.3 lists all formally concluded, full negotiated settlements between 1989 and 2005.[20] Negotiated settlements are formally concluded agreements to which the major parties of a conflict are signatories, and which include, at minimum, a provision for ceasing hostilities. This definition does not include simple ceasefire agreements. I draw on Doyle and Sambanis (2000, 2006) and Fortna's (2008) definition here, and report the year in which negotiations were concluded.[21] This definition excludes partial agreements and ceasefires, and it marks those settlements that included provisions for peacekeepers on the ground. There are fifty-eight settlements in total, of which exactly 50 percent (twenty-nine) include peacekeeping provisions. The pace of negotiated settlements with and without peacekeeping appears to be fairly consistent, with one gap from August of 1993 to November of 1994, when five settlements were negotiated with no peacekeepers. This gap tallies roughly with a generalized contraction of peacekeeping in those years. Eight negotiated settlements with peacekeeping missions failed, in comparison with ten negotiated settlements without peacekeeping missions, and those settlements that failed with no peacekeeping mission are concentrated in the 1993–1995 period.[22] This is the same period during which some of the UN's most notable peacekeeping failures took place.

In the most basic sense, the table reveals that negotiated settlements with peacekeepers are as common as negotiated settlements without peacekeepers, and that at first blush there is no dramatically different frequency of failure between these two kinds of settlements. The picture

---

[20] Data for Table 3.3 from Barbara Walter, *Committing to Peace: The Successful Settlement of Civil Wars* (Princeton: Princeton University Press, 2002); Doyle and Sambanis 2006; Howard 2008; Fortna 2008; and UCDP/PRIO 2010.
I include Somalia under failures in 1993 in accordance with Howard, but against Fortna's coding.

[21] The date of a case's peace agreement is reported in accordance with the protocol that Fortna established in *Does Peacekeeping Work?* (2008). Fortna's dates are cross-referenced against Doyle and Sambanis' data (2006), UCDP/PRIO's 2008 data on peace agreements, and Toft's data (Toft, 2010), and where Fortna provides no treaty date, I use the date that appears most frequently in these other sources.

[22] The discrepancy between this number and the number of peacekeeping failures I list in Table 1.1 stems from the inclusion in Table 1.1 of truces and ceasefires where peacekeepers are present.

Table 3.3 *Negotiated settlements, 1989–2005*[a]

| Country | Treaty date |
| --- | --- |
| Namibia | April 1, 1989* |
| Nicaragua | April 19, 1989* |
| Liberia | November 28, 1990* *(failed October 15, 1992)* |
| Mali | January 9, 1991 *(failed May 15, 1991)* |
| Angola | May 31, 1991* *(failed October 1992)* |
| Lebanon | September 15, 1991* |
| Cambodia | October 23, 1991* |
| El Salvador | January 16, 1992* |
| Mali (Azawad) | April 11, 1992 *(failed September 1994)* |
| Moldova | July 21, 1992* |
| Mozambique | October 4, 1992* |
| India (Bodoland) | February 20, 1993 |
| Afghanistan-Taliban | March 7, 1993 *(failed April 15, 1993)* |
| Rwanda | August 4, 1993* *(failed April 6, 1994)* |
| India (Tripura) | August 23, 1993 *(failed December 31, 1996)* |
| Israel-Palestinians | September 13, 1993 *(failed September 28, 2000)* |
| Chad | October 16, 1993 *(failed October 22, 1993)* |
| South Africa | April 26, 1994 |
| Chad | August 11, 1994 *(failed March 15, 1997)* |
| Angola | November 20, 1994* *(failed December 4, 1998)* |
| Bosnia and Herzegovina (Serb) | December 14, 1995* |
| Djibouti | December 26, 1994 |
| Mali | March 31, 1995 |
| Niger (Air and Azawad) | April 15, 1995 |
| Croatia (Serb) | November 12, 1995* |
| Chad | November 22, 1995 |

**Table 3.3** (*cont.*)

| Country | Treaty date |
| --- | --- |
| Bosnia | December 14, 1995* |
| Congo-Brazzaville | December 15, 1995 |
|  | *(failed June 25, 1997)* |
| Guatemala | December 31, 1996 |
| Liberia | August 17, 1996* |
|  | *(failed May 15, 1999)* |
| Philippines-Mindanao | September 2, 1996 |
|  | *(failed November 15, 2001)* |
| Sierra Leone | November 30, 1996 |
|  | *(failed May 15, 1997)* |
| Guatemala | December 29, 1996*[b] |
| Central African Rep. | January 25, 1997* |
| Tajikistan | June 27, 1997* |
| Bangladesh (Chittagong Hill Tracts) | December 2, 1997 |
| Angola | January 9, 1998* |
| U.K.–N. Ireland | April 10, 1998 |
| Guinea-Bissau | November 2, 1998* |
|  | *(failed January 31, 1999)* |
| Chad | July 3, 1999 |
| Sierra Leone | July 3, 1999* |
|  | *(failed May 2, 2000)* |
| Djibouti | February 7, 2000 |
| Burundi | August 28, 2000* |
| Djibouti | May 12, 2001 |
| Macedonia | August 13, 2001 |
| Papua New Guinea (Bougainville) | August 30, 2001* |
| Chad | January 7, 2002 |
|  | *(failed May 27, 2002)* |
| Democratic Republic of Congo | December 16, 2002 |
| Uganda | December 24, 2002 |
| Democratic Republic of Congo | April 2, 2003* |
| Liberia | August 18, 2003* |
| Burundi | November 16, 2003* |
| Comoros (Anjouan) | December 29, 2003* |
| Ivory Coast | July 30, 2004* |
|  | *(failed October 2004)* |
| Sudan (Southern Sudan) | January 9, 2005* |

Table 3.3 (*cont.*)

| Country | Treaty date |
|---|---|
| Colombia | February 15, 2005 |
| Indonesia (Aceh) | August 15, 2005 |
| Chad | August 18, 2005 |

Settlement's failure date (if any) listed in parentheses. Asterisk indicates the settlement provided for the deployment of a peacekeeping operation.

[a] Sources: Fortna 2008; Harbom, Högbladh, and Wallensteen 2006; Doyle and Sambanis 2000; UN Department of Peacekeeping Operations.

[b] PKO listed at DPKO but neither in Fortna nor UCDP/PRIO, given its status as a UNGA-mandated mission. Despite being mandated differently than many missions, MINUGUA was operationally quite similar to many other early peace operations. See Chapter 5 for details.

of negotiation and peacekeeping that emerges from this catalog is mixed: Peacekeeping scholars have focused on efficacy, and have found that peacekeeping on the balance prevents recidivism back into war,[23] but their careful analysis sits apart from the more shallow observation that the raw number of agreements that fail without peacekeepers present is not significantly greater than the number of agreements that fail with peacekeepers present.[24] If we are interested in the way that combatants perceive peacekeeping efficacy, then we must consider this simpler observation alongside our knowledge that, *ceteris paribus*, peacekeeping prevents backsliding into conflict.

These three charts, taken together, allow us to develop a sequence of civil war negotiations and peacekeeping outcomes between 1989 and 2004: They highlight how mission failures clustered in the 1990s as negotiations in other cases continued briskly, and they reveal three critical periods of time in which we would expect a guarantor's reputation for failure to matter if combatants concern themselves with the strength of a security guarantee.

[23] Fortna 2008; Howard 2008; Michael J. Gilligan and Ernesto J. Sergenti, "Do UN Interventions Cause Peace? Using Matching to Improve Causal Inference," *Quarterly Journal of Political Science* 3, no. 2 (2008): 89–122.

[24] This is of course in part because of the different ways in which success and failure are defined: A failure could occur at any point, whereas a mission cannot be accounted successful until it is formally concluded. This skews my accounting in favor of failure, but this bias accords with the findings of scholars working on prospect and learning theories.

## Negotiation Despite Failure

To begin with, the timeline indicates that formally concluded negotiations outpace both success and failure: There are more agreements negotiated, with or without guarantors, than there are either major mission failures or notable mission successes. This underscores findings about the increased prevalence of negotiated settlements globally,[25] and it broadly indicates that either there are overall international pressures or incentives to negotiate, or that negotiation is a phenomenon driven primarily by domestic concerns that have little to do with the credibility of a guarantee.

Second, the timeline indicates that the UN's touchstone peacekeeping failures in the 1990s – Somalia, Rwanda, and Srebrenica – apparently did not stay the progress of negotiations across civil war cases. Official reports and Security Council members refer to these three cases again and again; they inform the Brahimi report, the debates on the Responsibility to Protect, and the framing of mission mandates throughout the 1990s.[26] The broad-brush effect failure has on combatants' incentives to negotiate, however, is less immediately clear.

## Critical Time Periods

The sequence of post-Cold War events also reveals three critical time periods for considering why combatants negotiate after peacekeeping failures. These are key junctures at which combatants ought to consider

---

[25] Virginia Page Fortna, "Where Have all the Victories Gone? Peacekeeping and War Outcomes," paper presented at the Annual Meeting of the American Political Science Association, September 2009; Lise Morjé Howard and Alexandra Stark, "How Civil Wars End: The International System, Norms, and the Role of External Actors," *International Security* 42, no. 3 (Winter 2017/18): 127–171.

[26] There is clear evidence that the United States and UN failures in Somalia certainly structured the *supply-side* response to events in Rwanda (Michael Barnett, "The UN Security Council, Indifference, and Genocide in Rwanda," *Cultural Anthropology* 12, no. 4 [1997]: 551–578). See also S/PV.4035; Michael Tiernay, "Which Comes First? Unpacking the Relationship between Peace Agreements and Peacekeeping Missions," *Conflict Management and Peace Science* 32, no. 2 (April 2015): 135–152. Indeed, the UN Secretariat established an entire program to "mobilize civil society for Rwanda genocide victim remembrance and education in order to help prevent future acts of genocide" (A/RES/60/225 (2005) (United Nations, www.un.org/en/preventgenocide/rwanda [accessed July 2012]).

failure as they make their calculations: If the UN's reputation as a security guarantor matters, it ought to matter at these time periods. Put another way, these time periods should provide us with most-likely instances in which to observe the reputational process of interest. If I do *not* see reputational effects in these time periods, I am unlikely to see them anywhere.

The first of these junctures is between the second half of 1992, when missions in Angola and Liberia failed and a settlement was negotiated in Mozambique, and August of 1993, when the Rwandan government and the RPF concluded the Arusha Accords. The UN began 1992 with the huge success of the Chapultepec Peace Accords, which concluded the decade-long civil war in El Salvador. But this success was tempered by a quick series of peacekeeping failures, including brutal agreement collapses and killings in Liberia and Angola, continuing through February 1993 with the failure of truces in Rwanda and Croatia. Formal negotiations in Rwanda began during this period, as well.[27] This period offers us variation in exposure to success and failure for combatants negotiating agreements in both Mozambique and Rwanda, including within-case failure in Rwanda, and it is notable for the movement between cases of negotiators with experience in Cambodia, Liberia, Namibia, Angola, and Mozambique. Early negotiators in Rwanda, for example, traveled to Zimbabwe and Nicaragua "to compare notes with previous negotiation experiences."[28] This is a pattern that continued as peace operations evolved, producing greater exchanges of ideas and individuals across conflict cases.

A second critical time period is from October of 1993, when United States and UN troops were killed in Somalia in the "Black Hawk Down" incident that precipitated the mission's eventual disintegration, through the summer of 1994, when the Arusha Accords collapsed into genocide with UNAMIR on the ground, and when combatants in Chad negotiated a settlement without a provision for peacekeepers on the ground, but with the mediation and implementation oversight of the Central African Republic, France, Gabon, and the United Nations High Commissioner for Refugees (UNHCR).[29] Examining this period should afford insights about what lessons, if any, the

---

[27] Bruce D. Jones, *Peacemaking in Rwanda: The Dynamics of Failure* (Boulder: Lynne Rienner, 2001), 32.

[28] Jones 2001, 70. I return to this point in Chapter 4.

[29] Harbom, Högbladh, and Wallensteen 2006.

powerful spoilers to the peace in Rwanda drew from Somalia as they abandoned their settlement for renewed conflict and a strategy of mass atrocity. First-hand accounts of the meetings that determined UNAMIR's mandate and capabilities reveal that peacekeeper casualties in Mogadishu weighed heavily on the Security Council as they contemplated intervention in Rwanda.[30] That peacekeeping failures might have had a similar effect on combatants at this juncture seems, at the very least, a possibility.

A third critical period for investigation is the months between June 1995 and December 1996, between the failures at Bosnia and Croatia – including the massacres at Srebrenica – and the conclusion of negotiated settlements in Bosnia, the Republic of the Congo (Congo-Brazzaville), and Guatemala. Agreements in Bosnia were concluded with multilateral international involvement; agreements in Congo-Brazzaville were concluded with no international involvement; and agreements in Guatemala were concluded with heavy UN involvement, and in the shadow of the successful negotiations in El Salvador four years earlier in January 1992. The lessons the UN took from these failures are fairly consistent and enshrined within the Brahimi Report, but this consistency in the organization's policy changes was not matched by consistency in outcome across these three cases. Indeed, these cases represent three different paths in the wake of peacekeeping failure: Bosnia, the site itself of a failed UN peacekeeping mission, negotiated a settlement with involvement from the European Union (EU) , France, Germany, Great Britain, Russia, the United States, NATO, and the Organization for Security and Co-operation in Europe (OSCE), among others. Congo-Brazzaville, geographically proximate to several of the 1990s largest failures, concluded an internally enforced agreement.[31] Guatemala, on the other hand, which borders El Salvador – the site of the UN's single most unambiguous peacekeeping and negotiation success in the 1990s – negotiated an

---

[30] Michael Barnett, *Eyewitness to a Genocide: The United Nations and Rwanda* (Ithaca and London: Cornell University Press, 2003); Walter Clarke and Jeffrey Herbst, "Somalia and the Future of Humanitarian Intervention," *Foreign Affairs* 75, no. 2 (March–April 1996): 70–85; Jon Western, "Sources of Humanitarian Intervention," *International Security* 26, no. 4 (Spring 2002): 112–142; Samantha Power, *A Problem from Hell: America in the Age of Genocide* (New York: Basic Books, 2002).
[31] Harbom, Högbladh, and Wallensteen 2006.

agreement with the UN's oversight, despite the very recent failures in the Balkans.

To summarize, then, these three most-likely time periods for reputational effects are: (1) from 1992 to August of 1993, a period bookended by the peacekeeping successes in El Salvador and the conclusion of the Arusha Accords in Rwanda, with variation in the success of peace operations during that time; (2) from October 1993, when the Black Hawk Down incident in Somalia took place, to August 1994, when the Rwandan genocide concluded; and (3) between June 1995 and December 1996, eighteen months that were framed by failed missions in the Balkans and successful negotiations in Guatemala. These are times in which the UN's performance is likely to be visible and clear to parties in ongoing peace processes. Although actors may of course draw lessons from cases at other times, we *should* see evidence of it in these periods; if we do not, we are unlikely to find it elsewhere.

The Rwandan and Guatemalan cases are drawn from these time periods. Following the broad logic of most-similar case selection, both cases straddle the end of the Cold War; both peace processes unfold in small countries that experienced genocide during the course of civil war; both conflicts had ethnic dimensions; and both cases include both United States and regional organizations' involvement in negotiation processes alongside UN involvement. In both cases, conflicts between states and rebel forces with broader regional support produced effectively internationalized civil wars. Rwanda is a critical case, given its role in informing the reform of contemporary peacekeeping and peace-making policy. Guatemala, meanwhile, is a most likely case for the credible commitment hypothesis, given the success of the UN's mission in El Salvador.

The subsequent chapters present evidence from the Rwandan and Guatemalan negotiation processes. Chapter 4 addresses the Arusha peace process and UNAMIR in Rwanda, which not only is an intrinsically important case that has heavily informed institutional reactions to, and popular perceptions of, peacekeeping failure, but also allows me to examine the effects of both international and within-case failures on negotiation processes. I look at the effects of, first, a peacekeeping failure in Somalia, and second, the failure of UNAMIR itself, on the decisions to negotiate with UN involvement, and on the decisions to request UN peacekeeping assistance after the disastrous failure of

UNAMIR during the genocide. Chapter 5 focuses on the Guatemalan negotiations, which offer variation in exposure to success and failure: Here, I evaluate the countervailing influences of geographical proximate peacekeeping success (in El Salvador) and temporally proximate failure (Srebrenica) on the warring parties' willingness to negotiate, demobilize, and disarm under the UN's aegis.

## Process Tracing Cases

I evaluate the Rwandan and Guatemalan peace processes using process tracing tools: I am looking for procedural indicators for both the credible commitment and the distributional hypotheses within the available evidence about each set of negotiations. In Rwanda I focus on the period from July 1992 through August 1994, which encompasses the timeframe between the beginning of the Arusha negotiations and the end of the genocide. In Guatemala I examine the period from 1989 to 1997, which includes the beginning of the peace process, the transition from regionally led negotiations to UN-mediated negotiations, and the ultimate conclusion of the peace agreements.

Implicit in influential accounts of UN peacekeeping is the claim that good peacekeeping and bad peacekeeping should have different effects on combatants' willingness to strike a bargain: Combatants who expect to receive bad peacekeepers will not expect these peacekeepers to alleviate the credible commitment problem that plagues civil war termination. Combatants should therefore, by the internal logic of this theory, pursue other courses of action; they should either continue fighting, or they should attempt to make other arrangements to ensure the credibility of their bargain for peace.[32] The theory I propose hinges on combatants' strategic situations – whether they are desperate negotiators who must seek peace above all else, hardliners who prefer securing the material, tactical, and symbolic benefits of negotiation to a guarantee for the peace, or spoilers who are not genuinely interested in the success of agreements – and their beliefs about why past missions succeeded or failed. We should see these actors drawing different lessons from different cases. When negotiations with UN involvement

[32] James D. Fearon, "Rationalist Explanations for War," *International Organization* 49, no. 3 (Summer 1995): 379–414; Barbara Walter, "The Critical Barrier to Civil War Settlement," *International Organization* 51, no. 3 (1997): 335–364; Walter 2002; Fortna 2008.

seem unlikely from the observer's standpoint, we should see desperate negotiators insisting, in word and in action, that this time will be different, and we should see hardliners and spoilers pursuing ends other than peace, invoking past UN operations in accordance with their goals and preferences. We should see combatants either actively working to secure a better guarantee from the guarantor; to secure one of negotiation's other benefits, such as legitimacy, statebuilding, or refugee resettlement; actively indicating that their case, this time, is different from past peacekeeping failures; or using negotiation periods to regroup and rearm.

If there is no evidence of these processes during the Rwandan and Guatemalan negotiations and their aftermath, then my theory is wrong, and the security concerns that credible commitment theorists emphasize dominate the negotiating table: We should see evidence that the parties to these civil wars sought the strongest possible security guarantee from the UN in an effort to alleviate the credible commitment problem of war termination. We should see evidence that they invoke peacekeeping failures as cautionary lessons, that they do not seek a UN peace operation after a UN failure, and that they privilege the contribution that international actors can make to the post-conflict security environment over other benefits the UN could bring to the post-conflict space. In the Rwandan case, we should see past failures invoked as a source of security concern; in Guatemala, we should see evidence that, if parties to the conflict invoke other instances of UN peacekeeping operations, they focus on emulating success in El Salvador in their own negotiations, or on guarding against disasters like those in the Balkans.

## Evidence

The causal process observations I am most interested in hinge on actors' perceptions and interpretations of international events, and the effects these events might have on their own conflicts. Trying to determine what actors thought at some past juncture requires a plurality of reasonably persuasive evidence from diverse sources.[33] Accordingly, I triangulate

---

[33] Andrew Bennett, "Process Tracing: A Bayesian Perspective," in *The Oxford Handbook of Political Methodology*, ed. J. Box-Steffensmeier, H. E Brady, and D. Collier (Oxford: Oxford University Press, 2008), 217–270.

using multiple archives, interviews, and journalistic and scholarly accounts of the conflict and negotiation process.

To investigate the Arusha peace process in Rwanda, I consulted four primary sets of documents: the UN's official document center; the National Security Archive (NSA) of declassified US government documents housed at George Washington University;[34] the International Criminal Tribunal's documentation center; and the Rwandan parliamentary archive. Each set of documents had its own strengths and purposes.

Although the UN Secretariat was not an official party to the negotiations, the Secretary-General's office was a witness to the accords; the UN's aid agencies were on the ground for the entire duration of the conflict; and the UN emerged during the course of the negotiations as the implementing authority for the peace agreements, despite its comparatively limited involvement in the peace process. Accordingly, the UN's official documents, both those that were publicly available during the period under consideration and those that were written confidentially and subsequently declassified, catalog the negotiation and the deployment of the peace operation, and capture the day-to-day challenges of implementing the Arusha peace process from October 1993 to April 1994. The International Criminal Tribunal's documentation center provided analyses of the peace accords, as well as an accessibility guide to the genocide tribunal's massive stores of evidence.

The United States, along with France, was heavily involved in the actual negotiation of the peace agreement. United States negotiators were largely regarded as honest, neutral brokers,[35] and American

[34] I drew extensively on the "#Rwanda20yrs" project cosponsored by the National Security Archive at George Washington University and the Center for the Prevention of Genocide at the United States Holocaust Memorial Museum. The project made a slew of classified diplomatic communications, reports, and UNAMIR "sitreps" (daily messages to UN headquarters from the field) available to researchers in commemoration of the twentieth anniversary of the Rwandan genocide.

[35] See, for example, Jones 2001; see also statements from Paul Kagame to Deputy Chief of the US Mission to Rwanda Joyce Leader in declassified State Department document from the US Embassy in Kigali to the US Secretary of State, December 10, 1993 on the RPF Perspective on the Peace Process, available at www2.gwu.edu/~nsarchiv/NSAEBB/NSAEBB469/docs/DOCUMENT%2034.pdf.

diplomats therefore interacted extensively with both sides of the conflict. The declassified diplomatic cables from the negotiation period thus provide a rich, full account of the bargaining dynamics at Arusha, as well as the challenges of the implementation period; while the accounts may overstate the American role in the processes I examine, their initially confidential nature makes them invaluable for their candor about the actors involved. The complementary French archives were finally fully declassified by court case in June 2020, and unfortunately were not available in time for me to consult them for this analysis – but I would not expect their contents to contradict the findings from other archival sources, even as they fleshed out the French role in negotiations.[36]

Finally, the Rwandan parliamentary archive ultimately provided very little information about either the peace process, its implementation, or the RPF's subsequent decision-making. Despite the many documents that tie the state's current constitution directly to the Arusha Peace Accords, there are almost no documents from the 1990 to 1994 period in its entire collection. Proceeding from the understanding that silence is also data for the reconstruction of conflict narratives,[37] the omission of these documents, either by destruction or by secondment to the RPF's private archives from the Rwandan national records, may also tell us something about the peace process and the agreement's role in post-war Rwanda.

A series of semi-structured elite interviews in Washington, DC, and Kigali, Rwanda complemented my archival research. Most interviews in Washington, DC were background interviews not conducted for attribution, but these interviews were instrumental in understanding the details of the Arusha peace process.[38] Interviews in Kigali, Rwanda were conducted using snowball sampling, with a focus on identifying the key officials involved in the actual negotiation of the peace

---

[36] "France Grants Researcher Access to Mitterrand's Archive on Rwandan Genocide," *France24*, June 12, 2020, www.france24.com/en/20200612-france-grants-researcher-access-to-mitterrand-s-archive-on-rwandan-genocide.

[37] Lee Ann Fujii, "Shades of Truth and Lies: Interpreting Testimonies of War and Violence," *Journal of Peace Research* 47, no. 2 (2010): 231–241.

[38] I am grateful to Rick Ehrenreich of the Office of Analysis for Africa (INR/AF) at the US Department of State for his detailed recollection of the negotiation process, and for suggesting both which documents had already been declassified through FOIA and which parts of the National Security Archive's document collection might be most useful.

agreement and speaking with them. All interviews with actors involved in the negotiation process followed the same order of questions, proceeding from questions about the negotiations, to questions about their perception of the international community's commitment to their peace process and their capability to maintain peace, and finally to questions about their perceptions of other peacekeeping failures.[39] Whenever possible, in order to avoid the validity concerns that can plague interview research – particularly interview research about events in the distant past that actors may recollect imperfectly[40] – I complemented my interviews with published accounts, oral histories, memoirs, and interviews carried out by journalists and other scholars. When I find evidence of the processes I am interested in, even in interviews or oral histories conducted by other analysts for different purposes, I am confident that these processes are at work. The interviews I cite here are interviews I conducted with RPF actors who were directly involved in the negotiations at Arusha, and I triangulate their statements against the United States and UN accounts of the RPF's conduct during the negotiation process.[41] I could not interview former

---

[39] The project is filed under two separate Institutional Review Board (IRB) protocols with Georgetown University (IRB #2013-0021 and IRB #2013-0202). All interviews for actors involved in the negotiations follow the same order of questions:

(1) Questions about the dynamics of negotiations, including what the primary motivations for negotiation were, the major hurdles to the agreement, and the viability of the agreement;

(2) Questions about perceptions of the commitment and abilities of the international community. What did the actor want the international community to bring to negotiations? What did he or she want the UN to bring to negotiations? What did he or she expect them to bring to negotiations?

(3) Questions about international events and peacekeeping failures, framed in general terms at first and then later in specific terms if they volunteered a specific international event they had considered. Did they consider these events while they were negotiating? How did these events affect their perceptions about their agreement? Did these events affect what they thought about the international community? Did these events affect what they thought about the UN?

(4) Do they have any advice for ongoing peace processes?

(5) Was there anything I forgot to ask them that they would like to share?

[40] Layna Mosley, ed., *Interview Research in Political Science* (Ithaca: Cornell University Press, 2013).

[41] For reasons related to the political climate in Rwanda, alongside other considerations, I do not offer the full number of interviews I conducted in Rwanda or offer a full list of my interlocutors, and the only interviews from

Government of Rwanda (GoR) officials, as these actors were un-
available to me – in some cases, because they were under indictment
for genocide or dead. Here, I rely on the declassified evidence of the
International Criminal Tribunal for Rwanda (ICTR) and the American
diplomatic accounts of the negotiation processes alongside UNSC
documents – Rwanda, represented by the genocidal government, sat
on the UNSC for the duration of the genocide, and accordingly the
UNSC's official records include some information about this government's motivations and strategic choices.

I support this empirical research with journalists' and scholars'
accounts of the same time period. There are few scholarly accounts
of the Arusha peace process in its own right – the only book-length
study of the negotiations is Bruce Jones's *Peacemaking in Rwanda: The
Dynamics of Failure* (2001) – but I draw on the rich literature that
documents other dimensions of the successive Great Lakes crises from
the 1960s to the present.

To investigate the Guatemalan peace process, I triangulated between
multiple archives, oral histories, and journalistic and scholarly accounts
of the Guatemalan peace process for evidence of these perceptions and
how they informed negotiations.

First, I consulted archival material from the UN and the National
Security Archive. The UN's records on the Guatemalan Accords
encompass its role as observer to the regional conflict resolution processes of the late 1980s; its subsequent role as observer to the
Guatemalan peace process itself; and then its role as the formal mediator and implementer of the accord. My research drew primarily on
publicly available UN documents, reports, letters, and meeting records,
and on documents in Kofi Annan's personal papers, made available
through CUNY's archives.[42]

Kigali that are referred to directly or cited in this book are interviews with
officials who were directly involved in the negotiation process or who were in the
Rwandan government when I conducted interviews – genuine elites with
prominent positions and established records of government and diplomatic
service. Any other evidence I acquired in interviews is established in this chapter
using archival evidence.

[42] I did not consult the MINUGUA mission archives, which are not publicly
available, but rather drew extensively on William Stanley's recent work in these
private documents for the International Peace Institute's "official history" of
MINUGUA (William Stanley, *Enabling Peace in Guatemala: The Story of*

I also consulted the extensive declassified body of US government material available through the National Security Archives' Guatemala Document Project.[43] This project worked alongside the Guatemalan Truth Commission, provided expert assistance to domestic Guatemalan archivists and forensic anthropologists, and targeted the US Defense Intelligence Agency, the CIA, SOUTHCOM, the Agency for International Development, the US Department of State, and presidential documents for Freedom of Information Act (FOIA) requests to develop a portrait of both the Guatemalan security forces and the domestic human rights situation. Given the nearly continuous, often close association between these US agencies and the Guatemalan government during the Guatemalan Civil War, the Guatemala Document Project was intended not just to illustrate the US's role, but to provide the Historical Clarification Commission of Guatemala with as much documentation as possible about the Guatemalan's government's actions and motivations. The NSA's Guatemala Project provided the commission with more than five thousand pages of documents, and continues to work alongside Guatemalan prosecutors trying former members of the government for genocide – including, most famously, former dictator Efraín Rios Montt.[44]

*MINUGUA* [Boulder: Lynne Rienner, 2013]). CUNY's holdings of Kofi Annan's documents are listed here: http://ccnydigitalscholarship.org/kofiannan/.

[43] I consulted both digitized documents available through the Guatemala Document Project and physical documents that the National Security Archive holds offsite and which are not included in the digitized archive.

[44] On the NSA's work in Guatemala, see *Granito: How to Nail a Dictator*, directed by Pamela Yates, 2011; Priscilla B. Hayner, *Unspeakable Truths: Confronting State Terror and Atrocity* (New York: Routledge, 2002); Kate Doyle, *The Pursuit of Justice in Guatemala: National Security Archive Electronic Briefing Book No. 373* (Washington, DC, 2012), www2.gwu.edu/~nsarchiv/NSAEBB/NSAEBB373/index.htm#note_02. Hayner writes, "Beginning years in advance of the commission's start-up, and in consultation with other rights groups focused on Guatemala, the Archive submitted FOIA requests for information on over three dozen key cases that they expected the commission would investigate. In addition, once the commission was established, the commission made a direct request to President Clinton for the declassification of specific information pertaining to its investigations. The United States set up an interagency group to process its requests, which pertained to materials from the Department of State, Department of Defense, Central Intelligence Agency, National Security Council, and the Agency for International Development (regarding AID's public safety programs in the 1960s). In accordance with the commission's request, copies of the documents released were first given to the National Security Archive for processing" (Hayner 2002, 242). The process was intensive: "The director of the

Second, I drew on interviews and oral histories of key participants in the peace process, most of which were conducted by scholars, journalists, and UN staff either during the negotiation process itself or soon afterward, and are accessible through the United Nations Oral History Collection of the United Nations Dag Hammarskjöld Library.[45] Relying on published accounts, oral histories, memoirs, or others' interviews of elite actors has a number of clear advantages over any interviews I could have conducted myself in the 2010s, given that negotiations in the Guatemalan Civil War had started over thirty years ago by the start of this research.[46]

Finally, I drew on scholarly and journalistic accounts of the peace process. The Cold War-era Central American conflicts have long been of interest to political scientists, historians, sociologists, anthropologists, and legal scholars interested in civil war, American foreign policy, counterinsurgency, dictatorship, human rights, and transitional justice. Although Guatemala's conflict attracted less attention than its neighbors' struggles, researchers still documented and analyzed its peace process intensely. This wealth of material provides the foundation for the account in Chapter 5.

## Generalizability

Taken together, Chapters 4 and 5 constitute a theory-probing and a theory-testing endeavor: The analysis that follows tests the extent to which security concerns drive combatants to seek out the UN's services

Guatemala Project at the National Security Archive, Kate Doyle, was responsible for gathering and processing this material over a five-year period, beginning with the submission of the Archive's FOIA requests in 1994. At any given time, two to six people were working on the project at the Archive, reading and organizing released documents and helping to interpret them for the commission. When Doyle traveled to Guatemala, she provided detailed instructions to the commission on how the documents should be read. 'It is important to remind researchers that declassified documents are fallible. In addition to often richly detailed and valuable information, they can also contain factual errors, misinformation, or lies,' said Doyle" (Hayner 2002, 242).

[45] The oral histories are recordings and transcripts of interviews with participants in or witnesses to key UN events between 1945 and 2005 conducted by UN staff and Yale University researchers. More information is available at www.unmultimedia.org/oralhistory/. Page numbers refer to the audio recordings' posted interview transcripts.

[46] Mosley 2013.

in Rwanda and Guatemala, and it builds a theory of what combatants seek from the UN if they are *not* primarily concerned with security. Accordingly, although I would anticipate similar incentives operate in most cases where participants in a peace process expect they might receive peacekeepers, the analysis should be understood as a proof of concept, not as a perfectly generalizable set of lessons. As the final chapter in this book argues, changes in contemporary peace operations themselves – the post-2000 shift toward nearly ubiquitous protection of civilian mandates, frequent authorizations to use force, and the greater prevalence of both peace enforcement and counterinsurgency operations – might change the *specific* expectations that combatants have about the UN's presence on the ground. But the ideas the following cases introduce are still worth considering: peace and security are rarely the *only* motives at stake for participants in peace processes, and accordingly are rarely the only thing that participants will seek from international actors. The politics of peacemaking abide even when specific contexts change.

# 4 | *The Arusha Negotiations, 1990–1994*
*UNAMIR in the Shadow of Somalia*

## Defining the Puzzle

The Rwandan Civil War began in 1990, just as UN peacekeeping in civil wars was beginning in earnest. The Government of Rwanda (GoR) and the Rwandan Patriotic Front (RPF) began formal negotiations in July 1992 and reached a negotiated settlement in August 1993 after substantial international and regional peacemaking efforts. The Security Council authorized the United Nations Assistance Mission to Rwanda (UNAMIR) in October 1993, literally days after peace operations in Somalia crumbled in October 1993, and in April 1994 Rwanda collapsed into swift, brutal genocide.

The Rwandan genocide is emblazoned in popular consciousness and in the UN's institutional memory as the paradigmatic peacekeeping failure.[1] It is an intrinsically important case for scholars interested in peacekeeping by dint of both the introspection it provoked at the UN and by the sheer, catastrophic scale of the violence that tore through Rwanda while Blue Helmets looked on.[2] From a policy perspective, Rwanda's role in ordering and informing many subsequent interventions makes it a necessary case for assessing the long-term and across-

---

[1] See, for example, Samantha Power's *A Problem from Hell: America in the Age of Genocide* (New York: Basic Books, 2002); "Report of the Panel on UN Peace Operations [Brahimi Report]," August 2000; Max Boot, "Paving the Road to Hell: The Failure of UN Peacekeeping," *Foreign Affairs* 79, no. 2 (March/April 2000): 143–148.

[2] By any standard, the scale of atrocity in Rwanda is shocking. Jones (2001, 2) notes that the percentage of the Rwandan population killed in a single day of genocide was greater by at least a factor of ten than the percentage of the US population killed during the course of the Vietnam war, and that, "scaled to the size of the population, the daily death rate in Rwanda exceeded ... by at least a factor of three" the WWI Battle of Paschaendale, where 35,000 soldiers died in a single day, "repeated day in and day out for more than ninety days" (Bruce D. Jones, *Peacemaking in Rwanda: The Dynamics of Failure* [Boulder: Lynne Rienner, 2001]).

case effects of intervention. But what are the effects of other peace-keeping failures *in* Rwanda? Was a negotiated settlement surprising in Rwanda, and how did the UN's failures elsewhere affect the course of the civil war? We know failure in Somalia made UNSC members unwilling to commit resources to UNAMIR, and we know that failure in Rwanda prompted policymakers to reconsider the traditional pro-hibition on UN peacekeepers using force,[3] but we do not yet know what effect, if any, the UN's past performance had on the Rwandan peace process; how the peacekeeping failures in Somalia and Burundi may have conditioned the course of the conflict in the crucial months between the Arusha Accords and the genocide; and what lead the RPF to invite a second UN peace operation into Rwanda following the cataclysmic failure of the first mission.

Examining the Arusha peace process reveals that the parties to conflict had diverse motives for seeking out UN involvement – and that the statebuilding, refugee resettlement, legitimating, and economic dimensions of intervention that peacekeepers enable with their pres-ence overrode the concern these parties had about UN peacekeepers' ability to guarantee their peace agreements. This finding complicates credible commitment accounts of peace operations: Combatants turned to the UN after peacekeeping failures in search of the alternative benefits of bargaining that only the international community can pro-vide, even when they neither expected nor sought a credible, neutral security guarantee.

This section of the chapter defines the geographic, temporal, and thematic scope of the analysis. Next, I provide a brief background to the Arusha peace process, framing the Rwandan Civil War that pre-cipitated the negotiation, peace operation, and genocide. Then I turn to the evidence, asking: Why negotiate after peacekeeping failure? What do combatants seek from international intervention when they do not expect peace and security? I examine the processes by which the Arusha Accords were negotiated; the effects that peacekeeping failure had on combatant perceptions of UN credibility; and why the GoR and the RPF sought the UN's services through UNAMIR and UNAMIR II.[4]

---

[3] Michael Barnett, *Eyewitness to a Genocide: The United Nations and Rwanda* (Ithaca: Cornell University Press, 2003); Brahimi Report 2000.

[4] UNAMIR and UNAMIR II bookended the genocide, but the UNSC authorized a third operation, the French-led Operation Turquoise, during the genocide. This operation very rarely appeared in the evidence I evaluated, although it must also

Scholars and policy analysts have frequently examined the genocide and the shortcomings of the peacekeeping operation, but have far less frequently turned to the elaborate peace process that preceded both. The UN's failure in Rwanda is often regarded as the exemplary instance of international indifference,[5] where powerful states stood by as a preventable disaster they easily could have stopped convulsed a tiny, strategically unimportant country. There were, in fact, extensive international efforts underway *prior* to the genocide to mitigate and contain civil war, with heavy involvement from the Organization of African Unity (OAU) , the precursor to the AU), the United States, France, and Tanzania, in particular. These international efforts were designed to prevent the crisis from escalating, to negotiate a peace, and to build a democratic society, not specifically to prevent a genocide. Although these efforts ultimately failed, the Arusha peace process merits consideration in its own right: The international community was heavily invested in the process; negotiations sheared the extremists in the GoR's coalitions from the moderate Hutu leaders who signed the accords, sharpening their commitment to a genocidal strategy; and even today, the Arusha Accords serve as the basis of the RPF's constitution for Rwanda, enabling it to claim before the international community that it pursues a strategy of governance brought about by consensus.

There is substantial scholarly and political disagreement about the periodization of what some scholars have called the Second Rwandan Civil War, and in particular about its end date.[6] I understand the war

---

have conditioned the RPF's actions and decision-making processes. None of my interview subjects brought it up, perhaps because the RPF largely viewed it as a military operation and not as a peace operation. Indeed, its absence from the process I describe here is most likely a function of focusing on American diplomatic records and RPF interviews to illuminate the negotiation process. French documents on the genocide and the peace process had not yet been publicly released when I was working on this book, and my research systematically underplays the French role in the conflict resolution process as a result of this evidentiary bias, but this does not, of course, mean it was irrelevant to the processes under consideration. On Operation Turquoise, see Gérard Prunier, "Opération Turquoise: A Humanitarian Escape from a Political Dead End," in *The Path of a Genocide: The Rwanda Crisis from Uganda to Zaire*, ed. Howard Adelman and Astri Suhrke (New Brunswick: Transaction Publishers, 2000), 281–306.

[5] Barnett 2003.

[6] Doyle and Sambanis code two wars in this period: one between the GoR beginning in 1990 and concluding in August 1993 with victory for the

as beginning in October 1990, receding with the negotiation of the Arusha Accords in August 1993, resuming in April 1994 with the assassination of President Juvénal Habyarimana and genocide, and concluding in July 1994 with an RPF victory. Violence certainly continued throughout the 1990s with incursions into Rwanda from the Democratic Republic of the Congo (DRC) by Hutu rebels and retaliatory killings by the GoR that affected thousands of Rwandans and Congolese; indeed, the regional dimensions of the conflict continue to reverberate violence throughout the African Great Lakes today.[7] Other accounts cite the war's definitive conclusion at the genocide's end in July 1994, when the RPF defeated the GoR. Proceeding with the understanding that violence certainly continued after July 1994, for the purposes of this analysis, I define two periods of conflict termination for the war: a negotiated settlement in 1993 with a provision for UN forces, and a military victory in 1994, followed by the arrival of a second UN force by invitation.

First, the Arusha Accords were a lengthy, elaborate comprehensive peace agreement that began in July 1992 and concluded thirteen months later after substantial international peacemaking efforts.[8] Although the Accords themselves were never formally implemented, they were an important pause in the war. In evaluating this period, I examine the strategic situations of the actors negotiating the agreement; what these actors wanted from the negotiation process; and what they wanted the international community to bring to their negotiations. Second, I evaluate the period from Arusha's conclusion

government and various Tutsi groups, and another between the GoR and the RPF beginning in April 1994 and concluding with a victory for the RPF (Michael Doyle and Nicholas Sambanis, *Making War and Building Peace: United Nations Peace Operations* [Princeton: Princeton University Press, 2006]). Fearon and Laitin code a continuous war from 1990 to 1999 (James D. Fearon and David Laitin, "Ethnicity, Insurgency, and Civil War," *American Political Science Review* 97, no. 1 [February 2003]: 75–90.). Gleditsch et al. code a war ending in 1998 and then intermediate armed conflict from 1998 to 2001 (Kristian Skrede Gleditsch, "Transnational Dimensions of Civil War," *Journal of Peace Research* 44, no. 3 [May 2007]: 293–309). Hilterman 2002 et al. cite hundreds of civilians killed by Hutu rebels from the DRC and thousands of civilians killed in retaliation by the Rwandan government through at least 1999 (Joost Hilterman et al., *The War within the War: Sexual Violence against Women and Girls in Eastern Congo* [New York: Human Rights Watch, 2002]).

[7] Gérard Prunier, *Africa's World War: Congo, the Rwandan Genocide, and the Making of a Continental Catastrophe* (Oxford: Oxford University Press, 2011).

[8] Jones 2001.

through the full-scale return of war in April 1994 and ending with the genocide's conclusion and the RPF's victory at the end of that summer. In assessing this time period, I ask: What lessons, if any, did the RPF and the GoR draw from the Somalian peacekeeping failure and from a coup in Burundi in October 1993? What effect did international peacekeeping and peacemaking successes and failures have in pushing the different actors involved toward abandoning the Arusha Accords and adopting the strategy of mass atrocity? And what drove the RPF to seek the assistance of UNAMIR II once they had experienced the massive failures of UN peacekeeping efforts during the genocide, taken control of the country, and declared a unilateral ceasefire?

I argue that the negotiating table at Arusha was populated by desperate negotiators who had to settle because they could no longer fight; by hardliners, who used the negotiation process to pursue tactical, material, and symbolic goals other than peace; and by spoilers, who ultimately strove to break the peace. In this context, the international community's unique ability to assist in demobilization and refugee resettlement, as well as their ability to confer legitimacy upon political groups, were important dimensions of the negotiations. I also find that the parties to the conflict had a mixed picture of the UN's efficacy as a guarantor at the start of the negotiations, but often held onto earlier unfavorable impressions from the decolonization period, as well; and that they were aware of peacekeeping failure in Somalia, but they interpreted that failure in accordance with their own strategic situations, either assuming that they were different than the warring parties in Somalia or calibrating their strategies to upend the peace process according to the UN's observed vulnerabilities. Finally, I find that, despite the UN's massive failures during the genocide, the RPF returned again to seek the UN's help after the genocide because they required its statebuilding, refugee resettlement, and legitimacy-conferring capabilities; security goals were secondary to this decision. Considered together, the evidence in this chapter affirms that internationally led negotiations take place in a shared strategic and social environment and can be desirable to combatants for reasons that are distinct from security guarantees.

## Arusha and UNAMIR in Context: The Rwandan Civil War

The Rwandan Civil War was a conflict precipitated by a rebel invasion; exacerbated by economic crises, domestic political reform, ethnic politics, and a peace process that neglected powerful spoilers; and then marked by the choice of genocide as a specific policy decision in the context of civil war violence, despite the presence of international guarantors to the peace.

Rwanda in the 1990s was what Peter Uvin has called a "structurally violent" society: A state marked by perhaps the highest proportionate rate of crushing poverty in the world, by development efforts that centered on elites,[9] and by rising inequality, discrimination, corruption, and a frayed justice system.[10] The country had two large ethnic categories – "Hutu" and "Tutsi" – with historical, society-wide resonance first as a result of colonial divide-and-rule policies and then as a result of a series of wars and expulsions of Tutsis beginning in the 1960s. European colonizers supported a Tutsi monarchy until a revolutionary movement of Hutu nationalists came to power at independence, came to dominate the state and military, and ruled Rwanda as a single-party state under the National Republican Movement for Democracy and Development (MRND) and President Juvénal Habyarimana. During this period, the Rwandan government faced recurrent threats from Tutsi exiles operating from safe havens in Burundi. Governmental attacks on Tutsi civilians in this period were serious, although not yet genocidal in scale, and were correlated with the degree to which the Rwandan government felt threatened by insurgents.[11] Even during this period, majority Hutus and minority Tutsis spoke the same language, often intermarried, and, when they were distinguished, were distinguished primarily by occupation.[12]

In October 1990, a movement of Tutsi Rwandans in exile united under the RPF banner attacked Rwanda from southern Uganda, beginning a civil war in which the RPF quickly demonstrated their ability to take and control territory within the country: The RPF waged a fairly

---

[9] Peter Uvin, *Aiding Violence: the Development Enterprise in Rwanda* (West Hartford: Kumarian, 1998).

[10] Andy Storey, "Structural Violence and the Struggle for State Power in Rwanda: What Arusha Got Wrong," *African Journal of Conflict Resolution* 12, no. 3 (2012).

[11] Scott Straus, *The Order of Genocide: Race, Power, and War in Rwanda* (Ithaca: Cornell University Press, 2006), 353.

[12] Alison L. Des Forges, *Leave None to Tell the Story* (New York: Human Rights Watch, 1999); Filip Reyntjens, *Afrique des Grands Lacs en crise: Rwanda, Burundi: 1988–1994* (Paris: Karthala, 1994); Gérard Prunier, *The Rwanda Crisis: History of a Genocide* (New York: Columbia University Press, 1995).

classic guerilla campaign that hamstrung the Rwandan Armed Forces' (FAR) offensive options while also disrupting economic activity throughout the north of the country.[13] There was nearly immediate international involvement: Habyarimana was in the UN at the time of the RPF invasion, and flew to Europe to request military support from Belgium and France. Six hundred French army officers eventually arrived in Kigali by the end of 1990, and the OAU became involved in mediating between the two sides during that same time period.[14]

The negotiation process, which I detail further in the causal process observations, can be understood as comprising three phases: a regionally led set of efforts that began within days of the invasion; a formal negotiation phase that began in June 1992 under the aegis of Tanzania with heavy involvement from the United States and France and concluded with the signing of a peace accord in August 1993; and an implementation phase, led by the UN. The implementation phase technically followed the formal signing of the peace agreement, but required further negotiations to establish the transitional government that the Arusha Accords called for.[15] There were two formal delegations: the GoR's negotiating coalition and the RPF. Formal negotiations lasted thirteen months, shifting between Arusha, Kigali, and Kampala, and cycling between agreement and deadlock on multiple issues.[16] Tanzania set the agenda, and negotiations covered the following issues: a ceasefire agreement, the rule of law, powersharing, army integration, and refugee repatriation. The parties arrived at a ceasefire agreement comparatively quickly. Other key issues, including refugee return and the integration of the armed forces, held negotiations up.[17]

Two features of the prewar period are particularly salient for understanding the dynamics of the war and the Arusha negotiations: first, economic crisis – both in the form of declining land productivity and a worldwide fall in coffee prices, both with attendant unemployment and austerity – preceded the civil war and exacerbated the existing

---

[13] Jones 2001, 28–31.
[14] Renaud Houzel, *L'ONU et les operations de maintien de la paix: Rwanda 1993–1997* (Paris: Montchrestien, 1997), 25–26.
[15] Bruce D. Jones, "The Arusha Peace Process," in *The Path of a Genocide: The Rwanda Crisis from Uganda to Zaire*, ed. Howard Adelman and Astri Suhrke (New Brunswick: Transaction Publishers, 1999).
[16] Jones 2001.      [17] Jones 2001, 79.

economic disaster in the country.[18] These crises made the GoR unable
to sustain war for an indefinite period of time. Second, the end of the
Cold War and pressure from France precipitated the end of the
MRND's single-party rule and gave rise to a large, primarily Hutu
opposition movement, which encompassed both militant ethnic parties
and more broadly based moderate parties.[19] This political movement
produced a fractious negotiating coalition on the GoR's side at Arusha –
political elites allied with the government jockeyed among themselves
for power both in the domestic arena and at the negotiating table, often
explicitly trying to undercut the president's bargaining positions.

The Accords called for a Neutral International Force (NIF) to oversee
the security dimensions of the agreement. The UN emerged as this security guarantor in a process I describe in the next section. Accordingly,
UNAMIR was authorized in October 1993 and deployed by December
1993. From the beginning, the mission was staggeringly underresourced
and poorly supported by UN headquarters in New York.[20] From
October 1993 through March 1994, the GoR, the RPF, UNAMIR's
commander Roméo Dallaire, the OAU, United States, Belgian, French,
and German delegations to Rwanda, the World Bank and IMF, and UN
staff on the ground – including multiple aid and humanitarian agencies –
all struggled to implement the agreement, given both the contentious
coalitional politics unfolding in the country and UNAMIR's low logistical capacity.[21] Then, in April 1994, President Juvénal Habyarimana
was assassinated in a plane crash alongside the President of Burundi, and

---

[18] Jones 2001.        [19] Storey 2013; Prunier 1995.        [20] Barnett 2003.

[21] On the roles of the World Bank, the IMF, the United States, and the European States,
see the following declassified diplomatic cables: Document dated March 26,
1993 from US Embassy, Dar-es-Salaam, to US Secretary of State; Subject: Background
to Rwanda Talks Concerning Military Force Size, www2.gwu.edu/~nsarchiv/
NSAEBB/NSAEBB469/docs/DOCUMENT%209.pdf; Document dated February 2,
1994 from US Secretary of State Warren Christopher, to US Embassy in Kigali,
Subject: Official-Informal, www2.gwu.edu/~nsarchiv/NSAEBB/NSAEBB469/docs/
DOCUMENT%2037.pdf; and Document dated February 7, 1994, from US
Secretary of State Warren Christopher to US Embassy in Kigali, Subject Official-
Informal, www2.gwu.edu/~nsarchiv/NSAEBB/NSAEBB469/docs/DOCUMENT%
2038.pdf. For information about the specific UN agencies on the ground, see Houzel
1997, 27. The language in this section is very similar to the language in my 2018 piece
"Beyond Do Something: Revisiting the International Community's Role in the
Rwandan Genocide" in *War on the Rocks* (Anjali Dayal, "Beyond Do Something:
Revisiting the International Community's Role in the Rwandan Genocide." *War on
the Rocks*, October 5, 2018. https://warontherocks.com/2018/10/beyond-do-
something-revisiting-the-international-communitys-role-in-the-rwandan-genocide/).

extremist factions within the GoR's negotiating coalition undertook a concerted campaign of exterminating moderate factions of the GoR alongside mass killings of Tutsis.

Most scholars of the Rwandan genocide agree that genocide emerged as a specific policy decision in the context of civil war violence, not as a war of all-against-all in the wake of state collapse. This consensus highlights the elite-driven nature of the mass atrocity, emphasizing that the outcome of mass civilian killings was not the product of state collapse or of violent tribalism, but rather the product of specific state policy in the context of civil war, with violence's ethnic nature stemming from both colonial legacies and the rise of majoritarian ethnic nationalism following independence. This elite-driven model emphasizes the role of spoilers and hardliners in escalating violence toward genocide.[22] The context of civil war produced a "cumulative radicalization model"[23] in which eliminating the Tutsi population was framed as the national answer to threats against the state. The escalation was not one-sided; the RFP also escalated its targeting of civilians in the lead-up to the genocide[24] and there is evidence that the RPF shares culpability for deaths in the genocide itself.[25] In this understanding, Habyarimana's assassination provided Hutu extremists with the opportunity to eliminate moderates in the government and military

---

[22] Straus 2006, 40. See also Prunier 1995, 2011, and Lee Ann Fujii, *Killing Neighbors: Webs of Violence in Rwanda* (Ithaca: Cornell University Press, 2011). For a discussion of the multiple forms of violence unfolding in Rwanda during the war years, see Christian Davenport and Allan Stam, *Rwandan Political Violence in Space and Time*, unpublished Paper, http://bc.sas.upenn.edu/system/files/Stam_03.26.09.pdf.

[23] Straus 2006.    [24] Ibid., 30.

[25] Alan J. Kuperman, "Provoking Genocide: A Revised History of the Rwandan Patriotic Front," *Journal of Genocide Research* 6, no. 1 (2004): 61–84; Philip Verwimp, "Testing the Double-Genocide Thesis for Central and Southern Rwanda," *Journal of Conflict Resolution* 47, no. 4 (August 2003): 423–442; Judi Rever and Benedict Moran, "Exclusive: Top-Secret Testimonies Implicate Rwanda's President in War Crimes," *Mail & Guardian*, November 29, 2020, https://mg.co.za/africa/2020-11-29-exclusive-top-secret-testimonies-implicate-rwandas-president-in-war-crimes/. Rever and Moran's piece includes leaked, redacted statements about the RPF's targeting of civilians given to UN war crimes investigators but only first published in November 2020, after this book was well into its publication process. The leaked testimonies indicate additional support for the argument that the RPF would have reason to seek out the UN's legitimacy to certify its good intentions in the immediate aftermath of the genocide.

who had been party to the Arusha Accords that had granted concessions to the RPF.[26] These extremists were potential losers from the
Arusha Accords, and have been understood as classic spoilers to the
peace.[27]

The genocide and the relapse into full-scale war lasted just over three
months, ultimately ending with an RPF victory and unilateral ceasefire in
July 1994. A French-led, UNSC-authorized mission was deployed from
June until August 1994 with the mandate to provide safe haven for
refugees fleeing the conflict; in practice, the safe zone also sheltered fleeing
genocidaires; after the RPF victory, another enormous outflow of
refugees swept across the Great Lakes region.[28] This period was apoca-
lyptic: By its end, between 550,000 and 800,000 Rwandans were killed,
including approximately 75 percent of the Tutsi population and nearly
the entirety of the country's moderate political elite;[29] two million
refugees fled the country; one million Rwandans were internally
displaced; the infrastructure was largely destroyed; there were nearly no
civil servants still alive in the country; and, in the midst of this post-
conflict chaos, Tutsi refugees who had fled the country in the 1960s began
returning.[30] The RPF quickly followed military victory with establishing
a unity government that adopted the Arusha Peace Accords as the basis of
its constitution. UNAMIR II remained on the ground until May 1996,
and was followed by an extraordinary influx of foreign aid, statebuilding
resources, and internationally led reconstruction programs.[31]

---

[26] Des Forges 1999.
[27] Stephen Stedman, "Spoiler Problems in Peace Processes," *International Security*
22, no. 2 (1997): 5–53.
[28] Prunier 2000.
[29] The standard estimate in many journalistic and UN accounts of the genocide is
800,000 dead (cf. "Report of the Independent Inquiry into the Actions of the
United Nations during the 1994 Genocide in Rwanda," December 1995, and
"Report of the Panel on UN Peace Operations [Brahimi Report]," August,
2000). By historian Alison Des Forges's more conservative estimates, the death
toll amounts to at least 500,000 Tutsis – still approximately 75 percent of
Rwanda's pre-genocide Tutsi population (Des Forges 1999, 15–16). More
informal estimates place the number of Hutu dead – mostly moderates and
Hutus who refused to participate in the genocide – at approximately 10,000
(Straus, 2006, 51). Des Forges estimated another 25,000–60,000 Hutus were
killed by the RPF as they advanced.
[30] Filip Reyntjens, "Rwanda, Ten Years On: From Genocide to Dictatorship,"
*African Affairs* 103 (2004): 177–210.
[31] Scott Straus and Lars Waldorf, *Remaking Rwanda: State Building and Human
Rights after Mass Violence* (Madison: University of Wisconsin Press, 2011).

Credible commitment theories of peacekeeping anticipate that the warring parties sought the services of a third-party security guarantor to ease the credible commitment problem that might plague the implementation of the Arusha Accords. Accordingly, we must explain why these warring parties turned to the UN despite strong indications that the UN would be unable to uphold their agreement. My analysis indicates that factions within the GoR and the RPF turned to the UN despite clear signals of UN weakness in part because they were warweary and desirous of *any* guarantor, but that this is not the *only* explanation. To fully understand the dynamics of UN involvement in Arusha and its aftermath requires we incorporate the alternative benefits of bargaining into our explanation of these events: The extent to which parties to the Rwandan Civil War sought international involvement in negotiations to further their tactical, material, and symbolic goals is as consequential a story as the desperate struggle for a lasting peace during the conflict.

## The Arusha Peace Process

The following evidence covers the period from the start of the Arusha negotiations through the end of the Rwandan genocide, focusing broadly on two periods: the successive rounds of negotiation that concluded in August 1993 with the signing of the peace agreement, and then the implementation and genocide period, which began in October 1993 and ended in August 1993. The evidence is organized into four sets of questions: (1) Why did the Rwandan belligerents negotiate? What were their strategic positions and goals? (2) What did they want out of negotiation? What did they think international actors could bring to the negotiations? (3) What did they think of the UN? Were they aware of its past failures and limitations? How did they interpret these failures? (4) How did the failure in Somalia affect the implementation of the Arusha Accords? I begin by returning to the three types of actors I outlined in Chapters 1 and 2.

### *Why Did the Warring Parties Negotiate?*

My theory specifies three broad factions in many negotiations – desperate negotiators, hardliners, and spoilers – that crosscut the major parties involved in the conflict. All parties, rebels and government alike, may include desperate negotiators, who lack the capacity to return to war and have few options outside of negotiations; hardliners, who privilege securing their goals over striking a bargain; and spoilers, who ultimately have no interest in actually reaching a bargain.

There were two formal negotiating parties throughout the Arusha peace process: the GoR, a fractious, shifting coalition that represented both the president and his party, as well as the domestic opposition parties that were slowly being incorporated into the state's governing bodies; and the RPF, which had a taut negotiating team with direct links between the battlefield and the negotiating table. There is evidence that there were hardliners on both sides, with hardliners dominating the RPF's negotiating stance; there is also evidence of both desperate negotiators and powerful spoilers to the peace on the GoR side.

## Coalitional Politics and the Government of Rwanda

The GoR was conducting simultaneous negotiations with the RPF abroad and domestically with opposition parties. The largest of these parties were represented at Arusha, resulting in members of three different political parties sitting at the table for the GoR, with separate chains of command to the negotiations at Arusha from the president, the prime minister, and the armed forces.[32] The office of the president was particularly embattled: As Joyce Leader, the Deputy Chief of the Mission at the American Embassy in Kigali, characterized the period, "Democratization was being used inside the country by the opposition to gain inroads, to make inroads into the power of the president, to break his monopoly. The peace process was being used particularly by the RPF but also the opposition parties to make inroads again into the power of the president and his party."[33] Facing not just military pressure from the RPF and political pressure from newly empowered opposition parties, but also an economy teetering on the verge of collapse[34] and external pressure from major Western donors and

---

[32] Jones 2001, 72.

[33] Joyce Leader, interview by Michael Dobbs, Impact of Democratization and Peace, National Security Archive Oral History (Washington, October 29, 2013), www.youtube.com/watch?v=YRQ-UWnbAAI.

[34] The country was apparently nearly bankrupt by the middle of 1993 (Des Forges 1999, 94).

financial institutions,[35] the president and the moderate factions of his party, the MRND, most closely resembled the desperate negotiators implicit in credible commitment theories of war termination: They *had* to negotiate to end the war because they could not finance and wage a war of indefinite length. Assessments of this faction of the Rwandan government coalition vary: American observers to the peace process perceived them as pacifist and honest, willing to put all issues on the negotiating table in pursuit of a negotiated solution to the conflict.[36] Other analysts note that the extremist wing of the president's party

---

[35] Rick Ehrenreich, "INR/AA's African Trends-9/18/92 (No. 19)," *National Security Archive Electronic Briefing Book No. 458* (Washington, DC: US Department of State, September 18, 1992).

[36] See, for example, Lawrence Eagleburger, "Subject: Rwandan Minister of Defense on Integration of Forces, from US Secretary of State to US Embassy in Kigali," *State Department Electronic Reading Room, Accessed through National Security Archive* (Washington, DC, November 16, 1992), 5–6, www2 .gwu.edu/~nsarchiv/NSAEBB/NSAEBB469/docs/DOCUMENT%205.pdf; US Embassy Dar-es-Salaam to US Secretary of State, "Background to Rwanda Talks Concerning Military Force Size," National Security Archive Declassified Document (March 26, 1993), 5–6 www2.gwu.edu/~nsarchiv/NSAEBB/ NSAEBB469/docs/DOCUMENT%209.pdf; Ehrenreich 1992, 3; Ambassador Robert Flaten for US Embassy in Kigali to US Secretary of State, "Subj: GOR Outlines Strategy to Negotiations to End War," *Department of State Document Accessed through National Security Archive* (May 13, 1992), 2, www2.gwu .edu/~nsarchiv/NSAEBB/NSAEBB469/docs/DOCUMENT1.pdf. Lawrence Eagleburger, writing on behalf of the US Secretary of State, notes, for example, that "The Minister and Director General seemed serious about solving the integration questions, but very concerned about the percentage of participation the RPF might demand at Arusha"; Anthony Marley, writing on behalf of the US Embassy at Dar-es-Salaam, states that "The two government ministers have been open to the idea of compromise," in contrast with the other coalitional members. Rick Ehrenreich notes that "Habyarimana's side has been pushed harder and more successfully to compromise." Jones (2001) by and large shares the diplomatic cables' assessment of the MRND. Although these declassified diplomatic cables have necessary biases, including likely (logical) overreporting of the US role in various discussions, the United States is overwhelmingly regarded by the two negotiating bodies as a fair, neutral, and honest broker during the peace process (in contrast to France, which was seen as favoring the GoR [on this point, see Jones 2001, Storey 2013]); moreover, although some RPF fighters had trained in the United States as part of the Ugandan army, as subsequent events would bear out, the United States itself had no strategic interests in the conflict that would likely bias its assessment of the negotiating parties (on the United States's lack of strategic interest in Rwanda, see Barnett 2003 and statements made by National Security Advisor Anthony Lake in PBS Frontline's document *The Ghosts of Rwanda*). Accordingly, I place confidence in the validity of the US diplomatic assessments of the various factions.

trained the largest group of the genocidaires; that Habyarimana almost immediately disavowed the Accords after signing them, calling them "a scrap of paper" as early as November 1993[37]; and that by some accounts, in fact, Habyarimana spent nearly all of 1993 attempting to find some way *not* to sign the agreement.[38] While some members of president's party seemed genuinely interested in a positive peace,[39] much of the coalition had to seek a negotiated settlement and to grant heavy concessions in the name of peace because their strategic situation left them with no other options.

Domestic opposition parties were extremely influential at Arusha and constituted important parts of the negotiating coalition. In fact, the GoR's negotiating coalition was led by a member of an opposition party: Minister of Foreign Affairs and Cooperation Boniface Ngulinzira of the Democratic Republican Movement (MDR). This opposition party was the largest in the country and was pro-negotiation; although it included a Hutu-chauvinist wing, observers at the time noted "its core leadership is far more liberal [than the MRND] and is actively seeking a solution that would end the war and accommodate the RPF."[40] Other opposition parties were heavily involved as well, often as part of their efforts to pressure the president into accepting domestic political reforms. Indeed, the negotiations often took on the characteristics of a two-level game: Because any agreements reached in negotiations with the RPF would take legal precedence over the existing constitution and legal codes,[41] the peace process became a way to modify the constitution and extract concessions from the government. These concessions may otherwise have been impossible to win.[42] In this sense, while the president and his party were negotiating to end the war, the opposition that led the negotiating coalition constituted a hardline faction with political goals for the negotiating process that were distinct from terminating the conflict. "The opposition," wrote James Gasana, who was first the GoR's Minister of Agriculture and Environment and then Minister of

---

[37] Des Forges 1999, 40, 80.        [38] Ibid., 95.
[39] The internal jockeying within the MRND does indicate that some influential members of the party *were* perceived as more genuinely pacifist in the traditional sense of the word and in favor of accommodating the RPF (Des Forges 1999, 84, 90, 91).
[40] Ehrenreich 1992, 10.        [41] Ehrenreich 1992, 11.
[42] Reyntjens 1994; Jones 2001, 73.

Defense during the civil war and negotiations, wanted "to enjoy the fruits of the RPF's war effort so as to not have to shed the blood of its own members. This total opportunism [led] to the government's total polarization of how to conduct negotiations. Polarization continued to increase throughout the process until the signing of the Arusha Agreement."[43] Gasana also reported that factions within the government's negotiating coalition objected to the transitional government, on grounds that it was a way for domestic factions to assume power undemocratically and in contradiction to the will of the Rwandan people.[44]

There were also important spoilers on the GoR's negotiating team. Indeed, the architects of genocide were also at Arusha, ostensibly working toward the peace, as well. Led by Colonel Théoneste Bagosora, who was later convicted of genocide and crimes against humanity by the International Criminal Tribunal for Rwanda, these actors viewed the peace process as being driven by political parties with short-term political interests that were contrary to the national interest. Internal memos on negotiating strategies suggest that the army, in particular, preferred violent tactics to the political accommodation underway at Arusha; other sources report far more heterogeneity of opinion about the RPF and the peace process within the armed forces, but the upshot of these communications is clear: There were powerful actors who were very unhappy with the course of action that the GoR's negotiating team at Arusha had chosen.[45] Crucially,

---

[43] James K. Gasana, *Rwanda: Du parti-état à l'état garnison* (Paris: L'Harmattan, 2002), 113; author's translation. The original reads: "Cette opposition veut jouir des fruits de l'effort de guerre du FPR pour ne pas devoir verser le sang de ses propres membres. Cet opportunisme total débouche sur la polarisation du gouvernement quant à la façon de mener les négociations. La polarisation ne cesse pas de s'accentuer tout le long du processus jusqu'à la signature de l'accord d'Arusha."

[44] Gasana 2002, 175.

[45] Colonel Théoneste Bagosora To: Rwandan Minister of Foreign Affairs, "Subj: Negotiation Strategy," *Evidence from the International Criminal Tribunal for Rwanda, Accessed through the US National Security Archive* (June 1, 1993), www2.gwu.edu/~nsarchiv/NSAEBB/NSAEBB469/docs/DOCUMENT%2013 .pdf; Ambassador David Rawson for US Embassy Kigali to US Secretary of State, "Subject: The Military and the Transition to Peace," *US Department of State Declassified Document Accessed through the National Security Archive* (Kigali, February 17, 1994), www2.gwu.edu/~nsarchiv/NSAEBB/NSAEBB458/ docs/DOCUMENT%205.pdf; Lt. Col. Nsengiyumva Anatole to Army Chief of Staff, Rwanda Defense Ministry, "Subject: Mood of the Military and Civilians,"

however, these spoilers were not driving the agenda at Arusha,[46] and scholars trace the colossal failure of the peace process to the significant distance between the final peace agreement and the preferences of the far-right Hutu-chauvinist factions within the GoR's negotiation delegation.[47]

The GoR's negotiating team thus contained desperate negotiators who had weak outside options, hardliners who were using the process for political and tactical ends that were distinct from the peace, and spoilers whose vision of Rwanda could only be realized by ethnic cleansing, not by negotiation. This produced a weak, chaotic, internally quarrelsome coalition that was unable to maintain secret positions[48] or a unified chain of communication and command. The political differences among the different factions of the GoR negotiation delegation were so marked that the RPF became almost an arbiter between them, and, rather remarkably, was framed as such

*International Criminal Tribunal for Rwanda Evidence Accessed through the National Security Archive* (Kigali, June 27, 1992), www2.gwu.edu/~nsarchiv/ NSAEBB/NSAEBB469/docs/DOCUMENT%203.pdf; Ambassador Robert Flaten, US Embassy Kigali, to US Secretary of State, "Subj: Integration of the Armies and Demobilization," *Department of State Document Accessed through National Security Archive* (Kigali, November 20, 1992), www2.gwu.edu/ ~nsarchiv/NSAEBB/NSAEBB469/docs/DOCUMENT%207.pdf. Bagosora writes to the GoR's chief negotiator: "Considering that, once made, your statements during the negotiations are final, and that they engaged the responsibility of the entire nation, we had already asked you ... to consult the delegation you lead, and above all, the Strategy Group, before making any concessions on pre-agreed positions. That was in reaction to your unnecessary offer of 1,200 posts for the RPF in the *gendarmerie* at a time when the discussions were at the stage of dealing with the principles and modalities of the RPF joining that corps. Again yesterday, you cannot imagine how astonished we were to hear you express satisfaction with the Facilitator's proposed proportions for the army ... in front of the Observers and especially the RPF delegation." As for heterogeneity of opinion within the army, in 1992 the US embassy reports that "Rwandan thinking on the integration question has made tremendous strides onward in the past six months. The idea and principle is now accepted by the military and even by the ... right wing CDR party. Minister of Defense Gasana told me proudly this afternoon that the military is solidly behind the concept of integration as a result of a series of seminars he has sponsored" (3). By the implementation period, Rawson notes that mid-level officers' support for democracy is strongest, and that military forces on both sides blame politicians for the impasse (2).

[46] Ehrenreich 1992.      [47] Stedman 1997, 5–53; Jones 2001.
[48] Jones reports that "Observer team members would occasionally have GoR official negotiating papers, stamped 'Secret,' faxed to them via an unknown number in Brussels" (Jones 2001, 72–73).

within the GoR's own internal assessments of the negotiation process.[49] Indeed, Ngulinzira, the lead negotiator for the GoR, reportedly claimed it was easier to negotiate with the RPF than it was to negotiate with his own coalition.[50]

The various goals these different members of the coalition brought to the negotiation table indicate that the GoR was pursuing a multiplicity of goals during the course of the Arusha peace process. Only one faction – the president and his party – was likely to pursue *any* form of security guarantee because they had few options other than negotiation. The other factions were likely to view international intervention through lenses other than simply security guarantees, and to consider the UN's past record in peacekeeping accordingly.

## The Hardline RPF

Three men led the negotiation process for the RPF: Théogène Rudasingwa, Paul Kagame's "eyes and ears" at the talk; Pasteur Bizimungu, the future president of the postwar republic; and Patrick Mazimpaka (or Mazimhaka), the vice chair of the RPF and the principal negotiator.[51] Observers to the negotiation process framed the RPF as a disciplined, hierarchical negotiating team with a clear chain of command from Rudasingwa to the battlefield[52] and a firm ideological line, in contrast to the flailing dynamics of the GoR's team. The RPF was also viewed as the more intractable of the two teams, in part because, although it had much to gain from the peace process, it did not *have* to negotiate: The RPF enjoyed foreign backing from Uganda,

---

[49] Colonel BEMS Bagosora, et al. to Juvénal Habyarimana, "Subj: Negotiations in Arusha from 22 November 1992 to 9 January 1993," *International Criminal Tribunal for Rwanda (ICTR) Evidence Accessed through the National Security Archive* (January 15, 1993), www2.gwu.edu/~nsarchiv/NSAEBB/NSAEBB469/ docs/DOCUMENT%208.pdf. Bagosora writes, "The political differences that were prevalent in the country made themselves felt in Arusha, seriously clouding the atmosphere of the negotiations. This was a direct consequence of the composition of the delegation that carried with it all the [sensitivities] of the political parties. The members of the various political parties present in Arusha zealously vied with each other for behind the scene discussions with RPF on partisan issues so much so that RPF [believes] itself to be and conducted itself like an arbiter. In the future, the delegation should comprise a smaller number of delegates and the politics therein kept to the minimum possible" (3).

[50] Jones 2001, 72.    [51] Ibid.    [52] Ibid.

foreign sanctuary across the border, and the military upper hand. According to internal US Department of State documents from the time, "the government is vulnerable to military pressure from the RPF and to political and economic pressure from major Western donors. The RPF leadership by contrast enjoys sanctuary in Uganda and is not so heavily pressed by Kigali, outsiders, or the costs of a war which is fought on Rwandan soil. It is likely, therefore, that the RPF will maintain a more intransigent negotiating position."[53] Indeed, early in the war, Habyarimana offered the RPF reentry into Rwanda to participate in the new multiparty democratizing system; the RPF rejected the offer, preferring instead to concentrate on a guerrilla effort that pushed the government toward the bargaining table on terms more favorable to the RPF.[54]

The RPF negotiation strategy throughout was one that sought to capture the state to the fullest extent possible, and even the most moderate of the GoR's negotiators viewed the RPF's negotiation strategy as an extension of its military strategy and an effort to assume state positions at a proportion larger than the likely return from its constituencies' vote share in a democratic election.[55] Despite the perception, however, the RPF was clear in its political demands, and accordingly was nearly universally regarded as a sincere party that wanted the agreement to succeed.[56] The specificity of the resulting accords, which include such banal but hard-fought minutiae as provisions about the transfer of pensions for returning Tutsi refugees, certainly seems to indicate that – despite the suspicion with which it viewed the GoR, and despite its continued recruitment of young men into its military ranks throughout the negotiation process[57] – the RPF did expect to actually

---

[53] Ehrenreich 1992, 3.      [54] Ibid., 13.

[55] Ibid., 14; Houzel 1997, 53. Houzel is quoting James Gasana, the moderate GoR minister who fled the country under threat from extremists early in Arusha's implementation period. For further information, see J. K. Gasana, "Guerre, paix, et démocratie au Rwanda," in *Les crises politiques au Burundi et au Rwanda* (1993–1994), sous le direction d'A.Guichaoua, Université des Science et Technologies de Lille, 1995, 211–237.

[56] Jones 2001, 73; Ambassador Robert Flaten for US Embassy in Kigali to US Secretary of State, "Subj: GOR Outlines Strategy to Negotiations to End War," *Department of State Document Accessed through National Security Archive* (May 13, 1992), www2.gwu.edu/~nsarchiv/NSAEBB/NSAEBB469/docs/ DOCUMENT 1.pdf.

[57] Des Forges 1999, 98.

execute the agreement in the event that it was signed.[58] According to American records of the negotiation process, it classified only one of its political demands – the right of refugee return – as non-negotiable.[59] Given the tremendous number of Tutsis in neighboring countries whom the RPF considered refugees with the right of return, and the extent to which their return would alter the demography of Rwanda, this demand was both logistically complicated and politically barbed for the GoR coalition, as the next section of the chapter explores in further detail.

Thus, we can understand the RPF as hardliners for whom negotiation served tactical and material benefits: Given the comparatively intractable nature of its demands, and given that it had the ability to continue fighting, the peace process for the RPF was not a desperate necessity, but rather primarily an exercise in political dealmaking. To summarize, then, the Arusha peace process was one in which there were desperate negotiators, hardliners, and spoilers in the GoR's negotiating coalition, and primarily hardliners on the RPF's side. I therefore anticipate the warring parties' interest in negotiation with international involvement to be a mixture of security, material, tactical, and symbolic goals, instead of only security goals.

Given the various motivations of the parties at Arusha, we need a clearer sense of precisely which issues dominated negotiations, what the warring parties wanted to take away from the negotiating table, and what they believed the international community could bring to their settlement. Analysis of the negotiation process and the resulting

---

[58] See, for example, Section 5, Article 25 of the Protocol of Agreement between the Government of the Republic of Rwanda and the Rwandese Patriotic Front on the Repatriation of Rwandese Refugees and the Resettlement of Displaced Persons in the Arusha Accords: "Returnees who have contributed to the Social Security in Rwanda may claim their dues, either for themselves or their beneficiaries. As for those who have been contributing to the Social Security abroad, the Rwandese Government shall negotiate with the countries concerned as to arrange for the compensation or transfer of their dues" (S/26915, Annex to Letter dated December 23, 1993 from the Permanent Representative of the Republic of Tanzania to the United Nations addressed to the Secretary General, p. 65).

[59] Flaten 1992, "Subj: GOR Outlines Strategy to Negotiations to End War." Flaten is reporting on United States Assistant Secretary of State for African Affairs Herman Cohen's meetings with the RPF from May 10 to 11 of 1992. He also reports that Cohen believes the RPF is ready to negotiate, but has its doubts about whether the new GoR is truly free to negotiate, given the competing political dilemmas it faces.

accords reveals that parties to the Rwandan Civil War wanted the negotiation process to yield peace and security, tactical benefits, material benefits, and both domestic and international legitimacy, and that they wanted and expected the international community to contribute to these potential peace process outcomes. I take each of these potential benefits of bargaining in turn before turning in greater detail to the discussions between the GoR and the RPF and the nature of the international force that they envisioned to implement the Arusha Accords.

## Peace and Security

Some parties to Arusha clearly saw the accords primarily as a vehicle to end the war. The Habyarimana coalition within the GoR's negotiating group, pushed to the brink by economic crisis and war, needed the Arusha peace process to end the RPF's armed offensive within the country and, as noted earlier, pursued peace above other goals. The broader coalition and the RPF, however, also demonstrated their concern with security during the critical disarmament period that was slated to follow negotiations. This is clear in the twelve-page document that the two sides presented to observers following difficult negotiations over the integration of the Gendarmerie. The warring factions outlined their agreed-upon positions and the outstanding issues:

One stems from government resistance to an RPF demand that the gendarmerie be subject to the same integration process as the army, including disarmament, confinement to assembly points, and integration. The government challenged the RPF to demonstrate how the RPF goal of security for itself and the population could be assured under such circumstances. The RPF believes security will be assured during this process by the international force supervising force integration. Resolution of this dispute has been deferred until after agreement is reached on the nature and mission of the international supervisory force.[60]

---

[60] US Embassy Nairobi to US Secretary of State, "Subj: Arusha Talks: Status Report," *Department of State Document Accessed through the National Security Archive* (Nairobi, May 3, 1993), 1, www2.gwu.edu/~nsarchiv/ NSAEBB/NSAEBB469/docs/DOCUMENT%2010.pdf. This document is declassified, but unfortunately much of the actual sections that discuss the warring parties' preferences on the nature and mission of the international force remain redacted.

This document indicates that, one year before the genocide and halfway into the long negotiation process, the GoR had concerns about the security of the RPF and the population, while the RPF believed that the international force supervising force integration would assure its security. These concerns, at least, are what the parties shared with US diplomats: They were willing to publicly state their faith in the international community. This discussion was before the signing of the Accords or deep discussion of the specifics of the international force that was to be deployed, but the warring parties put off resolving the dispute on the Gendarmerie until they reached agreement on the nature and mission of the international supervisory force. This suggests that the warring parties, to some extent, viewed peacekeeping in much the same way that standard accounts of peacekeeping view it – as a tool that backs agreements with credible, neutral force to protect both sides as they disarm. The document *also* indicates, however, that these warring parties had clear preferences about the specifics of the intervention force, a point I return to later in the chapter.

I found evidence of pervasive mistrust between the parties throughout the negotiation process, particularly on the issues of demobilization and integration,[61] although negotiations under international auspices continued despite this pervasive mistrust. As Tito Rutaremara, the RPF's political activities coordinator and the party's General Secretary from 1993 to 1994, said, "As a movement, we trusted them; as individuals, no. When you are negotiating and you have gotten an agreement and you have found someone who will provide you security, you're not going to stop and say, we don't trust these people."[62] Taken together, then, evidence indicates that peace and security were, in fact, key drivers of the peace process, and that the warring parties who sat down at Arusha did so in part because they hoped to secure a neutral international force to provide them with protection during their demobilization efforts.

Peace and security were not, however, the *only* drivers of the process. Given the diversity of goals within the two negotiating coalitions,

---

[61] Ambassador Robert Flaten, US Embassy Kigali, to US Secretary of State, "Subj: Integration of the Armies and Demobilization," *Department of State Document Accessed through National Security Archive* (Kigali, November 20, 1992), 3, www2.gwu.edu/~nsarchiv/NSAEBB/NSAEBB469/docs/DOCUMENT%207 .pdf.

[62] Tito Rutaremara, interview by Anjali Dayal, Kigali (July 31, 2013).

we should expect the tactical, material, and symbolic benefits that only the international community might bring to the bargaining table to drive negotiations as well. I turn to these next.

## Tactical Benefits

Negotiation can provide warring parties with the time and space to regroup, rearm, and relaunch attacks, and it can empower the factional leaders who represent their parties at the negotiation table.[63] The negotiating parties at Arusha seem to have sought both benefits from the peace process. In the most general sense, violence within Rwanda marked the entire negotiation period: Even as elites sat down in Tanzania to construct the agreement, actors within Rwanda were pursuing a simultaneous campaign of civil strife. As Joyce Leader wired back to the US Secretary of State, "It does appear that violence of one sort or another is most likely to erupt when tensions increase as the society struggles to reach consensus on the direction of its next step in the democratization or the peace process. Once the consensus, or semblance of general agreement, is reached, as is the case now, with almost all elements of the society ready to accept the nearly revolutionary Arusha Accord principles, calm is restored for a time."[64] This violence largely took place without attribution: "Many Rwandans are convinced that the internal security rampant in the country in the last six months is no accident, but they disagree on the source. Both sides in Rwanda's political dialogue believe the incidents of internal insecurity fit the plans the other has to destabilize the country in order to achieve its goals."[65]

In fact, both parties used the negotiation period to pursue military goals. Hardliners and spoilers within the GoR coalition – particularly the right-wing flank of the president's party and the right wing of the military – used the negotiation time period to arm and train the

---

[63] Christopher Clapham, "Being Peacekept," in *Peacekeeping in Africa*, ed. Oliver Furley and Roy May (Aldershot: Ashgate, 1998), 303–319.

[64] Joyce Leader for US Embassy Kigali to US Secretary of State, "Subj: Internal Insecurity: an Ongoing Problem," *Department of State Document Accessed through National Security Archive* (Kigali, August 21, 1992), 12–13, www2 .gwu.edu/~nsarchiv/NSAEBB/NSAEBB469/docs/DOCUMENT%204.pdf.

[65] Ibid., 8. Gasana also describes this violence and how it was perceived by factions within the GoR coalition (see, for example, Gasana 2002, 177–179).

*interahamwe*, youth militias who would become the core perpetrators of the genocide.[66] The RPF used the time to slowly press its military advantage, consistently preparing for the renewed outbreak of full-scale war[67] and training new recruits throughout the period of lessened conflict, ultimately breaking the N'sele ceasefire – the first-adopted part of the Arusha Accords – in February 1993, following massacres of Tutsi civilians in the north of the country.[68]

The negotiations were also the staging ground for domestic political tactics – in particular, as noted in the previous section, for accelerating the domestic process of political opening that the Rwandan government was undergoing in tandem to the war, and for placing the domestic opposition parties and their leaders on an international stage early in the process of political liberalization. The RPF also sought these political benefits: Despite rejecting the opportunity to operate as a parliamentary party early in the war, Patrick Mazimhaka, the RPF's chief negotiator, noted that the peace process was a way for the RPF to forge more contact with minority political forces within the country.[69] These tactical benefits to negotiation empowered new political leaders in ways that continued war would not have, were distinct from the successful termination of the conflict, and also animated the Arusha peace process.

## Material Benefits

I argue that peace negotiations may offer material benefits that are distinct from the material benefits of winning a war, and that particular material benefits – statebuilding, refugee resettlement, and the influx of cash that international actors bring to the postwar economy – are *only* available through negotiations with international involvement.

---

[66] Des Forges 1999, 82–83; Straus 2006.    [67] Jones 2001, 34.
[68] Des Forges 1999, 87. The details of this incident are disputed. The RPF claimed it was acting in reaction to the massacre of three hundred Tutsis in the north of the country in late January 1993 and international inaction in face of these massacres, but the timing of its military action, on February 8, 1993, nearly a week after the massacres, led some analysts to note that the action was designed primarily as a way to force Habyarimana's hand at the negotiating table (Des Forges 1999, 87). If the action was designed *primarily* as a way to force the conclusion of the Accords, then the tactical benefits of negotiation in this instance were not necessarily distinct from peace.
[69] Patrick Mazimhaka, interview by Anjali Dayal, Kigali (July 30, 2013).

Consequently, we would anticipate that negotiating parties are interested primarily in statebuilding assistance, either because they are seeking to convert foreign aid into rent or because they cannot reconstruct the state on their own, will seek a negotiated settlement overseen by an intervener that they know can assist them in this reconstruction, irrespective of whether this intervener has a good track record upholding negotiated settlements.

The implementation of the Arusha Accords centered on two processes – the integration of the RPF and the GoR's armies and the repatriation and resettlement of refugees – that the negotiating parties could neither finance nor manage themselves. These two issues had also been the most contentious parts of the negotiations.

The question of integrating the GoR's armed forces and the RPF's army nearly fractured the peace process at several points: "The government had a desire to ... keep things very much as they were, and to bring the RPF in small numbers, and the RPF idea was quite the contrary. They felt that for their own security, and for the security of the Tutsis in the country, they needed to have a larger presence in the security forces in the country."[70] After months of debate about the exact percentage of RPF soldiers that would be folded into the army, the Tanzanian facilitators of the talk sent all the parties home at the end of June 1993, convinced that no agreement was possible until the parties could see their ways to compromise.[71] The proposed figures – that the RPF would constitute one third of the armed forces and half of the officer corps – would have required large-scale demobilization from within both forces, but particularly from within the Rwandan Armed Forces. The armed forces had ballooned over the course of the

[70] Joyce Leader, interview by Michael Dobbs, "Military Power Sharing Negotiations," *National Security Archive Oral History Interview* (Washington, DC, October 29, 2013), www.youtube.com/watch?v=bayUJPxfHFg#t=27.

[71] Joyce Leader, interview by Michael Dobbs, "Military Power Sharing Negotiations," *National Security Archive Oral History Interview* (Washington, DC, October 29, 2013), www.youtube.com/watch?v=bayUJPxfHFg#t=27; S/ 26007, Letter dated June 28, 1993 from the Permanent Representative of the United Republic of Tanzania to the United Nations Addressed to the President of the Security Council. See also the statement from Minister of Defense James Gasana on page 4 in Ambassador Robert Flaten for US Embassy in Kigali to US Secretary of State, "Subj: GOR Outlines Strategy to Negotiations to End War," *Department of State Document Accessed through National Security Archive* (May 13, 1992), 4, www2.gwu.edu/~nsarchiv/NSAEBB/NSAEBB469/docs/ DOCUMENT 1.pdf.

war, and proposed integration therefore became the prospect of unemployment and hunger for a large number of soldiers facing an already constricted domestic economy. Rumors of demobilization sparked mutinies, violence, and fatalities among civilians and soldiers as early as 1992.[72] The compromise solution built aggressive pension and retraining plans for the demobilized soldiers into the Arusha Accords. Neither the RPF nor the bankrupt GoR could finance these programs, which would have cost an estimated US$200 million,[73] and these provisions of the negotiations thus hinged on international involvement. The difficult (and ultimately impossible) task of fundraising the pensions fell to United Nations Development Programme (UNDP) and the World Bank during the implementation period.[74]

Refugee return was the central plank of the RPF's negotiating platform, and, like integration and demobilization, its successful adoption as a measure of the peace settlement rested on the material dimensions of international involvement in Rwanda. This involvement was not just a neutral international force for the protection of the refugees, which certainly was a point of concern for the RPF,[75] but was also logistical involvement to coordinate the repatriation and reintegration of refugees. These tasks would fall to the UNHCR by specific provision of the peace agreement. As the US Embassy in Kigali cabled back to Washington immediately after the negotiations had concluded:

The costs associated with implementing Rwanda's peace accord will be enormous. Demobilization and integration of the armed forces, reinstallation of displaced persons, return and reintegration of refugees, will all have large price tags. . ... Rwanda cannot finance these activities without help from the international community. Although some fat cat rebels, who allegedly

---

[72] Ambassador Robert Flaten for US Embassy Kigali to US Secretary of State, "Subj: Tensions in Rwanda," *Department of State Document Accessed through the National Security Archive* (Kigali, June 1, 1992), 1–4, www2.gwu.edu/~nsarchiv/NSAEBB/NSAEBB469/docs/DOCUMENT%202.pdf.

[73] Reyntjens 1994, 225; Prunier 1995, 193.

[74] Brent Beardsley, interview by Michael Dobbs, "Disarmament, Demobilization and Reintegration (Extended)," *National Security Archive Oral History Interview* (Washington, DC, April 30, 2013), www.youtube.com/watch?v=xsV3qUIpOXg.

[75] Ambassador Robert Flaten for US Embassy in Kigali to US Secretary of State, "Subj: GOR Outlines Strategy to Negotiations to End War," *Department of State Document Accessed through National Security Archive* (May 13, 1992), www2.gwu.edu/~nsarchiv/NSAEBB/NSAEBB469/docs/DOCUMENT 1.pdf.

financed the RPF, might be convinced to invest their funds in peace instead of war, this will be insufficient. Multi-lateral and bilateral aid, over which Rwandans have no control, will be crucial to the process. Funds will be needed for budget support as well as for the projects associated with implementing the peace accord. Rwanda's traditional donors must remain engaged, but new sources of funding must be forthcoming as well. World Bank and IMF participation will be critical. [As] implementation proceeds, the Rwandans will [inevitably] have to lower their sights and alter their procedures [in accordance with] resource availability.[76]

Although the note that Rwandans would have to lower their sights and alter their procedures proved prescient, the centrality of these expensive demobilization, repatriation, and resettlement provisions to the conclusion of the peace process indicates that negotiations at Arusha rested in part on the potential material benefits that bargaining could bring to the Rwandan state.

## *Legitimacy*

Finally, negotiation may have symbolic benefits that reside in the process of negotiation and that are distinct from the conclusion of a conflict. These benefits include recognition from the international community as valid partners and legitimate political actors in the peace process; the discursive value of airing grievances; and appearing to favor the consultative process of mediation and bargaining over the battlefield.

In the Rwandan case, these benefits appear to have motivated the RPF in particular. When asked what they wanted out of the negotiation process, RPF actors involved in the negotiations cited the RPF's quest for both international and domestic legitimacy as drivers of the peace process. As Mazimhaka, the RPF's chief negotiator, said, "You start with challenging the government, but the government has no loss of powerful friends. If you are just a bunch of refugees sitting at refugee camps, you have no right to challenge the government, you have to pursue a two-track solution, first to wage war, to demonstrate to the

[76] Joyce Leader for US Embassy Kigali to US Secretary of State, "Subj: The Rwandan Peace Process: Problems and Prospects for Implementing the Peace," *Department of State Document Accessed through the National Security Archive* (August 19, 1993), 12–13, www2.gwu.edu/~nsarchiv/NSAEBB/NSAEBB469/docs/DOCUMENT%2018.pdf.

world the problem, and then to negotiation, where you might also win the war."[77] In this understanding of negotiation, sitting down to negotiate is a diplomatic task directed equally at your opponents in war and the international community – as Tito Rutaremara, who served as a liaison between the political and military wings of the RPF during the Arusha negotiations, explained, "You gain time sitting at the table, you see that this is another human being, not just a body that you're shooting at, you're able to see if your ideas have the capacity for convincing other people. And you gain contact with the big observer countries that see how serious you are. It's a big diplomatic job you're doing. That's when they started taking us seriously. Before they were thinking that we were a small group that wanted to fight, but then they saw we were serious."[78]

This search for political legitimacy had purely domestic components as well. Mazimhaka framed another dimension of the peace process as a quest for ideological support from the population: "It was difficult to have a very protracted war in Rwanda, particularly when the population believes the propaganda of the government – they can't hide you. That's why you negotiate – to convince the population to doubt the government by a process of conciliation."[79] The process of negotiation, in short, offered the RPF new international recognition and legitimacy as political actors: Observers to the process noted that the attention of the United States, France, and Belgium, in particular, had in fact granted the RPF a substantial degree of international legitimacy[80] as well as the potential to establish itself as a legitimate political actor with the Rwandan population.

To summarize, then, negotiations with international involvement at Arusha offered the GoR and the RPF the possibility of peace and security, but negotiations also provided tactical, material, and symbolic benefits that were distinct from the cessation of hostilities. These alternative benefits of bargaining can help us understand why we might see actors seeking out the services of failed security guarantors. In the next sections, I turn to the specifics of how the two warring parties at Arusha envisioned the international intervention they sought, how they perceived the UN as a guarantor to their agreement, and how

---

[77] Patrick Mazimhaka, interview by Anjali Dayal, Kigali (July 30, 2013).
[78] Tito Rutaremara, interview by Anjali Dayal, Kigali (July 31, 2013).
[79] Patrick Mazimhaka, interview by Anjali Dayal, Kigali (July 30, 2013).
[80] Jones 2001; Ehrenreich 1992, 16.

recent failures affected the implementation period of the Arusha Accords.

## What Did the Warring Parties Think the International Community Could Bring to the Negotiations?

What did the warring parties want the international community to bring to the negotiation process? What did they think the international community *could* bring to the negotiations? How did they envision the intervention force that the Arusha peace process stipulated? This section presents evidence from the negotiation process and from the Peace Accords that concluded it. I conclude that the RPF and the GoR had a preference over guarantors, and that, although the negotiating parties studied past UN interventions as part of the negotiation process, UN peacekeepers emerged late in the peace process as the available international guarantors for the agreement – but UNHCR was involved from an early stage as an important party to the settlement process, with an extensive role in conflict termination built into the Arusha Accords themselves. Taken together, this evidence indicates that, although the negotiating parties ultimately received a guarantor whose record of success and failure they were wary of, they did have specific preferences over the contours of their intervention, and they emphasized the aid and humanitarian dimensions of international involvement alongside the security dimensions.

### The International Parties Involved

The OAU, the United States, and France dominated the early international dimensions of the Arusha negotiations, presenting text to the UNSC once viewpoints had converged.[81] Tanzania provided both location and facilitation for the peace process. The United States provided technical advice and input to the negotiation process at the request of the RPF, apparently as a counterbalance to the presence of the heavily pro-GoR French assistance team; France was on hand because of its long-term strategic affiliation with post-independence

---

[81] US Mission to the United Nations to US Secretary of State, "Subj: Possible Peacekeeping Operation in Rwanda," *Department of State Document Accessed through National Security Archive* (July 14, 1993), www2.gwu.edu/~nsarchiv/ NSAEBB/NSAEBB469/docs/DOCUMENT%2015.PDF.

Rwanda.[82] Although their work is understandably overshadowed in later accounts by American unwillingness to act during the genocide, American diplomats were heavily involved in the negotiation process. The process was the OAU's first foray into peacemaking in earnest, and it remained the primary international organization involved in the peacemaking process for much of its duration, despite the high level of involvement from two permanent members of the UNSC in the negotiations. Indeed, although the UN became the primary executor of the Arusha Accords,[83] and although a representative for the Secretary-General signed the accords as a witness, the UN was not a primary party to the negotiations; it was, however, the primary executor of the accords. A similar dynamic had occurred in other UN peacekeeping cases,[84] and it is reasonable to think that the Rwandan parties may have anticipated that the UN would become guarantor to the peace agreement throughout the negotiation process.

Both the Americans and the OAU explicitly raised UN involvement with the warring parties at different stages in the negotiation process.[85] Despite the potential for UN involvement, during the negotiation phase the warring parties were concerned with other international actors. Both the GoR and the RPF were concerned with remaining in the "good books of our friends and partners, especially France and the United States,"[86] and with maintaining the OAU's high level of interest

---

[82] Jones 2001; Ambassador Robert Flaten for US Embassy in Kigali to US Secretary of State, "Subj: GOR Outlines Strategy to Negotiations to End War," *Department of State Document Accessed through National Security Archive* (May 13, 1992), www2.gwu.edu/~nsarchiv/NSAEBB/NSAEBB469/docs/DOCUMENT%2011.pdf.

[83] Houzel 1997, 66; Ami R. Mpungwe, "Crisis and Response in Rwanda: Reflections on the Arusha Peace Process," in *Whither Peacekeeping in Africa?* (Stockholm: Norwegian Institute for International Affairs (NUPI) and the African Centre for the Constructive Resolution of Disputes (ACCORD), 1999).

[84] Lise Morjé Howard, *UN Peacekeeping in Civil Wars* (New York: Cambridge University Press, 2008); Houzel 1997, 67.

[85] Flaten to US Secretary of State 1992 (Subj: GOR Outlines Strategy to Negotiations to End War); US Embassy Dar-es-Salaam to US Secretary of State, "Subj: Rwanda Negotiations: Texts from Arusha," *Department of State Document Accessed through the National Security Archive* (Dar-es-Salaam, May 14, 1993), www2.gwu.edu/~nsarchiv/NSAEBB/NSAEBB469/docs/DOCUMENT%2012.pdf.

[86] Lt. Col. Nsengiyumva Anatole to Army Chief of Staff, Rwanda Defense Ministry, "Subject: Mood of the Military and Civilians," *International Criminal Tribunal for Rwanda Evidence Accessed through the National Security Archive*

in the conflict.[87] The GoR was particularly concerned with the prospect of waning Tanzanian attention: An internal GoR memo notes
that "The observers accuse the Rwandan Government of NOT BEING
resolutely committed to the negotiation process. Tanzania may lose
interest in the Rwandan case."[88]

The UNSC, the office of the Secretary-General, and the UN
Secretariat were not important audiences or participants in the process
until the implementation phase of the accords, with the exception of
UNHCR, which had a delegate involved in the negotiation processes as
early as February 19, 1991, just a few months after the war began.[89]

(Kigali, June 27, 1992), 4, www2.gwu.edu/~nsarchiv/NSAEBB/NSAEBB469/
docs/DOCUMENT%203.pdf.

[87] The RPF sent Salim Ahmed Salim, SYG of the OAU, a letter thanking him for his
work on May 5, 1993; they were particularly thankful for his work on NMOG:
"We would like in particular, to thank you personally for your expeditious
demarches at expanding the NMOG even though the objective has not been
fully realised for reasons beyond your control. Secondly, we commend the work
NMOG continues to do in monitoring the ceasefire in spite of the fact that it is
stretched to near breaking point. We are grateful that in spite of its handicaps,
the NMOG has been able to coordinate and chair the meeting on the displaced
persons now underway as requested by the two parties in their communiqué of
19/04/1993" (1). The message to thank international actors for their work in
monitoring and overseeing the ceasefire, even as the RPF acknowledges that the
NMOG has limited technical capabilities because of overstretch, indicates an
interest in maintaining the OAU's continued attention (quoted in US Embassy
Dar-es-Salaam to US Secretary of State, "Subj: Rwanda Negotiations: Texts
from Arusha," *Department of State Document Accessed through the National
Security Archive* (Dar-es-Salaam, Document 12 Date: May 14, 1993), www2
.gwu.edu/~nsarchiv/NSAEBB/NSAEBB469/docs/DOCUMENT%2012.pdf.
From: US Embassy in Dar es Salaam To: US Secretary of State Subj: Rwanda
Negotiations: Texts from Arusha Source: Freedom of Information Act Request
(May 14, 1993). www2.gwu.edu/~nsarchiv/NSAEBB/NSAEBB469/docs/
DOCUMENT%2012.pdf.

[88] Lt. Col. Nsengiyumva Anatole to Army Chief of Staff, Rwanda Defense
Ministry 1992, 3.

[89] The text of the N'sele Ceasefire Agreement includes the following: "Mindful of
the fact that Presidents Pierre BUYOYA of Burundi, Juvenal HABYARIMANA
of Rwanda, Ali Hassan MWINYI of Tanzania, Yoweri MUSEVENI of Uganda
and Prime Minister Lunda BULULU of Zaire, assisted by the Secretary-General
of the OAU and a delegate of the UN High Commission for Refugees adopted
the Dar-Es-Salaam Declaration of 19 February 1991 mandating President
Mobutu SESE SEKO of Zaire to take urgent and immediate steps to usher in
dialogue which should culminate in a formal ceasefire agreement between the
Government of Rwanda and the Rwandese Patriotic Front." The N'sele
Ceasefire Agreement is included as part of the Arusha Accords in an annex to
UN document S/26915, "Letter dated 23 December 1993 from the Permanent

## Preferences over Guarantors

The two negotiating parties at Arusha had preferences about which organizations they preferred as mediators and guarantors. Meditation and facilitation were largely conducted by OAU leadership, and by American and French teams, with the GoR and the RPF demonstrating their preference between peacemaking by different national delegations quite clearly. Tanzania ultimately emerged from the Arusha peace process nearly universally lauded for the work of its chief facilitator, Ami Mpugwe, but it was the second regional facilitator for the peace process. Senegal preceded it in the role, and both the RPF and the GoR questioned Senegal's impartiality and skill as a facilitating country.[90] Following Tanzania's accession to the role, however, the process became far smoother.[91] The preference between facilitators demonstrates that the negotiating parties were interested in the specific contours and processes of the agreement, not simply in *any* agreement to end the war.

The warring parties also indicated a preference between security guarantors, although here their choice was more constrained by the international community's will and capabilities. The agreement's implementation rested on the creation of the NIF, but the accords themselves never specified which actors should constitute the NIF. The agreement was signed in August 1993, and as late as May 1993 there was substantial confusion about what kind of force was both most desirable and possible. Both the UN and the OAU were expected to be involved, with the OAU remaining on the ground after the signing of the Accords until a full UN force could be deployed (a time period envisioned as three months), and with the UN subsequently leading the implementation efforts. Internal US assessments of the process note first that "OAU involvement after the peace accord is by no means certain" and that "UN involvement before the peace accord is signed appears out of the question." There were, therefore, concerns about the commitment and availability of each of the

---

Representative of the Republic of Tanzania to the United Nations addressed to the Secretary General."
[90] Ehrenreich 1992, 6; Ambassador Robert Flaten for US Embassy in Kigali to US Secretary of State, "Subj: GOR Outlines Strategy to Negotiations to End War," 3.
[91] Jones 2001.

guaranteeing forces on opposite sides of the Accords' signing[92] – indeed, at
times even the final agreement assigned duties to *either* the NIF or to an
expanded version of the OAU's Neutral Military Observer Group
(NMOG), as though the agreement's drafters were still unsure which
international actors were available and willing to oversee the agreement.[93]

Accordingly, the two parties began petitioning the OAU to expand
its role within Rwanda, concentrating on NMOG, which had been on
the ground in Rwanda for much of the negotiation process. A UN
Observer Mission had arrived in the summer of 1993 (UNOMUR) to
monitor the Uganda-Burundi border, but the RPF and the GoR focused
on NMOG. In a May 1993 letter from Col. Alexis Kanyarengwe,
Chairman of the RPF, to Salim Ahmed Salim, the Secretary-General of
the OAU, Kanyarengwe wrote:

As the negotiations slowly draw towards a conclusion, we cannot help but look
ahead to the implementation of the peace agreement. We therefore see a
continued role of the OAU as the steward of the peace process to its conclusion.
This shall be realised when we have successfully and satisfactorily implemented
the peace accord. We are well aware of the difficulties facing the OAU but we
hope you can find a way to extend the operations of the NMOG to continue to
meet new challenges as the process evolves. To this end, the RPF hopes you will
seek and obtain any form of assistance you may require, particularly from the
UN. The spirit with which you personally recommended the participation of the
UN to the two parties, should continue to guide and inspire cooperation
between the two bodies. We, as a party to the process, shall always be guided
by your decisions on this particular question. The RPF, therefore, hopes that
you will soon get the necessary means to expand the NMOG not only to enable
it to perform its present mission successfully, but also with a view to helping in
the implementation of a peace accord. We also think that in the absence of the
international force envisaged in the Dar Es Salaam communiqué, the expanded
NMOG could take over its mission.[94]

---

[92] US Embassy Nairobi to US Secretary of State, "Subj: Arusha Talks: Status
Report," *Department of State Document Accessed through the National
Security Archive* (Nairobi, May 3, 1993), 1–2 (p. 1, paragraph 7 and p. 2,
paragraph 8), www2.gwu.edu/~nsarchiv/NSAEBB/NSAEBB469/docs/
DOCUMENT%2010.pdf. Irritatingly, the paragraphs that accompany these
sentences are entirely redacted.

[93] See, for example, Article 81 of the Arusha Accords.

[94] US Embassy Dar-es-Salaam to US Secretary of State, "Subj: Rwanda
Negotiations: Texts from Arusha," *Department of State Document Accessed
through National Security Archive* (May 14, 1993), 1, www2.gwu.edu/
~nsarchiv/NSAEBB/NSAEBB469/docs/DOCUMENT%2012.pdf.

Here, the RPF wanted the NMOG to stay on as an implementer of the accords with UN assistance, indicating that they had a preference for greater involvement by the OAU. Both parties, including the war-exhausted factions of the GoR, sought the increased involvement of the NMOG in the humanitarian dimensions of the NIF, beyond its existing ceasefire monitoring, in the round of negotiations that followed the May 1993 round.[95]

United States diplomats report other evidence that the GoR was in favor of a UN-led force, just as they report that the international community also preferred a UN-led force, largely because of the perception that the OAU-led NMOG had not done a particularly good job: Madeleine Albright wrote:

The OAU has been dragging its feet in proposing concrete ways to shore up its operation, despite a visit by a seconded officer from UN DPKO. There are complaints that the OAU is inexperienced, corrupt, incompetent, lacking in funds, etc. The UN has the expertise to be more effective. UN SYG Boutros-Ghali expressed this point of view to the permreps of France, Belgium and the U.S. in the spring. Of the P-5, the French are mostly strongly in favor of having a UN-led PKO, since they are staunchly against the OAU, which is also out of favor with the GoR.[96]

---

[95] The text of the agreement to consolidate the ceasefire, quoted here as well and signed at Arusha on May 7, 1993, notes that the UN will not arrive unless the parties sign a peace treaty: "Elles on en outre été informées de ce que les Nations Unies ne pourront intervenir dans la mise sur pied d'une quelconque force international neuter au Rwanda avant la signature de l'accord de paix." The memo notes that the two delegations, having learned this point, hoped to restart the next meetings at a high level with discussion of the following points: "(1) Examiner l'état d'avancement des démarches de l'OUA pour l'élargissement du GOMN, (2) Examiner l'état d'avancement des démarches menées en vie de la mise en place de la force internationale neutre a vocation humanitaire suivant les dispositions du communiqué conjoint de Dar-es-Salaam et examiner d'autres opinions possibles y compris l'extension des missions du GOMN élargi pour qu'en plus de la vérification et du contrôle du cessez-le-feu, il prenne en charge, partiellement ou totalement, les mission de la force international neutre a vocation humanitaire" (US Embassy Dar-es-Salaam to US Secretary of State, "Subj: Rwanda Negotiations: Texts from Arusha," *Department of State Document Accessed through National Security Archive* (May 14, 1993), 2, www2.gwu.edu/~nsarchiv/NSAEBB/NSAEBB469/docs/DOCUMENT%2012 .pdf.

[96] Madeleine Albright for the US Mission to the UN to the US Secretary of State, "Subj: Possible Peacekeeping Operation in the Rwanda," *Department of State Document Accessed through the National Security Archive* (New York, July 14,

Despite preferring a UN-led mission, the Western countries that Albright mentions did not actually want to finance a UN-led peace-keeping operation; accordingly, they discussed devising "an imaginative way for the UN to help the OAU undertake the major part of the peacekeeping task, allowing the OAU to tap into UN expertise, but avoiding paying for the PKO through assessments on UN member states."[97] Indeed, the Secretariat was concerned about providing troops for the mission. Ultimately, the P5 determined that the Tanzanians had accomplished much of the necessary peacemaking already, and that accordingly the NIF would be an uncomplicated, traditional peacekeeping operation: "This is one case where both parties actually seem to be displaying the will to lay down their arms and move towards a peaceful settlement, as opposed to other areas (e.g., Angola, Bosnia, Georgia) where the goodwill of the protagonists is questionable."[98] France, Belgium, and the United States remained reluctant to make contributions to the mission before the formal conclusion of the Accords. This early reluctance seems to have been common knowledge at the UN, and it is therefore not unreasonable to believe that the warring parties knew of this reluctance as they approached the conclusion of the agreement as well.

By the signing of the agreement, it was clear that the UN would be the implementing authority for the Accords. Habyarimana sent the UN Secretary-General a letter immediately after the signing of the Accords, noting he would

like to express the wish that the international community may guarantee strict respect for this Agreement by giving the former conflicting parties the proof their respective security is ensured. I am therefore grateful for all that you will do to ensure that our world organization can take appropriate and prompt steps to ensure that the Peace Agreement signed this day between the Rwandese Government and the Rwandese Patriotic Front is in no way disrupted but, on the contrary, strictly respected by all the parties.[99]

1993), 5, www2.gwu.edu/~nsarchiv/NSAEBB/NSAEBB469/docs/DOCUMENT 15.PDF.
[97] Albright 1993, 1–2.      [98] Ibid., 4.
[99] A/48/308, S/26295, pp. 2–3, Annex to Letter dated August 10, 1993 from the Chargé d'Affaires of the Permanent Mission of Rwanda to the United Nations addressed to the Secretary-General.

And in September 1993, one month after signing the accords, a joint RPF-GoR delegation traveled to New York to demonstrate their commitment to the agreement, and to request and note the importance of sending a UN mission to Rwanda; the Secretary-General received them.[100] Despite initial indications that they preferred the OAU, then, the warring parties ultimately signed the Arusha Accords with the knowledge that the UN would be their guarantor; they then attempted to secure the best possible guarantee from the UN that they could get.

These are all process-observations that accord with my theory: Although the *choice* among guarantors is not unrestricted for parties to a conflict, in cases where we see negotiation despite peacekeeping failures, we should see combatants demonstrate a preference over guarantors, and either actively working to secure a better guarantee from the guarantor, actively working to secure one of negotiation's other benefits, or actively indicating that their case, this time, is different from past peacekeeping failures.

## Preferences over the Form of the Mission

The GoR and the RPF both also had preferences over the *form* of the mission. The final shape of the NIF and the particularities of integration, demobilization, and monitoring roles that the Arusha Accords assigned to international guarantors were the result not just of intense negotiations – as previously noted, the integration of the armed forces was a huge point of contention between the warring factions – but also of direct modeling and study of other transitional and integration processes. The United States suggested a number of other recent cases to the Rwandan parties, including Nicaragua, El Salvador, Angola, and Namibia, as potential templates for integration and demobilization in Rwanda; other actors suggested Cambodia, Liberia, and Mozambique; and a delegation of Rwandan officials actually traveled to Nicaragua and Zimbabwe on fact-finding missions to inform their negotiations.[101] As a result, the parties were clearly

---

[100] Houzel 1997, 23.

[101] Jones 2001, 70; US Embassy in Dar-es-Salaam to US Secretary of State, "Subj: Arusha V: Going Ahead on Nov. 23, Military Integration to Top Agenda," *Department of State Document Accessed through National Security Archive* (November 20, 1992), www2.gwu.edu/~nsarchiv/NSAEBB/NSAEBB469/docs/DOCUMENT 6.pdf.

attentive both to the potential variation in internationally led security guarantees and to the UN's record abroad.

The delegation passed through Washington on its return from its week in Nicaragua in November 1992, and it seems clear that they had strong preferences about which models might work best in Rwanda. They rejected the Nicaraguan model; the US's military advisor for Rwanda, Tony Marley, suggested Zimbabwe might be a better model, while the delegation suggested they might look to El Salvador's recently implemented agreements. Notably, the first models the United States suggested were *not* UN cases, while the GoR delegation expressed a desire to visit a UN-led case, indicating attentiveness to the UN's performance as a guarantor elsewhere.[102]

Ultimately, the mission was primarily based on various elements of the UN Mandate for Mozambique (ONUMOZ).[103] It was given over to the responsibility and command of the UN, but the Accords specified that the warring parties retained approval over which national contingents would staff the mission.[104] In addition to a set of security and protection functions for the civilian populations and political figures, the Accords assigned to the force the responsibility of general assistance in the implementation of the peace agreement, particularly the integration of the armed forces. Its role in supervising the new National Army's process of formation was very clearly specified, and included supervising the demobilization and disengagement of forces; cross-checking inventories of armaments and ammunitions; supervising supply operations; participating in the "programme designed for the training of members of the new Armed Forces and [catering] for the security of Training Centres"; the duty of specifying the date for two forces to assemble after demobilizing heavy weapons[105]; and the authority, with NMOG, to allow the use of particular heavy

---

[102] US Secretary of State to US Embassy in Kigali, "Subj: Rwandan Minister of Defense on Integration of Forces," *Department of State Document Accessed through National Security Archive* (November 16, 1992), www2.gwu.edu/~nsarchiv/NSAEBB/NSAEBB469/docs/DOCUMENT%205.pdf.

[103] Houzel 1997, 67.

[104] Protocol of Agreement between the Government of the Republic of Rwanda and the Rwandese Patriotic Front on the Integration of the Armed Forces of the Two Parties, Article 53, Arusha Peace Accords.

[105] Article 54, Protocol of Agreement between the Government of the Republic of Rwanda and the Rwandese Patriotic Front on the Integration of the Armed Forces of the Two Parties, Arusha Peace Accords.

vehicles or aircraft for specified missions at the request of the Army Command High Council and the Command Council of the National Gendarmerie.[106] At times, the Accords specified a complicated separation between the NMOG and the United Nations Reconnaissance Mission, which would both demarcate Assembly Zones together, and then the NIF, which would subsequently identify assembly points for the two forces. The Accords devolved to the NIF, alongside the Army Command High Council, the duty of specifying the date for assembly after demobilizing heavy weapons.[107] The specificity of the functions assigned to various intervention forces indicates a clear preference over which international actors were tasked with guaranteeing different security dimensions of the agreement.

## UNHCR's Central Role

The accords assigned a central role to UNHCR: The agency was intimately involved in the provisions of repatriation and refugee management, and was invoked in the Accords in a way that other international actors were not. Annex V of the Arusha Agreement, "On the Repatriation of Rwandese Refugees and the Resettlement of Displaced Persons," fleshed out UNHCR's roles and functions, including identifying, registering, and repatriating refugees, and it established UNHCR's responsibility, alongside the OAU, as the lead implementing organization for funding refugee programs.[108] Other parts of the Annex referred more generally to "the International Community" and its role alongside the Rwandan government in providing food, health, and education, as well as domestic, farming, and building materials to returning refugees.[109] The Accords also cited general "international funding institutions" with which the Rwandan government would undertake negotiations for assistance to expand the public sector's hiring capabilities.[110] The task of UNHCR, however, was

---

[106] Article 67, Protocol of Agreement between the Government of the Republic of Rwanda and the Rwandese Patriotic Front on the Integration of the Armed Forces of the Two Parties, Arusha Peace Accords.
[107] Article 54, Protocol of Agreement between the Government of the Republic of Rwanda and the Rwandese Patriotic Front on the Integration of the Armed Forces of the Two Parties, Arusha Peace Accords.
[108] Arusha Peace Agreement, Annex V, Sections 4–6.
[109] Arusha Peace Agreement, Annex V, Section 4, Article 15.
[110] Arusha Peace Agreement, Annex V, Section 5, Article 23.

framed as being akin to the duties of sovereign states in the region with the agreement, even to the point of being a negotiating party itself: The Accords dictated that "within six (6) months after the establishment of the Broad-Based Transitional Government, tripartite agreements between Rwanda, the UNHCR, and individual countries in the Region, and the UNHCR shall have concluded on issues pertaining to the repatriation of refugees."[111] Thus, although the parties to the Arusha Accords did not necessarily lobby for a UN peace operation from the beginning of the process onward, and although they demonstrated at times a preference for OAU security guarantors, UNHCR was built into the very foundation of the peace agreement.

The precondition for the return of the displaced, however, was the deployment of a NIF.[112] In this understanding of what the parties wanted from a peace operation, international force was the prerequisite for the humanitarian activities, not merely a monitor of the ceasefire, and humanitarian agencies were accorded more authority than the NIF.

## What Did Combatants Think of the UN's Past Performance?

This book hinges on the idea that, given the finite number of potential third-party security guarantors in the world, parties to a conflict develop a sense of what to expect from intervention, and that they shape their conflict and negotiation strategies in part with these expectations in mind. Accordingly, this section asks what the parties to the second Rwandan Civil War thought of the UN's abilities and past performance, and how they thought of the UN's past peacekeeping failures. This section presents perspectives on the UN in general; the next section deals more specifically with concerns about the UN's ability to implement the Arusha Accords in light of the Black Hawk Down incident in Somalia and a coup in Burundi.

Most studies of UN peacekeeping take 1989 as their starting point, with the note that peace operations in civil wars began with the DRC in 1960. In this standard account – one which I, too, adopt elsewhere in this book – peace operations began in earnest when divisions at the UNSC thawed after the Cold War. By this account, there were not

---

[111] Arusha Peace Agreement, Annex V, Section 7, Article 34.
[112] Arusha Peace Agreement, Annex V, Article 26.

many operations with which combatants in Rwanda could assess the UN's performance as guarantor to civil war peace agreements when the war began in 1990: As Chapter 3 details, by 1990 the Namibian agreement had concluded successfully; by 1991 an agreement had been negotiated in Cambodia; by 1992 Nicaragua and El Salvador's agreements had been successfully negotiated while missions in Liberia and Angola had failed; and by the conclusion of the Arusha Accords the mission in Cambodia had concluded successfully. This is a mixed picture of efficacy, although the failures were proximate to Rwanda and the successes largely distant.

My interviews revealed, however, that 1989 was not the appropriate starting point with which to assess Rwandans' relationship with the UN system. The parties to the conflict did not view the end of the Cold War as a new beginning for UN intervention in Africa. Instead, the colonial period and its legacies loomed large in the warring parties' perceptions of the UN because the UN's presence in the Great Lakes region dates to the colonial period. Although Rwanda was administered by Belgium after WWI, it was territory held in UN trusteeship, and "under UN tutelage, the process of decolonization unfolded as a series of electoral reforms, beginning in 1952."[113] A string of UN decolonization missions arrived in Rwanda at least once every three years from 1949 onward. Mahmoud Mamdani notes these visits often precipitated reforms to property and governance laws that favored Tutsi elites and produced protests among the Hutu herders and farmers who felt increasingly (and continually) marginalized by these elites. The simplified story of trusteeship's political dynamics is that, following years of incremental political reform, UN-backed elections and referenda in 1962 ousted the Tutsi monarchy; Tutsi parties lost heavily; and the Tutsi political elite moved into exile with plans to retake power via arms.[114] A UN intervention, and then subsequently a formal announcement of state independence, produced a political dynamic that lasted in some measure until the RPF invasion in 1990 – persisting even through an earlier war in 1964 – in which the center of Hutu political power was in Kigali, and the center of Tutsi

---

[113] Mahmood Mamdani, *When Victims Become Killers: Colonialism, Nativism, and Genocide in Rwanda* (Princeton: Princeton University Press, 2001), 114. For a full account of this period, see Catharine Newbury, *The Cohesion of Oppression* (New York: Columbia University Press, 1993).

[114] Ibid., 126.

political power rested in exile. During those years, despite the inherent difficulty of refugee status, "its upside was a consequence of UN recognition. Those recognized by the UN as refugees were entitled to UN aid" in a way that the poor in-country were not, and "most of the younger people had taken advantage of UNHCR scholarships."[115]

The UN, then, had a long history with the very Rwandans who fought the second Rwandan Civil War and who were negotiating the Arusha peace process: The men and women who fought that war were the children of people who had lived through the trusteeship period, and they themselves may have remembered the UN as being either trigger for elite consolidation of land before independence, or the catalyst of exile, or the custodian of refugee camps. When I asked RPF members I interviewed what they expected the UN to bring to their negotiated settlement, they categorically – and often quite vehemently – said they expected very little from the UN, given their past experience with the UN's promises. In each case, they brought up the UN's history as colonial authority without my prompting, since the UN's role in decolonization was neither part of my theoretical framework nor my interview script. In that sense, the revealed importance of the UN's role in decolonization constitutes strong confirmatory evidence that the UN's past action informs the actions of parties to civil war negotiations: It was novel information I uncovered by testing the theory.[116]

One former senator and party commissioner described a song that was sung among Tutsi refugees after the 1962 referendum about how the UN abandoned the losers of the election.[117] Rutaremara, the RPF General Secretary during the negotiation period and the genocide, told me: "Since I was born, I have been living on the frustration of the UN. During independence, the Belgians and the *Parmehutu* massacred people and they ran away. We became refugees, and they were not doing anything to help us back to our communities. All of our parents, they had hope in the UN, but as I got older, even they became frustrated ... twice in my life, I have been frustrated by the UN. We remained in refugee communities and the UN forgot about us, the international community wasn't talking about us. The whole of my

[115] Ibid., 165.
[116] Alexander L. George and Andrew Bennett, *Case Studies and Theory Development in the Social Sciences* (Cambridge, MA: The MIT Press, 2005).
[117] Wellars Gasamagera, interview by Anjali Dayal, Kigali (July 30, 2013).

life has been a frustration with the UN."[118] Mazimhaka, the chief negotiator for the RPF, also harkened back to the colonial period, noting, "I wasn't surprised when the mission failed again. I'm not surprised when the UN fails – I don't know why we keep doing this. We have to keep doing it because that's our organization."[119]

Other specters of the colonial period marked the negotiation process. Belgium, the former colonial authority in Rwanda, was involved in the observer group to the Arusha peace process, and, of course, it was a troop-contributing country to UNAMIR. While Dallaire and the local media expressed some initial concerns about this,[120] neither of the warring parties raised formal objections to their presence on the force.[121] Nonetheless, in the early days of the mission, Dallaire moved to downplay the Belgian aspects of the intervention by emphasizing its multilateral nature.[122] This, to some extent, indicates that, despite the RPF's perceptions of the UN, the UN "brand" had greater cache in Rwanda than the Belgian one, perhaps in part because multiple UN aid and humanitarian agencies were already on the ground in Rwanda by the war's end.[123]

Thus, the parties to the Rwandan conflict did, in fact, have prior, largely negative beliefs about the UN's conduct, but these beliefs stretched back to their own experience during Rwanda's bloody passage from colonial trust territory to independent state. The next section asks how these negative perceptions, taken in combination with the fresh failures in Somalia and a coup in Burundi, affected the Arusha Accord's implementation period under UNAMIR's authority.

[118] Tito Rutaremara, interview by Anjali Dayal, Kigali (July 31, 2013).
[119] Patrick Mazimhaka, interview by Anjali Dayal, Kigali (July 30, 2013). The last part of Mazimhaka's statement – that the UN is "our organization" – is one I will return to in the next section.
[120] Dallaire/UNAMIR/Kigali to Annan/DPKO/UNations, "Subj: Interaction Force HQ/UNDP For Demobilization and Integration Process," *United Nations Internal Document Accessed through International Criminal for Rwanda Database (ICTR)* (December 26, 1993), 6, www2.gwu.edu/~nsarchiv/NSAEBB/NSAEBB469/docs/DOCUMENT%2019.pdf.
[121] Roméo Dallaire, *Shake Hands with the Devil: The Failure of Humanity in Rwanda* (New York: Carroll and Graf Publishers, 2003), 106. Dallaire notes that this is most likely because it was clear that no other major Western power wanted to donate troops, and because both sets of ex-belligerents knew how long it would take to recruit another set of similarly equipped soldiers.
[122] Dallaire/UNAMIR/Kigali to Annan/DPKO/UNations, 1993.
[123] Houzel 1997, 27.

## How Did International Peacekeeping and Peacemaking Failures Shape the Implementation of the Arusha Accords?

The Arusha Accords were signed in August 1993; UNAMIR was authorized in October 1993; and the first troops were deployed in December 1993. While the mission was formally charged with overseeing the implementation of the Arusha Accords, in practice it also was overseeing further negotiations over the precise form of the Broad-Based Transitional Government that the Accords stipulated. In this capacity, mission personnel functioned as mediators, facilitators, and security guarantors to combatants whose relationship to their agreement was at best wary and at worst openly hostile – there were persistent delays in swearing in the new transitional government, as well as continual efforts at facilitation between the various factions of this government by both Jacques-Roger Booh-Booh, the special representative of the Secretary-General to Rwanda, and Dallaire. Since the transitional government was the lynchpin of the agreement – nothing else, including the integration of the military forces, could take place until this government was in place – this process consumed a significant share of UNAMIR's already-stretched resources.[124] Moreover, the situation on the ground in Rwanda was one of widespread terror, insecurity, and violence for civilians, with one seventh of the population still displaced.[125] Nonetheless, it still seemed to many of the actors involved as though UNAMIR could be a classic, straightforward mission to oversee a negotiated settlement, with enough goodwill on both sides to eke out a stable peace.[126]

---

[124] J.-R. Booh-Booh, Kigali, to Annan, UNations, "SUBJ: Daily Sitrep 080600B Jan to 090600B Jan 94 No: MIR 053," *United Nations Document Accessed through National Security Archive* (Kigali, January 9, 1994), www2.gwu.edu/~nsarchiv/NSAEBB/NSAEBB455/documents/DOCUMENT05.pdf; J.-R. Booh-Booh, Kigali, to Annan, UNations, "SUBJ: Daily Sitrep 140600B Jan to 150600B Jan 94," *United Nations Document Accessed through National Security Archive* (Kigali, January 15, 1994), www2.gwu.edu/~nsarchiv/NSAEBB/NSAEBB455/documents/DOCUMENT10.pdf.

[125] ECOSOC Commission on Human Rights Report, "Extrajudicial, summary, or arbitrary executions [in Rwanda]," August 11, 1993. Rapporteur: Bacre W. Ndiaye. E/CN.4/1994/7/Add.1.

[126] Dallaire 2003, 71; Albright to US Secretary of State 1993.

## Somalia and Burundi

As the previous section argues, the UN's record during the Arusha peace process itself was mixed; combatants seeking to assess the kind of security guarantor they might get would have been able to draw from both successful and unsuccessful examples. The implementation – and partial renegotiation – of the Accords presented these actors with a very different picture. Two international events punctuated the mission's inception: first, on October 3, 1993, the United States suffered an enormous, globally broadcast blow to its UN mission in Somalia; three days later, the UNSC met to authorize the mission to Rwanda. The UNSC's reaction to the Black Hawk Down incident in Somalia is well documented: The P5 drew back from peacekeeping immediately.[127] As Des Forges writes,

Constrained by the relatively small size of the force as well as by a determination not to repeat the mistakes made in Somalia, the diplomats produced a mandate for UNAMIR that was far short of what would have been needed to guarantee implementation of the Accords. In a spirit of retrenchment, they weakened several important provisions of the Accords. Where the Arusha Agreement had asked for a force to "guarantee overall security" in Rwanda, the Security Council provided instead a force to "contribute to" security, and not throughout the country, but only in the city of Kigali. At Arusha, the parties had agreed that the U.N. peacekeepers would "assist in tracking of arms caches and neutralization of armed gangs throughout the country" and would "assist in the recovery of all weapons distributed to, or illegally acquired by, the civilians." But, in New York, diplomats conscious of the

---

[127] Barnett 2003. UNAMIR inherited more than a reduced mandate from the UN's time in Somalia: Dallaire notes that many of the Belgian soldiers who served in Rwanda had been recently stationed in Somalia, and Dallaire reports that they spoke of this experience on arrival in Kigali: "Many of the Belgian soldiers had completed a tour in Somalia, which was a chapter-seven mission, and they came to UNAMIR with a very aggressive attitude. My staff soon caught some of them bragging at the local bars that their troops had killed over two hundred Somalis and that they knew how to kick '[racist slur]' ass in Africa. I was compelled to call a commander's hour . . . I left them with no doubt that I would not tolerate racist statements, colonial attitudes, unnecessary aggression or other abuses of power" (Dallaire 2003, 113). Kigali is a small, heavily networked city, and Belgian soldiers boasting of their time in Somalia at a bar was a story that could certainly have circulated quickly among many Rwandan elite. Dallaire also reports that "Much of the Belgian equipment [in Rwanda] had been shipped directly from Somalia without being cleaned or serviced" (Dallaire 2003, 113).

difficulties caused by disarmament efforts in Somalia completely eliminated
these provisions. In the Accords, the peacekeepers were to have been charged
with providing security for civilians. This part of the mandate was first
changed to a responsibility for monitoring security through "verification
and control" of the police, but in the end it was limited to the charge to
"investigate and report on incidents regarding the activities" of the police.[128]

The repercussions of the peacekeeping failure in Somalia were therefore immediate, and immediately observable to the GoR and the RPF:
UNAMIR was specifically designed to fall short of successfully implementing the Arusha Accords. Its shortfalls were apparent from the
mandate down to the day-to-day details of integrating the armed
forces, and everyone from the elites who negotiated at Arusha
down to the soldiers who stopped UNAMIR officers to ask them
about progress securing funding for demobilization pensions knew
of them.[129]

Second, on October 21, 1993 – one day before Dallaire arrived in
Rwanda to establish UNAMIR there – the first democratically elected
president of Burundi, a Hutu, was overthrown by a primarily Tutsi
army. Nearly 50,000 people, most of them Hutu, were killed in the
violence that followed. This produced an unforeseen influx of
Burundian refugees into Rwanda and exacerbated the cleavages that
radically ethnic parties in Rwanda were playing upon.[130] International
pressure – including from Belgium, which was asked to provide troops
to secure the situation in Burundi, but did not[131] – compelled the army

[128] Des Forges 1999, 100.
[129] Brent Beardsley, interview by Michael Dobbs, "Disarmament, Demobilization
and Reintegration (Extended)," *National Security Archive Oral History
Interview* (Washington, DC, April 30, 2013), www.youtube.com/watch?v=
xsV3qUIpOXg.
[130] Houzel 1997, 48–49; Reyntjens 1994.
[131] US Embassy Brussels to US Secretary of State, "Subject: FONMIN Claes'
Interview on His Trip to Rwanda and Burundi and on Situation in Zaire,"
*Department of State Document Accessed through National Security Archive*
(Brussels, March 11, 1994), www2.gwu.edu/~nsarchiv/NSAEBB/NSAEBB458/
docs/DOCUMENT 10.pdf. Belgian Foreign Minister Willy Claes says: "We
were asked to send 2,000 soldiers but it was obvious that the army did not want
them. There was, therefore, a risk of a violent confrontation. In the aftermath, it
was decided to send a stabilization force composed of troops designated by the
OAU. Belgium was ready to participate in the financing of this force with a
contribution of Dols 2 million. But even this, the arrival of 180 men, the army
did not want. It then became a question of sending 65 engineering or medical

to return government control to civilians, but donor states did not pressure the army to hold anyone accountable for either the political assassinations or the killing of civilians.[132] These two events gave the parties to Arusha two strong signals: first that the international community's commitment to implementing the Arusha Accords was weak, and second, that civilian populations could be killed en masse without repercussion from the international community.

## Perceptions of Somalia and Burundi

How did the parties to Arusha interpret these events? Both parties were clearly aware of the failures. For the RPF, while Somalia and Burundi were notable, they did not immediately draw the conclusion that the implementation of their agreement would suffer as a result, partially because they viewed themselves as different "types" than the Somali recipients of intervention. Mazimhaka said, "I don't think we were savvy enough to realize the broader crisis … we said, Somalia was different. *This* was after an agreement broadly supported by the population, broadly supported by its neighbors … here we will have support."[133] To some extent, then, this interpretation of peacekeeping failure hinges on perceptions of where failure comes from: For at least some parts of the RPF, spoilers were responsible for the failure in Somalia, and because the RPF viewed themselves as committed to the agreement, their case would be different. Internal US documents frame Kagame's similarly optimistic assessment of prospects for Rwanda in the immediate aftermath of the crises in Somalia and Burundi; over a private lunch, and amid discussions over the stalled plans to integrate the armed forces, he told US diplomats he was planning a vacation to the United States, and he thanked them for their continued support of the peace agreement.[134]

officers. We were far away from a stabilization force. But the army of Burundi considered that this intervention was also humiliating" (4).

[132] Des Forges 1999, 102.

[133] Patrick Mazimhaka, interview by Anjali Dayal, Kigali (July 30, 2013).

[134] Joyce Leader for US Embassy Kigali to US Secretary of State, "Subj: RPF Perspective on the Peace Process," *Department of State Document Accessed through National Security Archive* (Kigali, December 10, 1993), www2.gwu .edu/~nsarchiv/NSAEBB/NSAEBB469/docs/DOCUMENT%2034.pdf. See also Philip Gourevitch, *We Wish to Inform You That Tomorrow We Will Be Killed with Our Families* (New York: Picador, 1998), 221. It is perhaps not surprising

For extremists within the GoR who wanted to collapse UNAMIR, however, the lessons of Somalia and Burundi seem to have been about targeting Western peacekeepers to make them withdraw. UNAMIR was targeted for violence from nearly the moment its soldiers began arriving in Rwanda,[135] but the targeting of peacekeepers in the early days of a mission is standard practice, designed in part to test the mettle of intervening forces and in part to rattle them.[136] In the case of UNAMIR, however, the targeting was more specific: Belgian soldiers, in particular, were singled out by extremists bent on foiling Arusha's implementation and collapsing the mission.

The role of Belgian soldiers in Rwanda bears unpacking a bit. Many of these soldiers had recently served in Somalia; they were in Rwanda as nationals of Rwanda's former colonial ruler; they were there representing the international community's commitment to implementing the Arusha Accords; and they were the only "Western" country with troops on the mission, as well as the best-equipped and best-trained of UNAMIR's troops.[137] Evidence indicates that they were specifically targeted *both* as representatives of the former colonial power *and* as the pivot on which the entire mission's capabilities swung.

Early evidence that Belgian soldiers specifically were targeted comes from the same informant, "Jean-Pierre," who first brought the impending genocide to UNAMIR's attention. Jean-Pierre told Dallaire and other mission leaders that a

that Kagame would express thanks to the United States at a meeting with the United States, irrespective of what he thought of the US's actual commitment to peace process. It is worth noting, however, that even in December 1993, after considerable on-the-ground work from Dallaire and the UNAMIR administration, it was still the US's input that was being celebrated and vaunted, not the UN's; there are no comparably glowing celebrations in the internal UN documents.

[135] J.-R. Booh-Booh, Kigali, to Annan, UNations, "SUBJ: Daily Sitrep 300600B Jan to 310600B Jan 94 No: MIR 220," *United Nations Document Accessed through National Security Archive* (Kigali, January 31, 1994), www2.gwu.edu/~nsarchiv/NSAEBB/NSAEBB455/documents/DOCUMENT17.pdf.

[136] Patrick Cammaert, interview by Anjali Dayal, New York (April 15, 2013); see also Nynke Salverda, "Blue Helmets as Targets: A Quantitative Analysis of Rebel Violence against Peacekeepers, 1989–2003," *Journal of Peace Research* 50, 6 (2013): 707–720.

[137] Canada had no troops on the ground; only Dallaire and Beardsley represented Canada in a military capacity (Dallaire 2003).

January 8 demonstration had been meant to provoke a confrontation with the Belgian UNAMIR soldiers, but that since no conflict had developed, he had never given the order to open fire. . . . The informant confirmed that the January 8 demonstration, which he had commanded, had been meant in part to create conditions for killing Belgian UNAMIR soldiers, in the expectation that this would cause Belgium to withdraw its troops from Rwanda.[138]

In the same period, "the militia were ordered to never obey orders from Belgian soldiers, to call Interahamwe from surrounding areas whenever confronted by Belgians, and to get as many local people as possible to witness the confrontation . . . after a long diatribe against UNAMIR, the radio station called on the population to 'take responsibility' for what was happening because otherwise the Belgian soldiers would give Rwanda to the Tutsi."[139] Here, we see a mixture of mission-collapse motives and invocations of Belgium's colonial legacy in Rwanda.

Once the genocide began, UNAMIR's Belgian soldiers were among the first killed, and evidence indicates this was specifically because of the UN's past performance. Multiple sources report that a government official explained the decision to kill Belgian peacekeepers was explicitly inspired by the Mogadishu ambush and calibrated to force UNAMIR's withdrawal.[140] In his memoirs, Annan writes:

[The GoR official] was referring to the lesson that they had garnered from Somalia the year before: that the death of just a few foreign peacekeepers would be enough to end the appetite for intervention and allow them to get on with their murderous plans. They were right. Five days after the grisly killing of its soldiers, the Belgian government announced that it would withdraw its troops – the core fighting capability of UNAMIR – from Rwanda immediately.[141]

Beyond the initial killing of these soldiers, which so effectively replicated the collapse of UNOSOM, the UN mission in Somalia, those on the ground in Rwanda throughout the genocide reported that genocidaires were very specific in their targeting of international actors. In some cases, the mere presence of observers was enough to

---

[138] Des Forges 1999, 118.    [139] Ibid., 122.
[140] Barbara Walter, *Committing to Peace: The Successful Settlement of Civil Wars* (Princeton: Princeton University Press, 2002), 155; Jones 2001, 80.
[141] Kofi Annan and Nader Mousavizadeh, *Interventions: A Life in War and Peace* (New York: The Penguin Press, 2012), 57.

deter killing, while in others, peacekeepers were targeted by nationality to be killed, indicating attentiveness to the vulnerabilities of particular national contingents. Both Phillippe Gaillard, the Red Cross's Director in Rwanda during the genocide, and the BBC's Mark Doyle indicated that they knew the genocide's architects were watching the international press during the genocide, and that they behaved accordingly.[142]

The genocide itself seems to have been envisioned as early as the end of 1992, although at this point it was limited to extremists;[143] events in Burundi allowed extremists to frame their slaughter of Tutsis in preemptive, self-protective terms, and were part of what allowed these extremists to recruit a broader base of genocidaires. While the UN's retreat from Somalia in the face of peacekeeper casualties provided GoR extremists with a template for actions to trigger Great Power retrenchment, the coup and consequent unchecked civilian casualties in Burundi provided genocidaires with an additional rhetorical frame in which to couch their call to exterminate Tutsis. Des Forges writes, "For the anti-Tutsi propagandists, the assassination of the Burundian president offered just the kind of tragedy most helpful to their cause ... the doubts about RPF intentions, sown by the February 1993 attack and fed by the extent of RPF gains at Arusha, ripened following the assassination in Burundi."[144] Events and international inaction in Burundi were by no means the primary spur or frame for the genocide, but UN inaction there did allow extremists to expand the scope and resonance of their arguments.[145]

---

[142] See the interviews of Gaillard and Doyle in *PBS Frontline: Ghosts of Rwanda*. Gaillard claims that the early publicity about Red Cross convoys being targeted by the *interahamwe* embarrassed the extremists into allowing the Red Cross free passage in Rwanda. Doyle said that he avoided reporting the story of the Senegalese Captain Mbaye Diagne, who rescued and hid people from the start of the genocide until Diagne's death at a roadblock explosion, out of fear that drawing attention to his actions in the international press would have gotten him killed. Finally, Bonaventure Niyibizi, a US Embassy employee, reports that unarmed Senegalese soldiers standing guard at the ICRC hospital and at the St. Famille Church were able to keep people safe and keep genocidaires out, whereas other unarmed soldiers at UN sites were targeted.

[143] Prunier 1995, 169.      [144] Des Forges 1999, 102–103.

[145] For comprehensive discussions of competing explanations for the Rwandan genocide, and for compelling explanations for the local and individual-level spurs to violence, see Straus 2006 and Fujii 2011.

To summarize, then, evidence indicates that the parties to the Arusha Accords were, in fact, aware of and concerned by the failures during the accords' implementation period, but that their interpretations of these failures varied. For the RPF, who viewed themselves as different kinds of recipients of intervention, failure in Somalia was distant. For extremist GoR actors who were already committed to upsetting the peace agreement, however, the UN's failure provided a tactical guide to action that precipitated both UNAMIR's swift breakdown and Rwanda's descent back into war and convulsive, totalizing mass atrocity.

## What Drove the RPF to Seek the Assistance of UNAMIR II after UNAMIR's Collapse?

The preceding evidence has indicated that a multiplicity of motives drove parties to the negotiating table at Arusha; that the material, tactical, and symbolic benefits that only the international community could bring to the Rwandan peace process were important to the negotiating actors alongside a sometimes genuine desire to end the war; that the parties to the conflict had a mixed picture of the UN's efficacy as a guarantor at the start of the negotiations, but often held onto earlier unfavorable impressions from the decolonization period; and that they were aware of peacekeeping failure in Somalia, but that they interpreted that failure in accordance with their own biases, either assuming that they were different than the warring parties in Somalia or calibrating their strategies to upend the peace process according to the UN's observed vulnerabilities. The final section of this chapter asks why, after the UN's spectacular institutional and operational failure in Rwanda itself during the genocide, the RPF turned again to the UN for UNAMIR II, which remained on the ground in Rwanda until 1996.[146]

---

[146] Noting UNAMIR's operational failure – which was effectively predetermined by its sheer lack of equipment, its lack of any common operational language among most of its battalions, and its progressive abandonment by both the UN Secretary-General and the UNSC – is not intended to dismiss the commitment or bravery of the UNAMIR peacekeepers who remained on the ground after the Belgian contingent withdrew. By all accounts, many of these soldiers committed astonishing acts of bravery, often while unarmed, to save people. Dallaire, for example, is largely viewed as a hero in Rwanda for staying to do what he could; Kagame, for instance, is reported to have said "that he appreciated General

The RPF's victory in July 1994 was as decisive as the UN's failure had been during the genocide: The RPF took Kigali and declared a unilateral ceasefire following a sweep through the country that followed the genocide's path.[147] It quickly established a unity government that adopted the Arusha Peace Accords as the basis of its constitution; in the most technical sense, it had no need for a demonstrably ineffective multilateral security force. Interviews with the RPF reveal that the exigencies of statebuilding and refugee resettlement, financial crisis, and legitimacy again required the UN's involvement, and that peace-keepers were part of this overall package of intervention.[148]

Rwanda became the poorest country in the world after the geno-cide.[149] The RPF, which had lacked the financial resources to pay for demobilization, certainly lacked both the technical and financial cap-acities to rebuild the state economy. In this framework, the UN was viewed as the only possible institution for the RPF to turn to. As Mazimhaka said, "We have to keep doing it because that's our organ-ization" and "if the Security Council doesn't step up, where are you going to go, to UNICEF only? To the refugee camps?"[150] Or, as another senior RPF official argued, "The international community is only the big powers – US, Russia, Germany, France, the ones who are leading – if the UN is there, it's those powers. What is the international community? Not small countries like Rwanda."[151] This is, to some

Dallaire as a man, but not 'the helmet he wore,' and that he had told Dallaire so directly" (Gourevitch 1998, 160).

[147] Prunier 1995, 2011.

[148] The Rwandan parliamentary archive includes no documents related to the civil war, the genocide, and the negotiation of the Arusha peace process; in fact, there are no documents related to the 1990–1994 period. It is possible these documents were destroyed; it is possible they were seconded to another archive that I could not access. The only conclusion I can draw from this absence is that it bolsters the RPF's ability to shape the narrative of this period in ways that affirm its claim of collaborative governance rooted in the compromise of the Arusha Accords.

[149] Gourevitch 1998, 270.

[150] Patrick Mazimhaka, interview by Anjali Dayal, Kigali (July 30, 2013).

[151] Tito Rutaremara, interview by Anjali Dayal, Kigali (July 31, 2013). Small powers can exercise significant bargaining power at the UNSC – the GoR, for instance, used its position on the UNSC to argue in favor of Operation Turquoise and delay the RPF's military advance through Rwanda (Prunier 2000). The perception that the international community is only big powers – or at least the frame that the international community is only big powers – is likely an estimation about financial assistance and military intervention.

extent, evidence in favor of the idea that actors in civil wars turn to the UN again and again because they are war-weary, exhausted, and have no other options *but* to turn to the UN for their security at the end of war, even when they believe the UN will fail again.

Again, however, the particularities of the UN's goods and services, beyond guaranteeing the peace, matter a great deal. Just as UNHCR was central to the Arusha negotiations, refugees were central to the decision to pursue UN involvement after the genocide, and just as the international community's presence at negotiations uniquely conferred legitimacy onto the RPF as a political party, so, too, was the UN's presence in postwar Rwanda a talisman against accusations that the RPF was waging a second war against the Hutu majority population in Rwanda after the genocide:

> When the worst was over, then they [the UN] decided to come back – we asked them to. When the RPF defeated the government troops and the militias, it resulted in about 2.5 million refugees running into neighboring countries. Now, Rwanda had another 1 million refugees already – out of a population of about 7 million – look at the numbers – what did we have left? We had to face the construction of the country, we needed the UN to support repatriation programs, and for confidence-building against the people we had defeated, and for human rights, to keep the government from revenge and to make the guys who were defeated feel secure. ... We had to make sure [peacekeepers] were visible, to help with some resources to help the refugees back, to help us observe that the defeated forces were not just running away, but that they were also fighting back.[152]

In this sense, then, the UN is not just the only port of call for combatants in need of security. Its participation in the post-conflict context helps construct the state anew, repatriate the war-scattered, and certify the good intentions of the victorious party in ways that are palatable to domestic actors and the international community alike. The security of the warring factions is just one category of action among many in this framework.

## Conclusion

The Rwandan case is intrinsically important for scholars who are interested in peacekeeping, negotiation, and international statebuilding

---

[152] Patrick Mazimhaka, interview by Anjali Dayal, Kigali (July 30, 2013).

and reconstruction processes. Most accounts of the Rwandan genocide address the Arusha Accords only fleetingly, despite these negotiations' centrality to the process by which political liberalization produced mass atrocity. By focusing on the Arusha peace process and its aftermath, this chapter reveals that the parties to the Rwandan Civil War were certainly interested in the UN's ability to guarantee their peace agreement, but they were far more interested in the UN's ability to assist them in demobilization, in refugee resettlement, and in crafting their identities as legitimate political actors. Given these goals, negotiation with the assistance of a failed security guarantor is not a puzzle, even when there are strong indications that UN peacekeepers will be unable to uphold the peace agreement at hand. The chapter also finds that the traditional focus on the post-1989 universe of peacekeeping cases neglects the very real, and comparatively recent, experiences with the UN as a decolonization authority that many of the parties to African civil wars had as young people. This experience is systematically underexplored in the contemporary literature on civil war intervention and the UN's role in post-conflict reconstruction.

Taken together, then, the evidence in this chapter finds that internationally led negotiations unfold in a shared strategic and social environment, that the warring parties in Rwanda were attentive to the UN's behavior elsewhere, and that they turned to the UN despite its failures because they were more interested in its ability to confer tactical, material, and symbolic benefits to the negotiation process than they were in its functions as a security guarantor. This is evidence in favor of the book's distributional hypothesis, and evidence that complicates credible commitment accounts of how peacekeeping works.

# 5 | *Guatemala, 1989–1996*
## *MINUGUA in Light of El Salvador*

When it ended in 1996, the civil war in Guatemala was the Western hemisphere's longest-running conflict, with each stage of conflict shot through with international intervention. Central America was a key theater in the Cold War, and external involvement linked each of Central America's civil wars together twice: first by the proxy dynamics of the Cold War, and then through the Esquípulas II regional conflict resolution process spearheaded by the region's presidents. Negotiating the end of the Guatemalan Civil War, Kofi Annan wrote to the Security Council, was "a milestone both for Guatemala, where it ends 35 years of internal conflict, and for Central America, where it ends the last war in the isthmus and thus completes the principal task which the Presidents of the region set themselves when they signed the Esquípulas II agreement..."[1]

This chapter examines the UN's engagement in Guatemalan negotiations from 1989 to 1997, asking how parties to the conflict assessed the UN's performance as the guarantor of agreements elsewhere. Specifically, it asks how these parties evaluated the concurrent, countervailing evidence of the UN's successful peacekeeping next door in El Salvador and the UN's failed peacekeeping at the same time in the Balkans. How did the GoG and the Unidad Revolucionaria Nacional Guatemalteca (URNG), the coalition of rebel groups fighting and negotiating with the GoG, perceive and interpret the UN's success as peacemaker next door in El Salvador at the start of their negotiations? How did they perceive and interpret the major peacekeeping failure at Srebrenica, which took place during the Guatemalan negotiations? In what ways did these perceptions shape both negotiations and the contours of the peace agreement that emerged from negotiations?

---

[1] Private letter from UN Secretary-General Kofi Annan to His Excellency Mr. Njuguna Moses Mahugu, O.G.W., President of the Security Council, February 5, 1997, http://ccnydigitalscholarship.org/kofiannan/items/show/4396.

What lessons did the parties draw from other cases of UN intervention, and what drove them to seek international assistance from the UN and MINUGUA, the observer mission that arrived in the midst of the peace process, amid competing signals about the UN's ability to verify the human rights situation in Guatemala and its ability to manage demobilization and disarmament?

I find that participants to the Guatemalan peace process looked nearly exclusively at El Salvador to make their assessments about UN behavior, but that they perceived the Salvadoran example as a *negative* one: Both sides believed their Salvadoran counterparts had given too much up during their negotiations, and despite lobbying for multiple forms of UN assistance during the course of negotiations, the GoG and URNG worked hard to guard against the same distributional losses and gains they saw the UN as having induced into the Salvadoran agreement. In this context, I find that both sides actively pursued UN intervention for the symbolic, material, and tactical benefits it brought to the negotiation process, even as the GoG actively sought to minimize the UN's role as security guarantor to the peace process. There is no evidence that the parties to the Guatemalan Civil War considered the UN's failures in the Balkans during the negotiation process, although there is substantial evidence that the GoG and URNG were attentive to the larger constellation of UN peacemaking and peacekeeping activities. These findings are surprising given credible commitment theories of peacekeeping, which, extended to their logical conclusions, would anticipate that the UN's success in El Salvador would enhance the Guatemalan parties' confidence in the UN as guarantor, instead of spurring them to limit the UN's role in Guatemalan peace and security.

This chapter draws on archival material from the UN and the National Security Archive; published interviews and oral histories of the primary actors involved on all sides of the conflict; and the extensive scholarly literature on the Guatemalan Civil War and peace process. Parties to the Guatemalan Civil War had multiple competing guides with which to forecast the likely effect of UN intervention on their peace process. Accordingly, in the analysis that follows, I investigate which of these guides they pursued, asking whether the alternative benefits of bargaining drove the warring parties to seek international involvement, or whether the desire for a strong security guarantor that could alleviate the credible commitment problem of war termination pushed the warring parties to seek the UN's assistance.

In the next section of this chapter, I outline both the context and conduct of the war and the dynamics of the negotiations. Then I turn to the evidence, asking how information about the UN's conduct abroad affected negotiations in Guatemala: first, I outline the strategic positions that the warring parties occupied; second, I examine what the negotiating parties hoped to get from the peace process, and what they hoped the international community would contribute to the peace process. Finally, I ask how the warring parties viewed the UN's past record of peacekeeping and peacemaking, and how the UN's conduct in Srebrenica and El Salvador informed the negotiation processes. The concluding section raises questions about geographic proximity and temporal simultaneity, asking why El Salvador exerts such a strong influence on the Guatemalan parties when the Balkans cases do not.

## Background to the Case

At the Cold War's end, UN peacemakers became involved in Central America's cluster of long-running conflicts. The Guatemalan Civil War was the longest-running and last-resolved of these conflicts: The war began in 1960 and reached its most brutal peak from 1978 to 1982, when genocide wracked the indigenous communities of the highlands. Negotiations, which would ultimately last nearly a decade,[2] began under the regional Equípulsas II umbrella in 1987, a series of dialogues that strove to resolve the Central American wars and involved the UN Secretary-General in the processes. The negotiations continued under civil society leadership and with assistance from interested countries, with the UN first as an observer beginning in 1989, and then as the formal mediator of the negotiations in 1994; verifier of the human rights provisions of the agreement in 1995; and then implementer of the agreement that was finally signed at the end of 1996. MINUGUA remained on the ground until 2004.[3]

---

[2] Accord: An International Review of Peace Initatives in association with the Latin American Faculty of Social Sciences, Guatemala City, *Negotiating Rights: The Guatemalan Peace Process* (London: Conciliation Resources, 1997), 5.

[3] On the history of the Guatemalan Civil War, see Susanne Jonas, *The Battle for Guatemala: Rebels, Death Squads, and US Power* (Boulder: Westview Press, 1991); David Stoll, *Between Two Armies in the Ixil Towns of Guatemala* (New York: Columbia University Press, 1993); Virginia Garrard-Burnett, *Terror in the Land of the Holy Spirit: Guatemala under General Efraín Rios Montt 1982–1983*(Oxford: Oxford University Press, 2011); Jennifer Schirmer, *The*

From its beginning, the conflict had the transnational qualities of many of Latin America's Marxist insurrections; it also acquired ethnic and class dimensions, given the fracture between the indigenous Mayan rural majority and the ruling, landholding *ladino* elite.[4] In 1954, a CIA-backed military coup removed a popularly elected leftist president from power and began decades of military dictatorship. The war itself began in 1960, after a nationalist uprising by military officers failed. Marxist insurgencies spread across the country, particularly to the largely indigenous highlands, which subsequently bore the brunt of the military's extensive counterinsurgency operations. Four large guerrilla groups emerged over the course of the conflict: the Ejército Guerrillero de los Pobres (EGP), Organización del Pueblo en Armas (ORPA), the Partido Guatemalteco del Trabajo (PGT), and the Fuerzas Armadas Rebeldes (FAR). There were significant differences between these major groups for much of the war,[5] but they ultimately united under the URNG banner.

Over the next thirty years, counterinsurgency operations defined Guatemala, turning the country into what its analysts call a "centaurized" civilian state dominated by a military counterinsurgency apparatus.[6] The counterinsurgency campaigns

exacerbated all the original causes of the conflict. On one hand, displacement and resettlement deepened an already desperate land problem. On the other, democratic space was at its most limited with the army and military commissioners the only state representatives in the highlands, and city authorities obliged to demand prior application for gatherings of more than two people.

---

*Guatemalan Military Project: A Violence Called Democracy* (Philadelphia: University of Pennyslvania Press, 1999).

[4] See "Guatemala: Reaction and Repression," in *Modern Latin America*, ed. Thomas E. Skidmore and Peter H. Smith (Oxford: Oxford University Press, 2001). The *ladino* population in Guatemala is the Spanish-speaking *mestizo* population that is not primarily ethnically indigenous. Members of the population, which is a recognized ethnicity in Guatemala, often trace much or part of their ancestry to continental European origin.

[5] On the wartime distinctions between the groups, see Iosu Pareles, *Guatemala Insurrecta: Entrevista con el Comandante en Jefe del Ejército Guerrillero de los Pobres* (Madrid: Editorial Revolución, 1990).

[6] Susanne Jonas, *Of Centaurs and Doves: Guatemala's Peace Process* (Boulder: Westview, 2000), 10. The centaur imagery itself is drawn from the Guatemalan writer Carlos Figueroa.

The rule of law was also grievously undermined . . . . Almost inevitably, the indigenous rural majority bore the brunt of these mounting injustices.[7]

War devastated the civilian population – by the late 1980s, estimates suggest that around 180,000 people had died; 40,000 people disappeared during the conflict; over four hundred villages had been entirely destroyed in the Rios Montt government's "scorched earth" campaign; and at least 100,000 people fled to Mexico as refugees.[8] By the end of the war, the World Bank estimated that approximately 75 percent of Guatemalans lived in poverty, and almost 58 percent lived in extreme poverty.[9] Cold War-era support from the United States for the military counterinsurgency operations had ebbed over the course of the war, and international investment in the country was scarce, following decades of war and instability.[10]

A controlled transition from military to civilian rule began from 1984 to 1985.[11] Initial talks between the new civilian Cerezo government and the unified command structure of the URNG began in 1986. They were largely conducted under the regional Equípulsas II framework, or the "Procedure for Establishing a Firm and Lasting Peace for Central America." A National Reconciliation Commission (CNR) – composed of the Guatemalan Bishop Rodolfo Quezada; the civilian government's Vice President; the head of a major civil society group; and a journalist – became facilitators between the two sides, cementing civil society's centrality to the negotiations in a dynamic that persisted for the next decade.[12]

The Equípulsas II agreement also created a role for the UN as a monitoring force across the region – the UN Observer Group in Central America (or ONUCA, Observadores de las Naciones Unidas en Centroamerica). "In principle, peace processes would occur simultaneously" across the region; in practice, however, the UN managed

---

[7] Accord 1997, 14.     [8] Ibid., 10; Jonas 2000, 35.     [9] Accord 1997, 76.
[10] See, for example, "Statement by Richard Boucher on Guatemala: Stopping Deliveries of Military Assistance," Office of the Assistant Secretary/Spokesman, US Department of State, December 21, 1990, Guatemala Documentation Project, National Security Archive, Washington, DC, Offsite Box No. 21, Folder "Arms Sales to Guatemala after 1990, 1989–1994."
[11] William Stanley, *Enabling Peace in Guatemala: The Story of MINUGUA* (Boulder: Lynne Rienner, 2013), 16.
[12] Ibid., 18–19.

these armed conflicts sequentially, beginning with Nicaragua (1989–1990), then El Salvador (1990–1994), and finally Guatemala (1994–1996).[13] Refugee return began in 1993 and continued through-out the rest of the negotiations.[14] The Salvadoran case served as a constant example for negotiators of Guatemala's agreement, who moved to correct what they viewed as errors in the Salvadoran process in their approach to Guatemala – focusing, for example, on "the necessity of coordination between the UN and the IFIs," to avoid the cross-purposes at which the UN, the IMF, and the World Bank had worked at the end of the Salvadoran negotiations.[15]

From their perspective at the long end of the UN's sequential Central American interventions, the warring parties would therefore have had substantial opportunity to observe the UN's behavior in these previous cases. El Salvador was not just the closest example from which the Guatemalan belligerents could draw – it was then the UN's most unambiguous peacekeeping and peacemaking success, "both in terms of implementing its mandate, and in terms of helping to reform and create domestic institutions that would ensure the future peaceful development" of the country.[16] Both parties to the Salvadoran conflict were strong, and relied heavily on the UN as third party security guarantor after they signed the Chapultepec Peace Accords in January 1992; both parties also made heavy concessions at the negoti-ating table – the Salvadoran negotiation process was centralized, with the UN Secretariat at the heart of the process, and the UN used a "single negotiating technique" in which "UN negotiators would draft the text of various aspects of the peace proposal, present the drafts to both sides, and then revise in light of suggestions. The parties did not generally draft their own documents, which meant the proposals often flowed from the UN Secretariat's agenda."[17] The UN peace operation in El Salvador, ONUSAL, had deep organizational ties to the office of the Secretary-General, as well.[18]

---

[13] Nicola Short, *The International Politics of Post-Conflict Reconstruction in Guatemala* (New York: Palgrave, 2007), 70–71.
[14] Roman Krznaric, "Guatemalan Returnees and the Dilemma of Political Mobilization," *Journal of Refugee Studies* 10, no. 1 (1997): 61–78.
[15] Short 2007, 70–71.
[16] Lise Morjé Howard, *UN Peacekeeping in Civil Wars* (New York: Cambridge University Press, 2008), 88.
[17] Ibid., 102.   [18] Ibid., 98.

The Guatemalan negotiations, by contrast, produced "the softest of soft peacekeeping,"[19] with a mission that had a General Assembly mandate, not a UNSC mandate, with limited exceptions for the military observer component that monitored rapid rebel demobilization. The final accords were expansive in scope, but included comparatively few measurable commitments by the parties, and they were not engineered by the UN, but were rather the result of broad-based civil society participation, which generated a negotiating agenda for the government and the rebels when direct talks between the two parties began in 1991.[20]

There were three broad stages to negotiations: (1) indirect talks; (2) direct talks mediated by the Archbishop Rodolfo Quezada, then Bishop of Zacapa y Santo Cristo de Esquípulas in Guatemala; (3) direct talks moderated by Jean Arnault for the UN. Negotiations had been running for six years by the time the UN moved to helm the process in 1994; as a result, although the UN actors involved in Guatemala drew heavily on their experience in El Salvador,[21] important negotiating precedents and dynamics had already been set.[22] Negotiations were stop-and-start, and resulted in a series of cumulative agreements, only one of which – the Comprehensive Agreement on Human Rights, signed on March 29, 1994 in Mexico City – entered into force immediately.[23] That agreement established the UN's verification mission and charged it with monitoring and verifying all human rights violations committed by either side after its inauguration, even before the conclusive end of the war.[24]

---

[19] Stanley 2013, 3.     [20] Ibid., 5.

[21] See Francesc Vendrell, interview by Jean Krasno, *Yale-UN Oral History Project* (New York, April 16, 1996), 29–30; Beatrice Rangel, interview by Jean Krasno, *Yale-UN Oral History Project* (New York, September 16, 1997), 45–46; Marrack Goulding, interview by James S. Sutterlin, *Yale-UN Oral History Project* (Oxford, June 20, 1998), 68–69.

[22] Stanley 2013, 6–9.     [23] Accord 1997, 84.

[24] A/RES/48/267, September 28, 1994, establishes "a Mission for the Verification of Human Rights and of Compliance with the Commitments of the Comprehensive Agreement on Human Rights in Guatemala with the recommendations contained in the report of the Secretary-General, for an initial period of six months."

Violence continued throughout the negotiation process,[25] even after
MINUGUA's deployment,[26] and international ultimatums were a central part of the negotiation process – "international pressure and
presence was required to overcome the convoluted, ideologically over-
determined logic of Guatemalan politics, the legacy of a thirty-six year
Cold War-era civil conflict. As one URGN leader acknowledged, 'We
couldn't have kept it alive among Guatemalans. Without the persist-
ence of the UN, the peace process would have been impossible.'"[27]
Finally, after concerted work by both the GoG and the URGN, as well
as the UN and the Group of Friends (Colombia, Mexico, Norway,
Spain, the United States, and Venezuela) that had consulted with the
UN and the warring parties throughout the negotiations, a definitive
ceasefire was signed to end the war on December 4, 1996.[28] The final
peace accords were signed on December 29, 1996.[29]

Extended to their conclusions, credible commitment theories of peacekeeping would predict that, given the nearby success in El Salvador, the
parties to the Guatemalan Civil War would seek a similarly strong
presence from the UN in its negotiations, and that they would lobby
the UN for similar commitments to those that the Government of El
Salvador and the Farabundo Martí National Liberation Front (FMLN)
received in the 1992 Chapultepec Peace Accords. In these theories of

---

[25] The US ambassador, in his internal assessment of the situation, noted that he
expected state-sponsored violence to be an integral part of the peace process:
"On the other hand, he [President Serrano] has failed to end 'selective violence'
and to make clear to the security forces that he will not tolerate such activity. In
fact, it is not clear the president openly opposes actions against the left,
particularly while there is a war on. He seems ambiguous on this topic, an
ambiguity that fuels such violence. He clearly has done remarkably well in
getting the military to abandon its long-standing opposition to negotiations with
armed guerrillas. There is more of a chance for a peace accord today than at any
other time in the past thirty years. However, part of the cost for such action
might be the tolerance of a covert war aimed at denying the left a chance for
power in peace that it could never get in war" (Ambassador Thomas Stroock to
US Secretary of State, "Secret Cable: Selective Violence Paralyzes the Left," *US
Department of State Document Accessed through National Security Archive*
(Guatemala City, May 10, 1991), 13, www2.gwu.edu/~nsarchiv/NSAEBB/
NSAEBB11/docs/doc26.pdf.

[26] Jonas 2000, 44. Just days after the Comprehensive Agreement on Human Rights
was signed, for example, the head of the constitutional court was assassinated in
broad daylight.

[27] *New York Times*, March 27, 1996; quotation is from Jonas 2000, 58.

[28] S/1996/1045, Add. 2.     [29] Accord 1997, 5.

peacekeeping, if the warring parties did not seek such guarantees and commitments in the course of their own negotiations, we might look for evidence that they had less faith in the UN's capacity to guarantee their agreement successfully given the simultaneous peacekeeping failures abroad. Instead, the following evidence indicates the GoG and the URNG continually sought the UN's assistance in mediating their agreements, and were particularly concerned with the symbolic, material, and tactical benefits that bargaining under UN auspices could bring – but that they simultaneously moved to correct against what they perceived as distributional losses their Salvadoran counterparts had sustained in negotiations, often actively seeking to weaken the UN's actual efficacy on the ground.

## The Guatemalan Peace Process

This chapter examines the negotiation period from 1987 to 1996, focusing on formal negotiations in the 1990s. The evidence is organized into three sets of questions: (1) Why did the Guatemalan belligerents negotiate? What were their strategic positions and goals? (2) What did they want out of negotiation? (3) What did they think of the UN's past performance? How did the GoG and the URNG perceive the UN's success as peacemaker next door in El Salvador? How did they perceive other major peacekeeping failures, including the failure at Srebrenica, which took place during the Guatemalan negotiations? How did these perceptions influence the course of negotiations under UN auspices? I begin with the actors' strategic positions and goals.

### The Warring Parties' Strategic Situations

Understanding the strategic positions of the two major groups that emerged over the course of the war – the GoG and the URNG[30] – vis-à-

---

[30] Multiple rebel groups early in the war eventually coalesced under the URNG umbrella. Tracking the shifting arrangement of various coalitions across the peace process's entire decade is beyond the scope of this project, but despite the unified negotiation coalition, there remained significant distinctions and divisions within the opposition to the GoG across both the armed opposition and Guatemalan civil society (see, for example, Norma Stolz Chinchilla, "Of Straw Men and Stereotypes: Why Guatemalan Rocks Don't Talk," *Latin American Perspectives* 26, no. 109[November 1999]: 29–37).

vis one another, with respect to their position on securing the peace, and in relation to the UN, is a critical part of understanding how these actors drew on the UN's past performance in the course of the peace process. Evidence indicates that both coalitions had few strategic options aside from negotiation; that both coalitions included factions who privileged goals other than peace in the negotiation process, and that the GoG coalition included a set of actors whose strategic goals lay entirely outside the peace process.

## Who Was Negotiating the Accords?

Two capacious, often poorly organized, and fractious coalitions negotiated the Guatemalan peace accords: the GoG, which encompassed both the successive new democratically elected civilian governments of the late 1980s and the powerful military actors who had previously ruled the country and still held a great deal of power within the state; and the URNG, which was internally divided in terms of strategy and approach, although more unified in terms of goals than the GoG coalition. Civil society organizations constituted a third group; they had an important observation role at the negotiating table.

Both of the warring parties made attempts to unify their bargaining positions. The GoG was a fractious, internally divided group that was prone to splits, with separate factions seemingly more concerned with internal power dynamics than with their relationship with the URNG.[31] On the GoG side, the army ran a series of internal purges as part of their efforts both to discipline the negotiating coalition and to keep its own internal politics off the negotiation table.[32] There was

---

[31] Jonas 2000, 65.

[32] Schirmer 1999, 272–273. Furthermore, internal USG documents reveal that the role of the army was complicated and required finesse for the Guatemalan Minister of Defense to manage, and that he was at pains to stress both to American army and intelligence personnel and other members of the GoG that the army was part of the GoG's negotiating coalition, not its own separate entity or veto player: "The MOD, General Samayoa, followed Conde and talked about the army and the peace process. Garcia was emphatic that the army had to demonstrates its willingness to be part of the dialogue while at the same time complying with its constitutional mission. According to Garcia, the army won in the military arena but has been losing in the political and ideological arena. Garcia stated that the members of the army were also representative of the people and that the army as an institution was part of the peace process as an integral part of the GoG, not as a separate entity" ("Members of the

also extensive internal jockeying among the civilian actors on the GoG side before the UN arrived as mediator of the peace accords: A self-coup[33] by President Serrano during the negotiation process early in 1993 upset the emerging, fragile dynamic between civilian and military leaderships. It was followed by a crisis on the center-right of the political spectrum, crowned in the unexpected ascendency of the GoG's Human Rights Ombudsman Ramiro de Léon Carpio to the Presidency in June 1993, and then followed by a move toward the military for Carpio, who had previously been perceived as being more open to dialogue with the URNG. Throughout, government negotiators claimed that they would not negotiate the army's postwar role with the URNG.[34]

The URNG's various rebel groups, on the other hand, operated under a common command structure that proposed negotiations as a unified front – their internal divisions had come earlier, as several of the organizations within the group had split throughout the 1980s "over the issue of whether to continue armed struggle or lay down their arms in the mid-1980s to prevent further bloodshed."[35] Even on this side, however, analysts and observers had questions about the coalition's organizational abilities, its cohesiveness and capacity to make concessions.[36]

A third set of actors – a broad civil society coalition whose member groups ranged from the far right to the far left – was granted formal consultative status during the negotiation process, and although this group was not a signatory party to the agreements, its inclusion produced a negotiation process heavily focused on consensus

---

Government Peace Commission Talk about the Peace Process," Memo from Department of Defense Joint Staff Washington DC to RUEKJCS/DIA WASHDC, RHLBAAA/USCINCSO Quarry Heights PM//SCJ2//info RUEHME/ USDAO Mexico City MX RUESHSN/USDAO San Salvador ES, December 1991. In National Security Archive Guatemala Documentation Project, Offsite Box 28, 1991 Folder, p. 0004).

[33] A "self-coup" or an "autogolpe" is a coup d'état in which the executive dissolves the parliament and grants him or herself extraordinary powers; see, for example, Maxwell A. Cameron, "Self-Coups: Peru, Guatemala, and Russia," *Journal of Democracy* 9, no. 1(1998): 125–139.

[34] Jonas 2000, 65.     [35] Ibid., 35.

[36] Stanley 2013, 28. Indeed, the URNG ultimately dissolved over dissatisfaction with the accord, and popular sectors were angry about the accord and the extent to which the URNG ceded its demands to the Arzú political platform (ibid., 43).

and characterized by many veto players.[37] The multiplicity of actors who were party to the negotiations led one former GoG negotiator to say "'We were not negotiating only with the URNG,' but with all sectors of Guatemalan society."[38] To set negotiation terms from the government's position alone required that this negotiator confer with different factions of the army, with the civil society groups, and with the legal political parties and their presidential candidates, all before approaching the URNG and the UN; indeed, the negotiator reported holding nearly twice as many meetings with these groups as with the URNG – forty-one versus twenty-six meetings.[39] By 1993, the unarmed opposition "had consolidated their own position, vocal and increasingly independent of the guerrillas. They had also helped shape the agenda for a negotiated settlement and established their representative, [Bishop] Rodolfo Quezada Toruño, as official 'conciliator' in the nascent talks" between the GoG and the URNG.[40]

## Stalemate: The Necessity of Negotiations

By the late 1980s, Guatemala was in a state of "chronic social crisis,"[41] although it was no longer either ungovernable or in a state of full-out insurrection, as it had been in the past. Scholars have framed the peace process as precipitated by the stalemate between the guerrilla and the military, neither of whom could win a conclusive military victory.[42] By the time peace talks began, the worst years of war were over; relatively few members of the Guatemalan public were directly affected by the fighting, and while the URNG's ability to carry out major attacks against the Guatemalan military was increasingly limited, the guerrilla retained their ability to fight indefinitely. For the GoG, newly transitioning to civilian rule from a long period of military dictatorship, even a low-grade war conducted indefinitely over many years carried high costs, including decreased investment and a heightened military presence in daily life.[43]

[37] Ibid., 9.   [38] Jonas 2000, 65.   [39] Ibid.   [40] Accord 1997, 7.
[41] Jonas 2000, 30.
[42] See Short 2007 for a historiography of this understanding, as well as an alternative reading of the "process as a (second) passive revolution of certain elites, assisted by the international community, both through official channels and civil society" (Ibid., 63).
[43] Ibid., 10–11.

Although the URNG had experienced a resurgence in the late 1980s, it now recognized both its inability to wrest full state power from the government and that continuing to pursue an exclusively armed strategy would come at an astronomically high cost to the civilian population, who had already endured repression and genocide in the course of the war. Regional developments also allowed the URNG to observe the Sandinista Revolution and its aftermath in Nicaragua, and to note that the United States was unlikely to allow another revolutionary party to assume power of a state in its backyard,[44] while the GoG was convinced the looming end of the Cold War had stripped the movement from its revolutionary roots.[45] The URNG began to press the new civilian government for political negotiations as early as 1986, the year the transition to civilian rule from military rule began. The government resisted, requiring that the URNG disarm before any negotiations, and by the first half of 1990, the war was again intensifying, with an uptick in guerrilla attacks, and a series of coups and power plays on the right that reflected the army's inability to definitively win the war.[46]

The GoG's side thus maintained a group of powerful spoilers to the peace, as well as some actors whose goals could only be achieved outside of the peace process. The URNG's coalition was primarily composed of actors who were committed to goals that they could achieve through the negotiation process. Both parties, however, found their strategic situations significantly circumscribed by the fact that they could not win the war outright and were required to negotiate – the GoG because its decades of counterinsurgency had failed to end the war, and the URNG because it acknowledged that it could no longer capture the state even with continued war.

## What Did the Warring Parties Want Out of Negotiation?

Given the various motivations of the parties to the conflict, we need a clearer sense of precisely which issues dominated negotiations, what

---

[44] Jonas 2000, 13.
[45] "Members of the Government Peace Commission Talk About the Peace Process," Memo from Department of Defense Joint Staff Washington DC to RUEKJCS/DIA WASHDC, RHLBAAA/USCINCSO Quarry Heights PM//SCJ2// info RUEHME/USDAO Mexico City MX RUESHSN/USDAO San Salvador ES, December 1991. In National Security Archive Guatemala Documentation Project, Offsite Box 28, 1991 Folder, pp. 0003–0004.
[46] Jonas 2000, 13.

the warring parties wanted to take away from the negotiating table, and what they believed the international community could bring to their settlement. Examining the negotiation process and the resulting accords reveals that parties to the Guatemalan Civil War wanted the international community to do many things in Guatemala: They wanted the negotiation process to yield peace and security, tactical benefits, material benefits, and both domestic and international legitimacy – and they wanted and expected the international community to contribute to these potential peace process outcomes. I take each of these goals in turn.

## *Peace and Security*

Factions within both parties were negotiating to end the war, but the parties had very distinct understandings of what conflict termination meant. The URNG's goals for the peace process were to establish a post-conflict peace that addressed the root causes of the conflict, while the GoG sought a more minimal outcome – a ceasefire and an end to guerrilla violence.[47] Negotiations were marked by swings between these two different conceptions of war termination, but the resulting peace accords were closer in line to the URNG's conception of full-scale social change in Guatemala: The incremental agreements the two parties struck between 1994 and 1996 slowly encompassed multiple points of the URNG's positive vision of the peace and ended finally with the GoG's desired comprehensive ceasefire.[48]

War centered on issues of land distribution, political organization, and the limits of state violence,[49] and ultimately the two parties signed twelve separate agreements that addressed all these root causes of the conflict: in order of their negotiation, the Framework Agreement for the Resumption of the Negotiating Process between the GoG and the URNG (January 1994), which committed both parties to the negotiation process; the Comprehensive Agreement on Human Rights (March 1994); the Agreement on a Timetable for Negotiations of a Firm and Lasting Peace in Guatemala (March 1994); the Agreement on Resettlement of the Population Groups Uprooted by the Armed

[47] Ibid., 31.
[48] For the full text of all the agreements, see www.usip.org/publications/peace-agreements-guatemala.
[49] Accord 1997, 5–6.

Conflict (June 1994); the Agreement on the Establishment of the Commission to Clarify Past Human Rights Violations and Acts of Violence that Have Caused the Guatemalan Population to Suffer, which established Guatemala's Truth Commission (June 1994); the Agreement on Identity and Rights of Indigenous Peoples (March 1995); the Agreement on Social and Economic Aspects and the Agrarian Situation (May 1996); the Agreement on the Strengthening of Civilian Power and on the Role of the Armed Forces in a Democratic Society (September 1996); and then finally, in December 1996, the Agreement on the Definite Ceasefire, the Agreement on Constitutional Reforms and the Electoral Regime, the Agreement on the Basis for the Legal Integration of the Unidad Revolucionaria Nacional Guatemalteca, the Agreement for a Firm and Lasting Peace, and the Agreement on the Timeline for the Implementation, Compliance and Verification of the Peace Accords.

The early rounds of negotiation alternated between substantive agreements and logistical agreements, in which the GoG jockeyed for commitments to a ceasefire, and, despite the GoG's efforts to attract international attention and involvement, rounds of talks in which the army "presented unrealistic proposals for negotiations that would have discarded previously signed agreements and, in essence, would have required the URNG to disarm without any substantive settlements."[50] Meanwhile, the URNG pushed what even sympathetic observers viewed as maximalist goals.[51] International mediation, time, and changes in GoG leadership eventually produced an overlapping bargaining range between the two groups of actors, but the resulting design of the accords was sweeping in scope, with comparatively few measurable benchmarks and commitments for the warring parties, partly as a result of this early dynamic and partly as a result of broad-based civil society participation in the agenda-setting process.[52]

Both parties were, therefore, committed to their particular conceptions of the peace, and committed to using the negotiation process to achieve the end of war. They clearly relied on international actors to provide the traditional functions that credible commitment scholars assign to third party guarantors: carrying information between war-

[50] Jonas 2000, 42.     [51] Ibid., 41.     [52] Stanley 2013, 5.

ring parties, verifying the human rights and security situation, and providing a guarantee to both sides about the credibility of the guarantee.[53] The international community also became a set of actors that could break internal deadlocks and add their weight to overcoming resistance on sticky issues, pushing the parties closer to ending war.[54]

Given the strength of UN response in El Salvador, credible commitment theories of peacekeeping would anticipate that belligerents in Guatemala should have sought the strongest possible mission they could have received in the service of guaranteeing the peace unless they noted other, competing signals of UN weakness. My theory asserts that other goals – tactical, material, and symbolic ends that combatants might pursue while negotiating a settlement with international actors present – might have driven the dynamics of negotiation, as well. And indeed, evidence indicates that these other goals not only motivated the warring parties in Guatemala, but actively led these parties to minimize the UN's efficacy as a security guarantor.

## Tactical Benefits

Negotiation can provide warring parties with tactical benefits that are distinct from war; it can grant them the time and space to regroup, rearm, and relaunch attacks; it can empower the factional leaders who represent their parties at the negotiation table;[55] or it can create political space for national policymakers to make domestically unpopular decisions and blame international actors for them.

There is evidence that both the GoG and the URNG used negotiations in service of tactical goals. Both sides were particularly interested in the instrumental use of the negotiation process to arrive at domestic political goals. Interview evidence indicates that URNG leaders initially viewed the negotiation process as "primarily a way to open up space for the popular movement, within a context dominated by counterinsurgency structures; at that time, they did not fully

[53] See, for example, "Framework Agreement for the Resumption of the Negotiating Process between the Government of Guatemala," Article V, Section I, A/49/610.
[54] Jonas 2000, 41–42.
[55] Christopher Clapham, "Being Peacekept," in *Peacekeeping in Africa*, ed. Oliver Furley and Roy May (Aldershot: Ashgate, 1998), 303–319.

see how Guatemala could be transformed through a peace process," although the arrival of MINUGUA shifted many of their viewpoints.[56]

On the GoG side, the new civilian leaders of the state appear to have used the negotiation process as a way to break domestic political impasses they held with the military. In January 1996, for example, Alvaro Arzú won the presidency and brought a fresh approach to negotiations; he met with the URNG several times before his inauguration, and he and his chief negotiator, Gustavo Porras, committed to working with the URNG despite the group's crumbling political and military leverage. Arzú and his team used the URNG's demands to their advantage; they "became a vehicle for Arzú's team to pursue reforms that they considered good for the country but would have had political difficulty pursuing were it not for the internationally sponsored peace talks."[57] Just as the domestic political opposition in Rwanda used the Arusha peace process to modify the Rwandan constitution, so too did the new civilian government of Guatemala use the Guatemalan peace process to enact political reforms that the military found objectionable.

## Material Benefits

Peace negotiations may offer material benefits that are distinct from the material benefits of winning a war, and particular material benefits – state building, refugee resettlement, and the influx of cash that international actors bring to the postwar economy – are *only* available through negotiations with international involvement. Evidence indicates that financial motivations drove the negotiating parties in Guatemala – particularly given that long years of war had drained state coffers, while the once-abundant military aid that the United States provided during the Cold War had diminished amid changing

---

[56] Jonas 2000, 62. See also Nicola Short's interviews with URNG leaders Noriega and Asturias (Short 2007, 72). Declassified US documents also include evidence the GoG thought this is how the URNG was using the negotiation process, as well ("Members of the Government Peace Commission Talk About the Peace Process," Memo from Department of Defense Joint Staff Washington DC to RUEKJCS/DIA WASHDC, RHLBAAA/USCINCSO Quarry Heights PM//SCJ2// info RUEHME/USDAO Mexico City MX RUESHSN/USDAO San Salvador ES, December 1991. In National Security Archive Guatemala Documentation Project, Offsite Box 28, 1991 Folder, pp. 0003–0004).

[57] Stanley 2013, 39–40.

global politics and rising attention to human rights within the United States. As early as 1990, for example, the US vice president noted in a briefing to Guatemala's president that

Guatemala's international image is deteriorating due to ... violence and the absence of investigative follow through. The lack of progress in the investigation of such major cases as the deaths of the San Carlos University Students and the stabbing of the Peace Brigadists is severely hampering our efforts to argue for assistance in Guatemala. We are already facing substantial cuts in our global level of economic and military assistance for FY90.[58]

In this context, negotiations became a way for the GoG to attract international investment and aid even as its international image was increasingly tarnished by allegations of mass atrocity and systematic human rights violations. Throughout the negotiations, it was clear that financial support from the donor countries and international financial institutions (IFIs) would be conditioned upon compliance with the peace process.[59] By the early 1990s, influential elements within the private sector began to support the peace process as part of a move to "gain access to free trade arrangements such as NAFTA, to foreign investment, and to international funding promised to Guatemala after the signing of the peace accords";[60] this support would have been important to the new civilian government as it attempted to distinguish itself from past military dictatorships.

International funders were involved throughout the negotiation process, and a major international funders' meeting in June 1995 made it clear that the largest part of international funding would be withheld from the GoG until the accords were finally signed.[61] Measures to attract private investment and appeal to international financial institutions were actually built into the Agreement on the Social and Economic Aspects and Agrarian Situation, the signing of which immediately preceded the donors' conference: for example, the agreement calls on the government to

promote, through all means possible, the development of a dynamic land market that would enable tenant farmers who either do not have land or

---

[58] US Department of State Briefing Paper, "The Vice-President's Meeting with Guatemalan President Vinicio Cerezo," *Declassified State Department Document Accessed through the National Security Archive* (January 19, 1990), 3, www2.gwu.edu/~nsarchiv/NSAEBB/NSAEBB11/docs/doc24.pdf.
[59] Jonas 2000, 60.      [60] Ibid., 61.      [61] Ibid., 45.

have insufficient land to acquire land through long-term transactions at commercial or favourable interest rates with little or no down payment. In particular, [to] promote the issuance of mortgage-backed securities guaranteed by the State whose yield is attractive to private investors, especially financial institutions.[62]

Attracting international aid and funding accordingly seems to have been an important driver of negotiations for the GoG.

## Legitimacy

Finally, negotiations may have symbolic benefits that reside in the process of negotiation and are distinct from the conclusion of a conflict. These benefits include recognition for warring parties from the international community as valid partners and legitimate political actors in the peace process and in domestic politics; the discursive value of airing grievances; and appearing to favor the consultative process of mediation and bargaining over the battlefield. These processes were particularly important goals for the parties to the Guatemalan negotiations given the GoG's internationally tarnished reputation and the URNG's status as a Cold War-era Marxist insurgency.

Interviews with URNG leaders reveal both their drive to be perceived as coherent, legitimate military *and* political actors by the UN and foreign governments, and that they refrained from spectacular acts of political violence in favor of negotiation as part of this drive.[63] This

---

[62] Agreement on the Social and Economic Aspects and Agrarian Situation, Section III, Part B, paragraph (e).

[63] See, for example, the book-length 1990 interview with Rolando Morán, the chief commander of the EGP, which includes the following: "Q: Sin embargo, altos mandos militares descalifican a la guerrilla guatemalteca que, por cierto, creo que es de las más Antigua de América Latina dicen que la URNG no tiene capacidad real" (85). "A: Como occure con las organizaciones populares guerrilleras, la URNG no puede competir con el estado en material de difusión, de comunicaciones ... pero hay querer también el otra lado de la medalla: nil as ayudas y asesorías israelitas, taiwanesa y norteamericana, han logrado aplastar a la guerrilla. En estos años no hemos llevada a cabo acciones espectaculares en la capital, que den la vuelta al mundo; pero nos hemos consolidado como una fuerza politico-militar coherente, con corporeidad, y reconocimiento de parte de las Naciones Unidas y muchas gobiernos. Está el hecho, además, de que Vinicio Cerezo cada vez tiene que referirse más a la URNG: y no solo él, también gobiernos de la region y fuerzas políticas internacionales. Y este hecho se da no ya porque seamos una fuerza a política de la oposicíon, sino porque somos además un poder militar con raigambre, un poder con el que hay buscar una

international recognition was not uncontroversial, and in the early days of the negotiations, the GoG moved to limit the international community's interaction with the URNG as much as possible. At one point, they only allowed an International Committee of the Red Cross (ICRC) vaccination program in war-stricken area to proceed on the conditions that the "(1) ICRC would not seek URNG permission of the program, thus implying URNG's control of the territory, and (2) the GoG ministry of public health would take part. [The] ICRC apparently violated the first stricture by contacting the URNG via the UN, re its plan, and the second by refusing GoG participation. The GoG prevented ICRC from executing the plan."[64] The URNG retaliated by making "the 'immediate application of international humanitarian law' to the internal armed conflict a 'non-negotiable' demand."[65] At another point, the GoG frantically lobbied to prevent indigenous rights and URNG activist Rigoberta Menchú from receiving the 1992 Nobel Peace Prize, going so far as to suggest a completely unknown Guatemalan businessman with GoG ties in her stead.[66]

However, both parties eventually made efforts to demonstrate how serious they were to the international community.[67] Ultimately, as UN Mediator Jean Arnault argued – in large measure because it required

salida al conflicto armado" (Pareles 1990, 85–86). The most relevant lines note that, despite the URNG's comparatively low technical capacity, and although they refrained from the kind of spectacular terrorist acts in the capital that would have given them global recognition, they consolidated themselves into a coherent political-military force acknowledged by the UN and many governments. Consequently, that the president, regional governments, and international political forces, found themselves required to constantly talk about the URNG indicated they were an opposition political force rooted in military power seeking to find a solution to armed conflict. Drawing on interviews with former URNG members, Michael Allison notes that the URNG had little political experience within the Guatemalan system, that it repeatedly lost its most politically savvy members to civil society organizations, and that it struggled to establish a political wing – all of which would center negotiations as a strategy for enhancing political legitimacy (Michael Allison, "The Guatemalan National Revolutionary Unit: The Long Collapse," *Democratization* 23, no. 6 [October 2016]: 1042–1058).

[64] US Department of State, "Confidential Cable: GOG Meets Most FMF Human Rights Benchmarks: Time for 'Small Steps' in Response to Big Ones," *US Department of State Document Accessed Through National Security Archive* (Washington, DC, November 22, 1991), 2, www2.gwu.edu/~nsarchiv/NSAEBB/NSAEBB11/docs/doc27.pdf.

[65] Ibid.      [66] Jonas 2000, 2–3.      [67] Ibid., 41.

the UN to help it rehabilitate its international standing[68] – the GoG accepted the UN human rights verification mission, indicating its shifting stance toward international recognition of the URNG. Later, in a similarly powerful signal, the URNG accepted the terms of the GoG's proposed police and military reforms, accepting, in the process, the state's legitimacy, after three decades of attempting to overthrow it.[69]

To summarize, then, negotiations with international involvement offered Guatemalan belligerents the possibility of peace and security, but they also provided tactical, material, and symbolic benefits that were distinct from war termination. These alternative benefits of bargaining can help us understand why we might see actors either seeking the services of a failed guarantor or working to minimize the efficacy of a successful guarantor. In the next sections, I examine what specifically the two warring parties sought from international intervention, how they perceived the UN as a mediator and guarantor to their agreement, and how the UN's recent successes and failures affected the negotiation process.

## Perceptions of Past UN Performance

This book argues that, given the shared social space of international peacekeeping and peacemaking, parties to a conflict develop a sense of what to expect from intervention, and that they shape their negotiation strategies in part with these expectations in mind. Accordingly, this section asks what the parties to the Guatemalan Civil War thought of the UN's abilities and past performance, which examples they drew upon in making their negotiation decisions, and how the UN's other interventions affected the Guatemalan peace process.

I argue that, despite a full range of competing examples about the efficacy of UN interventions, the GoG and the URNG drew nearly exclusively on the UN's success in El Salvador – but that they read this case for the lessons about distributional losses it offered, not for lessons

---

[68] Stanley 2013, 5.
[69] Jean Arnault, "Good Agreement? Bad Agreement? An Implementation Perspective,"(Princeton: Centre of International Studies, Princeton University, 2006), 16, https://gsdrc.org/document-library/good-agreement-bad-agreement-an-implementation-perspective/.

about the credibility of their guarantor. Consequently, they repeatedly moved to limit the UN's authority and scope as a security guarantor, despite still seeking its services as the verifier of its demobilization and human rights processes, while also seeking to engage its mediation capabilities, its political and humanitarian agencies, and its legitimating abilities. Indeed, the UN's success in El Salvador appears to have actually prolonged the Guatemalan negotiations,[70] as the parties monitored how the implementation of particular provisions of Chapultepec Peace Accords, such as demobilization and the release of the Truth Commission's report, affected their Salvadoran counterparts. This is evidence in favor of a distributional hypothesis, and it is surprising from the perspective of credible commitment theories of peacekeeping, which would anticipate that success next door in El Salvador would increase the Guatemalan parties' confidence in the UN as security guarantor, precipitating the conclusion of a peace agreement. I detail evidence for each of these explanations below.

## Other UN Examples

In assessing the UN's past performance as a guarantor to peace agreements, and as a potential provider of peace and security, tactical and material benefits, and legitimacy, the warring parties in Guatemala could have drawn on a number of potential examples from both their own region and other regions. As previously noted, the Guatemalan process was last-concluded of the three Central American negotiations, enabling Guatemalan actors to examine processes in Nicaragua and El Salvador, and to directly observe which of the high-level UN diplomats moved directly from one peace process to another. Negotiations in El Salvador concluded in 1992, enabling the GoG and the URNG to observe not just the UN's conduct as a negotiator but also its actions during the implementation phase of the peace accords, while they themselves were still negotiating.

The period of the Guatemalan negotiations also covered what was then to date the most rapid expansion of UN peacekeeping and peace-making, enabling the Guatemalan parties to observe the failures in Angola, Somalia, and Rwanda, as well, all of which occurred either shortly before or immediately after the UN assumed its formal role as

---

[70] Jonas 2000, 38 suggests this possibility as well.

mediator in Guatemala. The UN's successive failures in the Balkans took place during the negotiation period, along with a number of successfully concluded missions.[71] Indeed, the UN itself was in a more embattled position when it became deeply involved in Guatemala than it was in El Salvador, facing funding cuts and political crisis, and in particular faltering US support; in fact, late in the Guatemalan negotiations, the United States began to push for a greater role for the Organization of American States (OAS) in Guatemala as part of an effort to keep UN costs down.[72] There is almost no evidence, however, aside from a few passing references to the plight of rebels in Angola and Namibia,[73] that the negotiating parties in Guatemala considered these other cases of UN intervention when they made their own strategic decisions, or that they seriously considered shifting the process to the OAS umbrella.

Instead, El Salvador loomed large for both warring factions, despite the fact that the Salvadoran and Guatemalan conflicts were quite different.[74] International actors involved in the Guatemalan negotiations report that the Guatemalan parties were anxious to be treated differently from the Salvadorans. Jorge Montaño, the Mexican Ambassador to Guatemala and one of the UN's "Group of Friends" to the Guatemalan negotiations, reported that

in Guatemala obviously the example of El Salvador was a very important one ... the Guatemalans at the early stage in the process were always insisting that Guatemala and El Salvador were different. And they didn't want any similar kind of approach .... The first negotiation took place towards the end of 92 at the UN, the first encounter of the UN, and obviously, as I saw, the Guatemalans were reluctant to be treated like Salvadorians.[75]

Francesc Vendrell, the Secretary-General's first representative in Guatemala, made a similar observation:

---

[71] See Howard 2008 for a full account of the successful missions.
[72] Jonas 2000, 58–59.     [73] See, for example, Pareles 1990, 88.
[74] The ethnic dimensions of the conflict, as well as the lack of parity between the rebels and the government, in some ways made the Guatemalan case more comparable to concurrent African cases.
[75] Jorge Montaño, interview by Jean Krasno, *Yale-UN Oral History Project* (Mexico City, October 1, 1999), 54.

The Guatemalan government felt all along that, at least I should say the 'Guatemalan authorities,' that is the President and the armed forces, felt that they didn't want to suffer the fate, as they saw it, of their El Salvadorian counterparts, where they felt the army had been reduced, had been purified, had been removed from a role in civil society, and so on and so forth. Therefore we had always to be careful not to appear to be copying the El Salvadorian process. The UNRG, on its side, also felt that the FMLN had gone to [sic] far in concessions. As it turned out, of course, we all knew eventually they would follow a similar path, if they were going to reach an agreement at all. So anyway, the agreement is relatively similar.[76]

Both men's statements indicate that El Salvador, despite being a success for the UN, formed a largely *negative* example for the Guatemalan parties, who did not want to be treated like the parties to El Salvador's Civil War, and who felt as though their Salvadoran counterparts had made too many concessions or lost a great deal under the UN's negotiating auspices. Members of the GoG raised this concern explicitly, as well. As part of a panel of speakers addressing an American military audience in 1991, Manuel Conde, the Secretary of the Presidency and the chief of the government's peace commission, said "The GoG is very worried about the concessions given to the FMLN by the Salvadoran government, because the URNG would like to have the same concessions given to them here .... Conde finally concluded that he hopes the URNG does not use the peace in El Salvador in order to lengthen the process and demand other concessions."[77]

This concern for the distributional losses that the Salvadoran parties faced is apparent in five different facets of the Guatemalan negotiations: (1) the warring parties' preferences over the specific personnel who staffed the UN negotiation team; (2) the GoG's preference for a UNGA mandate instead of a UNSC mandate for MINUGUA; (3) the terms on which the Truth Commission was authorized; (4) the attacks that MINUGUA faced both before its deployment and on its arrival in

[76] Vendrell 1996, 32–33.
[77] "Members of the Government Peace Commission Talk about the Peace Process," Memo from Department of Defense Joint Staff Washington DC to RUEKJCS/DIA WASHDC, RHLBAAA/USCINCSO Quarry Heights PM//SCJ2// info RUEHME/USDAO Mexico City MX RUESHSN/USDAO San Salvador ES, December 1991. In National Security Archive Guatemala Documentation Project, Offsite Box 28, 1991 Folder, p. 0005.

Guatemala; (5) and finally, the GoG's move to appoint Spanish, instead of UN, personnel to reorganize its police and military forces. In each arena, one or both parties worked to minimize the UN's scope of authority in Guatemala, or to alter a provision that had been successfully implemented in El Salvador, often with specific reference to the perceived losses that their counterparts had sustained in the Chapultepec Peace Accords. I take each in turn.

## Preference over Personnel

First, the negotiating parties had a specific preference over the UN personnel who staffed the negotiating team. Initially, the Secretary-General appointed Francesc Vendrell as his observer to the process, but factions within the armed forces viewed Vendrell as pro-URNG, and the GoG requested he be removed for having overstepped his mandate as observer after he helped arrange a meeting between then-President Serrano and the URNG leadership, and after he helped draft some elements of the human rights agreement.[78] Although the GoG asked the UN to replace Vendrell with someone senior, Boutros Boutros-Ghali replaced him with the far more junior Jean Arnault. Over the course of the negotiations, the two sides converged – surprisingly, given their substantial disagreements on other issues – on Arnault as their choice for UN moderator. The position of moderator would usually have gone to someone much higher-ranking than Arnault, and the parties' preference for the relatively junior Arnault made UN headquarters uneasy, but UN diplomats ultimately supported the negotiating parties' choice.[79] This was a marked difference from the Salvadoran negotiation process, when high-ranking UN diplomats, including the Secretary-General himself, were heavily invested in the day-to-day proceedings of the negotiation process – and there were in fact times in the bargaining process when Arnault had to call on higher-ranking UN personnel to force the Guatemalan parties' hands.[80] The lobbying for Arnault indicates that the GoG wanted a

---

[78] Jonas 2000, 62; Vendrell 1996, 28; Stanley 2013, 22.
[79] Stanley 2013, 26–27.
[80] Ibid., 34–35. In February 1995, for example, after a long period with little movement on agreements and much foot-dragging from both parties, the UN Secretariat had Marrack Goulding issue a threat that indicated the UN would

*weaker* role for the UN than it had in El Salvador, and that the URNG supported this decision.[81]

## The UNGA Mandate

The GoG played a similar hand vis-à-vis the mandate for the UN verification mission to Guatemala. Most peace operations are given UNSC mandates; this was certainly true of the mission to El Salvador, which, like MINUGUA, began first as a human rights verification mission that then became a mission that supervised demobilization.[82] MINUGUA, however, was a mission that was, unusually, authorized and overseen by the UN General Assembly (UNGA). Various actors in New York jockeyed over whether the mission would be UNSC or UNGA-led: The Secretariat preferred a UNSC mandate, while the Mexican, Colombian, Venezuelan, and US governments all preferred a UNGA mandate; Mexico, Colombia, and Venezuela, in their capacity as members of the Group of Friends, wanted to retain their influence over the mission, which would have been much more difficult under a UNSC mandate, while the United States wanted to keep costs low, which called for UNGA supervision.[83]

Most critically, however, the GoG strongly preferred a UNGA mandate for the verification mission; they were concerned they would not be able to control a peace process anchored by a stronger, UNSC-mandated mission. As early as 1991, senior officials within the GoG were anxious to minimize the UN's role in peacemaking, emphasizing that its role was purely to observe, not to actively mediate. A US government document records Manuel Conde, the Secretary of the Presidency and the chief of the government's peace commission, telling assembled US military officers that "The peace process is Guatemalan,

---

not participate in the peace process if the parties did not sit down again in accordance with the UN's timetable (ibid.).

[81] Stanley suggests that Arnault was an easy person to work with, and that he was very respectful of the Guatemalan parties. We should not discount the likelihood that Arnault's personal characteristics played a strong role in the warring parties' decision to request he serve as the conflict's mediator. That he sometimes had to appeal to his higher-ups to issue ultimatums, however, seems to indicate that the parties were also aware that his presence as mediator gave them more bargaining latitude than negotiations that were more immediately tied to higher-ranking officials.

[82] Howard 2008.      [83] Stanley 2013, 32–33.

and while the GoG appreciates the presence of the U.N. as an observer, the process is one of conciliation – requiring a conciliator not a mediator."[84] At the same meeting, Ernesto Viteri, adviser to the president, "was very emphatic in stating that the [UN] Observer ((Vendrell)) had no role in the negotiations than observer."[85] Both senior advisers were at pains to minimize the UN's role from the outset, which is not what we would expect if the success of the Salvadorian negotiations or the credibility of the UN's guarantee were driving the desire for UN involvement in Guatemala.

Indeed, the GoG seems to have drawn specifically on ONUSAL as they decided to pursue minimal UN involvement: Stanley argues that "The Guatemalan political elite had by this point gotten a close look at the UN presence in neighboring El Salvador, and wanted to do whatever they could to reduce the authority of any UN mission."[86] Their preferences about the contours of the UN verification mission were directly tied back to their observation of ONUSAL in El Salvador, resulting in a mission that was far weaker than its successful counterpart next door.

## The Truth Commission

El Salvador's Truth Commission report was released in early 1993, during the Guatemalan negotiations, and shortly before the Guatemalan parties themselves began negotiating their own terms of accountability for past human rights violations.[87] The Salvadoran Truth Commission had held wide-ranging authority to investigate and report on atrocities, and it served as the main reference point for Guatemalan parties considering how to contend with their own history of violence.[88] "The idea of a truth commission attracted intense interest from civil

---

[84] "Members of the Government Peace Commission Talk about the Peace Process," Memo from Department of Defense Joint Staff Washington DC to RUEKJCS/DIA WASHDC, RHLBAAA/USCINCSO Quarry Heights PM//SCJ2// info RUEHME/USDAO Mexico City MX RUESHSN/USDAO San Salvador ES, December 1991. In National Security Archive Guatemala Documentation Project, Offsite Box 28, 1991 Folder, p. 0005.
[85] Ibid., 0004.     [86] Stanley 2013, 32.
[87] Victoria Sanford, *Buried Secrets: Truth and Human Rights in Guatemala* (New York: Palgrave Macmillan, 2003), 258.
[88] Priscilla B. Hayner, *Unspeakable Truths: Confronting State Terror and Atrocity* (New York: Routledge, 2002), 43.

society and victims groups in Guatemala, and they lobbied negotiators heavily in an attempt to influence its terms,"[89] while the URNG immediately put the idea of a commission to examine the abuses committed over the course of the war high on the negotiation agenda.[90] However, as Vendrell recalls,

The Guatemalan military was very opposed to the idea of a truth commission. First, it didn't want the name, of course, because it was the same as El Salvador's, but particularly it feared, to some degree rightly, that a commission to investigate the past would be used to really, completely, deprive the military of any legitimacy because the abuses committed in Guatemala during the 30-year war were far worse than the ones in El Salvador.[91]

In a similar vein, the Army's Deputy Chief of Staff, Brigadier General Mario Rene Enriquez Morales, told a 1992 breakfast gathering of attachés that "The URNG had copied this [the truth commission] from the Salvadoran peace process and believed that this would help polarize Guatemalan society," but that there was an agreement among the GoG that the truth commission's findings could not be used in judicial processes.[92] Indeed, their chief objection was the Salvadoran model of naming perpetrators of human rights violations:[93] "We didn't want what they did in El Salvador," Hector Rosada, the former chief of the GoG's negotiating team, told scholar Priscilla Hayner, also noting that "there was nothing they liked about that commission, but the fact that it named high-level perpetrators [was] probably the most unattractive aspect."[94]

Negotiations were tense and difficult, and ultimately the GoG's stronger bargaining position produced a Historical Clarification Commission (instead of a truth commission) entitled the Commission to Clarify Past Human Rights Violations and Acts of Violence That Have Caused the Guatemalan People to Suffer.[95] The two parties signed the commission into existence in Oslo in June 1994.[96] The

---

[89] Ibid., 46.     [90] Vendrell 1996, 32–33.     [91] Ibid.

[92] US Department of Defense, "IIR [Censored] Report on Breakfast for Attaches Hosted by Army Chief of Staff," July 1992, National Security Archive, Guatemala Documentation Project, Documents Not Included, Offsite Box 28, 1992 Folder, p. 0802.

[93] For a full internal account of the Historical Clarification Commission (CEH), see Christian Tomuschat, "Clarification Commission in Guatemala," *Human Rights Quarterly* 23, no. 2 (2001): 233–258.

[94] Hayner 2002, 124.     [95] Ibid., 45.     [96] Tomuschat 2001, 233–258.

agreement's final language prohibited the commission from attributing responsibility for violence to any individual in its work, recommendations, and report, and was specifically charged with investigating without any judicial aim.[97] Civil society reaction was initially fierce, and directed against the URNG for signing the agreement; indeed, participants to the negotiations believed the strong reaction to the agreement "came close to derailing the peace talks altogether."[98] Flexible interpretation of the agreement by the multinational commission charged with its execution, however, eventually won public support for the commission and its findings.[99] Indeed, despite the GoG's strong efforts to distinguish the Guatemalan and Salvadoran processes during negotiations, ultimately many of the Truth Commission's staff came directly from ONUSAL and from their work on the Salvadoran Truth Commission.[100]

## Attacks on MINUGUA

MINUGUA mission faced a series of attacks and threats from its arrival in Guatemala onward. These attempts to minimize the MINUGUA's influence also reveal the warring parties' efforts to produce different outcomes for themselves than those their counterparts in El Salvador had experienced. The attacks were both overt – including kidnappings, harassment, and shootings from the most vocal opponents to the peace – and passive, including a pattern of background resistance from the GoG to MINUGUA's work and recommendations.[101] The GoG had previously attempted to minimize MINUGUA's authority, presence, and mandate before its deployment, using the delay in its arrival to call its

---

[97] Acuerdo sobre el Establecimiento de la Comisión para el Esclarecimiento Histórico de las Violaciones de los Derechos Humanos y los Hechos de Violencia que Han Causado Sufrimientos a la Población Guatemalteca, Oslo, Norway, June 23, 1994, Funcionamiento III.

[98] Hayner 2002, 46.

[99] Ibid., 46; during the course of the commission's work, the commission chair, Christian Tomuschat, wrote that "The final report, although it shall not attribute responsibility to any individual, may have to mention the names of a considerable number of persons who, during the worst years of the conflict, held high positions in the Government or within the structures of the URNG .... Clearly, the report itself will not charge these persons individually with having committed human rights violations, but ... attentive observers will be in a position to draw the requisite conclusions from the facts displayed in the report" (ibid., 124).

[100] Sanford 2003, 258.        [101] Jonas 2000, 49.

staffing levels "elevated and excessive," to argue that it should not be empowered to investigate human rights abuses, and then erroneously announcing to the public that it was not in fact authorized to carry out investigations, all while criticizing the UN for delays in actually deploying the mission.[102]

In March 1996, the URNG called for an open-ended halt to offensive armed actions, and the GoG responded by halting offensive counter-insurgency operations.[103] Far from requesting the UN serve as neutral third party guarantor to this ceasefire, however, the GoG in particular moved to sideline the UN, claiming that the "new understandings" between the warring parties negated the need for such a strong inter-national presence in the negotiation process. This was a negotiation move that explicitly drew lessons from the UN's experiences in El Salvador – "According to top UN officials, the PAN, [then-President] Arzú's party, and CACIF[104] had been warned by their colleagues in El Salvador's rightist party, ARENA, to limit the UN role. It took a combination of the URNG's insistence on a central UN role and sensi-tivity by UN officials in dealing with the government to defuse open hostility."[105] Indeed, even during and immediately following the signing of the final peace accord, GoG officials, including the president, sug-gested that verification was either unnecessary or could be carried out by the OAS.[106] These dual moves to minimize the UN's role in security and verification while continuing to seek its presence along other fronts indicate that the GoG needed the UN's presence in post-conflict Guatemala, but that it sought to shape this presence with attention to the perceived losses its counterparts in El Salvador had sustained.

## Preference for Spanish Police and Military Training

Finally, the GoG made efforts to circumvent the UN and the URNG while negotiating the last agreement of the comprehensive accords, the

---

[102] Ibid., 45; Stanley 2013, 34.     [103] Jonas 2000, 51.
[104] The Coordinating Committee of Agricultural, Commercial, Industrial, and Financial Associations.
[105] Jonas 2000, 51. Jonas also notes that "Hence, some believe, both MINUGUA and the UN negotiating team assumed a 'lower profile' during the first part of 1996 – which coincided with the budget crisis of the UN General Secretariat and the attendant uncertainties about MINUGUA's future."
[106] Jonas 2000, 68.

Agreement on the Strengthening of Civilian Power and on the Role of the Armed Forces in a Democratic Society. These efforts again reveal their desire to guard against the kind of losses they believed UN peacemakers had visited on El Salvador's government.

The Arzú government pressured the URNG into signing the last of the agreements, which dealt with police and military reform – the URNG lacked the technical expertise to formulate their own policy on integration and security sector reform, and the GoG quickly moved to limit UN involvement in the process by negotiating a bilateral agreement with Spain: "Having observed the way international advice and assistance programs had shaped the development of a new civilian police force in El Salvador, the Arzú government had its own ideas," Stanley writes. He notes that

> the Salvadoran process had, according to [Guatemalan] Interior Minister Rodolfo Mendoza resulted in a cacophony of contradictory advice from different nations' police advisors. Mendoza also observed that the transition from the old police to the new PNC in El Salvador had created a security vacuum that had contributed to a postwar crime wave. As a result, within a week of taking office in January 1996, Mendoza told MINUGUA that he was in conversations with the Spanish government and that plans were already under way to bring a Spanish Civil Guard (GCE) advising team to redevelop the police.[107]

This move was controversial, not in the least because of the Spanish Civil Guard's perceived association with the Franco regime; Guatemalan human rights NGOs objected strongly, as did MINUGUA. International NGOs interested in demobilization were caught off guard by the speed and direction of the negotiations.[108] The Asamblea de la Sociedad Civil (ASC) – the civil society association that had been the third advisory party to the negotiating parties throughout the process – was rarely heeded at this stage in the negotiations, but it suggested the alternative Honduran model of demobilization and integration in lieu of either the Spanish or Salvadoran models.[109] The GoG moved swiftly to work with Spain despite these counterexamples and despite popular resistance, and it had strong preferences about which roles specific international actors should play in post-conflict Guatemala: Both pieces of evidence

---

[107] Stanley 2013, 47.     [108] Ibid., 49.     [109] Ibid.

underline how El Salvador serves as a constant reference point for the GoG's negotiation decisions.

Taken together, this evidence indicates that parties to the Guatemalan peace process were very attentive to other cases as they formed their negotiation decisions. That the parties to the Guatemalan Civil War, and in particular the GoG, read the UN's success in El Salvador as a largely cautionary tale, working to minimize the UN's authority on the ground while also still lobbying the UN to continue participating in Guatemala's post-conflict politics, indicates that these parties sought the UN's assistance because they were interested in the alternative benefits of bargaining – the tactical, material, and symbolic benefits that only international presence in negotiation could bring to the peace process and the post-conflict state – and not simply in the UN's capability as a credible third party guarantor to their agreement. Society wide security was one motive among many, and easily sidelined to a whole host of other interests.

## Conclusion

We can say, then, that participants in the Guatemalan peace process were very attentive to the UN's behavior in El Salvador, and to the consequences of UN intervention for their Salvadoran counterparts. Extended to their logical conclusions, credible commitment theories of peacekeeping predict that success in El Salvador would enhance the Guatemalan warring parties' confidence in the UN's capability as a credible third party guarantor, thus hastening the end of war and the conclusion of a negotiated peace. Instead, I find that the GoG and the URNG viewed the Salvadoran example in a largely negative light: Both sides believed their Salvadoran counterparts had conceded too much at the negotiating table. Accordingly, even while lobbying for multiple forms of UN assistance during the course of negotiations, the GoG and URNG moved to guard against the same UN policies and provisions they believed had cost their counterparts a more favorable settlement. Both sides actively pursued UN intervention for the symbolic, material, and tactical benefits it brought to the negotiation process, even as the GoG actively sought to minimize the UN's role as security guarantor to the peace process.

The UN's banner success in El Salvador thus first prolonged the war in Guatemala and then produced a weaker agreement, a degraded capacity to enforce the peace, and inferior human rights outcomes for the Guatemalan domestic public. Indeed, although the peace has miraculously held, it is bitter for many in Guatemala: The peace accords quickly deteriorated in the implementation period – in 1998, for instance, the coordinator of *Nunca Más*, the report which chronicled human rights violations during the war, was murdered; in 1999, constitutional reforms proposed by the negotiated agreement were rejected by popular referendum[110] – and in the years since the war, judicial impunity, drug trafficking, and organized crime, among other threats to the civilian population, have conspired to make Guatemala one of the most dangerous places in the world.[111]

Just as the Rwandan negotiations raise real questions about the relationship between UN peacekeeping and the UN as decolonization authority, the Guatemalan peace process raises questions about the salience of different examples. With a range of UN interventions to examine as they weighed how to proceed, the Guatemalan government in particular focused on the Salvadoran case. This bears further investigation by scholars, as does the contemporary salience of both the Rwandan and Guatemalan cases. What can these cases tell us about peacekeeping and peacemaking today? The next chapter turns to these questions.

[110] Jonas 2002, 10.    [111] Doyle 2012.

# 6 | Conclusion

This book's core argument is intuitive: The United Nations' central role in contemporary conflict resolution means peace operations have structural consequences for peace processes worldwide – and that participants in peace processes worldwide can observe the UN's peace-making and peacekeeping tools at work in other places as they make their own decisions. If we take peace operations' structural dimensions seriously when we examine negotiation processes, then we learn parties to negotiation are interested in international involvement for a full range of material and symbolic benefits that extend well beyond peace – and indeed, even parties with little interest in peace may still seek out the UN's post-conflict intervention. Governments and rebels alike who seek out UN intervention may do so because the UN's involvement in peacemaking and peacekeeping affords them benefits that *only* the international community can bring, some of which may have nothing to do with actual settlement of the conflict. Some parties to conflict will want little more than to strike a deal, end bloodshed and suffering, and mitigate the costs of war. But for other parties to conflict, distributional and legitimacy concerns are paramount, and international involvement in conflict termination may also bring tactical, material, and symbolic benefits.

First, meeting with international mediators and negotiators can buy belligerents time by affording them time away from the battlefield to regroup, rearm, and launch unexpected attacks.[1] Negotiation may also offer tactical benefits by empowering factional leaders, who represent their parties at the negotiation table,[2] or by granting domestic political

---

[1] Scott Wolford, Dan Reiter, and Clifford J. Carrubba make a similar point in "Information, Commitment, and War," *Journal of Conflict Resolution* 55, no. 4 (August 2011): 556–579, 561.
[2] Christopher Clapham, "Being Peacekept," in *Peacekeeping in Africa*, ed. Oliver Furley and Roy May (Aldershot: Ashgate, 1998), 303–319.

parties a way to "launder" domestic political reforms that they would otherwise be unable to enact.[3]

Second, intervention may also have straightforward material benefits. International involvement can be a way of securing future rents, either because intervention will reconstitute the local economy in a way that benefits elites, or because international intervention in conflict-torn states can evolve into state-building, or can help desperate parties to conflict undertake expensive, vital, and otherwise impossible projects like refugee resettlement and integrating armed forces.

Finally, UN involvement in conflict termination may also have symbolic benefits for parties to a conflict, including recognition from the international community as valid partners and legitimate political actors in the peace and post-conflict processes.[4] Combatants who turn to the UN to secure aid and economic assistance from third parties, or to cultivate their images and identities as appropriate, equal parties in conflict resolution and international recognition may have goals beyond successfully implementing their peace agreements.

In Rwanda, the UN's massive peacekeeping failure during the genocide would have made turning back to the UN for a second peacekeeping mission after the genocide seem like an unlikely choice – and yet the postwar Rwandan government did precisely that, in an effort to bring legitimacy to its postwar reconstruction efforts through multilateral involvement. In Guatemala, parties to the conflict actively worked to minimize the UN's role as a security guarantor while using the UN's presence to pursue domestic political goals – the new civilian leaders of the state, for example, appear to have used the negotiation process as a way to break domestic political impasses they held with the military, which had long ruled the country as a dictatorship. When it became clear that donor countries would condition financial support on compliance with the peace process, UN involvement in peacemaking, peacebuilding, and peacekeeping also became a way for the

[3] Kenneth W. Abbott and Duncan Snidal, "Why States Act through Formal International Organizations," *Journal of Conflict Resolution* 42, no. 1 (February 1998): 3–32.

[4] Klaus Schlicte and Ulrich Schneckener, "Armed Groups and the Politics of Legitimacy," *Civil Wars* 17 (2015): 409–424; Lee J. M. Seymour, "Legitimacy and the Politics of Recognition in Kosovo," *Small Wars & Insurgencies* 28, no. 4–5 (2017): 817–838; Reyko Huang, "Rebel Diplomacy," *International Security* 40, no. 4 (Spring 2016): 89–126.

Guatemalan government to attract international investment and aid even as its international image was increasingly tarnished by allegations of mass atrocities and systematic human rights violations.[5]

This book began with a simple idea: Failures have consequences – and if those consequences are unclear, we should ask why. UN peacekeeping in civil wars became a frequent policy tool at the end of the Cold War, and its early days were rocky. Between 1992 and 1995 alone, upward of 782,000 people died in places where UN peacekeepers were on the ground to keep the peace.[6] For combatants and civilians alike, this astonishing number of casualties should have cast doubt on the UN's ability to protect them and uphold any peace agreement they struck: Who could have deep faith peacekeepers would protect them when they had repeatedly failed to forestall catastrophes?

Interrogating the consequences of failure is particularly important because influential scholarly accounts of external involvement in civil wars frame mistrust as a central problem that international actors must solve to help end civil wars. Following this logic, these accounts of how UN peacekeeping works assume that peacekeepers help resolve credible commitment problems that prevent negotiated settlements, that parties to conflict are similarly motivated at the negotiating table, and that parties to conflict should seek the assistance of external actors who can guarantee their security. In this account, international actors' involvement in peace processes is desirable because they mitigate mistrust by credibly, impartially upholding negotiated settlements. Factions in a conflict need not trust each other to uphold their end of the deal. They need only trust that the UN will prevent the other side from breaking the agreement. Similarly, policymakers often frame peacekeeping as the solution to a range of security problems – and

---

[5] US Department of State Briefing Paper, "The Vice-President's Meeting with Guatemalan President Vinicio Cerezo," *Declassified State Department Document Accessed through the National Security Archive* (January 19, 1990), 3, www2 .gwu.edu/~nsarchiv/NSAEBB/NSAEBB11/docs/doc24.pdf; Susanne Jonas, *Of Centaurs and Doves: Guatemala's Peace Process* (Boulder: Westview, 2000), 60.
[6] I detail the calculations for this estimate in Chapter 3. Sources: M. J. Anstee, *Orphan of the Cold War: The Inside Story of the Collapse of the Angolan Peace Process, 1992–1993* (Basingstroke: Macmillan, 1996); Alison L. Des Forges, *Leave None to Tell the Story* (New York: Human Rights Watch, 1999); Lise Morjé Howard, *UN Peacekeeping in Civil Wars* (New York: Cambridge University Press, 2008); Bethany Lacina and Nils Petter Gleditsch, "Monitoring Trends in Global Combat: A New Dataset of Battle Deaths," *European Journal of Population* 21, no. 2–3 (2005): 145–166.

indeed, increasingly peacekeepers are asked to perform military tasks.[7] But if combatants do not believe peacekeepers can uphold agreements or provide security, do they turn to the UN out of desperation, in search of absolutely any international assistance, or does something else drive them to seek UN intervention even when they assume it will fail?

The book suggests that the credible commitment theory of war termination – the architecture underpinning many influential accounts of peacekeeping – is an insufficient foundation for understanding the UN's involvement in peacemaking. Scholars have focused on whether peacekeepers can prevent peace agreements from collapsing back into war by leveraging information, technical support, and credible force. But if we invert the question – if we ask what parties to conflict want from the UN even when they *don't* believe they'll get a credible, neutral force that can help them uphold the terms of their peace agreement – then our explanations shift as well: Concerns about what combatants want and need, and questions of material benefits and international status and legitimacy come to the fore, while concerns about peace and security recede.

This is not an argument that credible commitment theories are wrong, but rather that they are consequentially incomplete – that peace operations are desirable to warring parties for all kinds of reasons that may have little to do with security, and that may be more tightly bound to the political dynamics of negotiation than to cycles of mistrust and fear. Previous scholarship tells us that peace agreements flourish when combatants are committed to them[8] – and this book argues that the demand for peace operations reflects the same political dynamics that drive negotiation.

Accordingly, my findings also call into question a dominant account of how peacekeeping works. I contend that parties to conflict envision peacekeeping as a solution to a range of distributional and ideational problems – and, indeed, given that they may be more concerned with issues of statebuilding and legitimacy than with mistrust, that they

---

[7] Carlos Alberto dos Santos Cruz et al., "Improving Security of United Nations Peacekeepers: We Need to Change the Way We Are Doing Business," December 19, 2017, https://peacekeeping.un.org/sites/default/files/improving_security_of_united_nations_peacekeepers_report.pdf.

[8] Suzanne Werner and Amy Yuen, "Making and Keeping Peace," *International Organization* 59, no. 2 (Spring 2005): 261–292.

sometimes view peacekeeping as a necessary process that is incidental to solving these distributional and ideational problems. This is fundamentally different from primarily security-based accounts of what peacekeepers do, of how peacekeeping works, and of why belligerents seek out the assistance of international actors. If the account I offer is correct, then scholars should examine the social dimensions of peace operations as they consider the assumptions, mechanisms, and processes through which peace operations work.

My account focuses on what elite parties to conflict – the people literally at the negotiating table – want from the UN. It leaves what civilians want from potential interveners unaddressed. News reports reveal that – even when combatants do not – civilians in conflict zones often expect the UN will protect them.[9] Systematic research about what civilians want and expect from peacekeepers remains a vital undertaking for future researchers, particularly since nearly all peacekeepers today operate under civilian protection mandates,[10] and particularly since important research illuminates the vital local-level dimensions of peacemaking, peacebuilding, and stability.[11]

## Implications of the Arguments

What else do this book's two core insights – that peace operations have structural properties, and that parties to negotiation seek out the UN's

---

[9] Patrick Cammaert, interview with Anjali Dayal, New York (April 15, 2013). Cammaert noted that, at the first signs of trouble, civilians in conflict zones often fled toward the UN base, expecting protection. News reports relay this dynamic, as well. See, for example, this Reuters report in 2015 on Darfur: "Despite their complaints, civilians have been increasingly seeking out UNAMID team sites in Darfur for protection … Khadija Ismail, a 26-year-old mother of five, is haunted by the attack on her village and says that when she reached Zam Zam, already jammed with some 150,000 people reliant on aid agencies, she and her children received no food or shelter. But she still felt the United Nations was her only hope. 'If the government expelled UNAMID, we would have to leave Sudan with them, because no one else will protect us,' she said" (Khalid Abdelazi and Louis Charbonneau, "Question Marks Hang Over Flawed Darfur Peacekeeping Force," *Reuters*, March 11, 2015, www.reuters.com/article/us-sudan-unitednations-darfur-insight/question-marks-hang-over-flawed-darfur-peacekeeping-force-idUSKBN0M70ZV20150311).

[10] Lise Morjé Howard and Anjali Kaushlesh Dayal, "The Use of Force in UN Peacekeeping," *International Organization* 72, no. 1 (Winter 2018): 71–103.

[11] Sarah B. K. von Billerbeck, *Whose Peace? Local Ownership and United Nations Peacekeeping* (Oxford: Oxford University Press, 2017); Autesserre 2010.

post-conflict presence for a whole range of non-security concerns even when they are not primarily concerned with peace – tell us about the world? I argue the book's arguments have implications for both scholars of peace operations and for policy debates on peace operations. For scholars of peace operations, the evidence I advance in this book should make us reconsider both the stark conception of individual conflicts as independent units and an easy historicization of peace operations as two periods bisected by the end of the Cold War. For policymakers and practitioners, this book joins an ongoing debate about the future of peace operations with more evidence in favor of peacemaking as a locally grounded political process – not an externally engineered military undertaking. I outline each set of implications in turn below.

## Implications for Scholarship

First, my research indicates that internationally centralized conflict resolution processes complicate attempts to box conflict processes neatly into independent national cases. Scholars of peacekeeping and peacemaking ought to systematically account for the ways international interventions anywhere might affect domestic conflict processes everywhere. This book accordingly joins other scholarship that evaluates the unintended consequences of peacekeeping,[12] and that contends that global processes of cooperation and hierarchy meaningfully shape domestic security processes.[13] At the very least, scholars should be mindful of the often reflexive methodological assumption that individual conflicts or individual peace processes are independent

---

[12] Séverine Autesserre, "Hobbes and the Congo: Frames, Local Violence, and International Intervention," *International Organization* 63, no. 2 (April 2009): 249–280; Séverine Autesserre, *The Trouble with the Congo: Local Violence and the Failure of International Peacebuilding* (Cambridge: Cambridge University Press, 2010); Séverine Autesserre, *Peaceland: Conflict Resolution and the Everyday Politics of International Intervention* (Cambridge: Cambridge University Press, 2014); Alan J. Kuperman, "The Moral Hazard of Humanitarian Intervention: Lessons from the Balkans," *International Studies Quarterly* 52 (2008): 49–80.

[13] Stathis N. Kalyvas and Laia Balcells, "International System and Technologies of Rebellion: How the End of the Cold War Shaped Internal Conflict," *American Political Science Review* 104, no. 3 (2010): 415–429; Tanisha Fazal, *Wars of Law: Unintended Consequences in the Regulation of Armed Conflict* (Ithaca: Cornell University Press, 2018).

units; at most, they should extend their assessments of conflict diffusion effects beyond refugee and rebel movement to include norms of conflict resolution and potential lessons about the material, tactical, and symbolic benefits of international intervention. Future research should consider these lessons alongside other measures of conflict diffusion.

Second, scholars of peace operations should consider the UN's role as decolonization authority in their analyses. Scholars of UN peace operations tend to be begin their analyses in 1989, when the post-Cold War thaw in US-Russian relations produced a flurry of peace operations; that year serves as a systemic line of demarcation even though many long-running missions were initially authorized before that date. The Rwandan case here complicates that crisp dateline; parties to negotiation in Rwanda considered their relationship with the UN not just in light of concurrent or recent peace operations, but in light of their own personal experiences with the UN during decolonization. Scholars of UN peacekeeping – particularly those interested in case study research and in African cases – should also ask how the UN's role as the decolonization authority shaped its role as the post-Cold War guarantor of a peace throughout the 1990s and 2000s. Critics of humanitarian intervention highlight its neo-imperialist characteristics,[14] while thoughtful research on both the imperial origins of international law and on decolonization's role in shaping international organizations lays bare the continuity between imperial forms of international order and contemporary Atlantic-led institutions of liberal internationalism.[15] Left still unexplored is how these decolonization dynamics shape the expectations, ideas, and strategies that the local

---

[14] See, for example, Mohammed Ayoob, "Humanitarian Intervention and State Sovereignty," *The International Journal of Human Rights* 6, no. 1 (Spring 2002): 81–102.

[15] Adom Getachew, *Worldmaking after Empire: The Rise and Fall of Self-Determination* (Princeton: Princeton University Press, 2019); Jennifer Pitts, *Boundaries of the International: Law and Empire* (Cambridge, MA: Harvard University Press, 2018); Lauren Benton and Lisa Ford, *Rage for Order: The British Empire and the Origins of International Law* (Cambridge, MA: Harvard University Press, 2018); Antony Anghie, *Imperialism, Sovereignty and the Making of International Law* (Cambridge: Cambridge University Press, 2007); Mark Mazower, *No Enchanted Palace: The End of Empire and the Ideological Origins of the United Nations* (Princeton: Princeton University Press, 2013).

recipients of peace operations, both civilian and combatant, have of and about the UN.

At least, peacekeeping merely echoes the trusteeship dynamics of decolonization; at most, peacekeeping embodies the latest stage of a lived experience with multilateral intervention that began decades before the end of the Cold War for many in Sub-Saharan Africa. Some of the rebel leaders of civil wars in the 1980s and 1990s grew up in postindependence UNHCR camps, and many others came of age during the period when the UN Trusteeship Council was managing the local transition to independence. Viewing peacekeeping's post-Cold War period as divorced from these earlier dynamics risks missing a key factor shaping how both negotiating elites and the local population view the UN.

## Implications for Policy

Peace operations today are different than the older peace operations I cover in this book. In fact, they are different *because* of the peace operations detailed in this book; UNAMIR's collapse amid genocide was one of a series of spurs toward civilian protection mandates and the Responsibility to Protect doctrine in the late 1990s and early 2000s. Because my theory emphasizes the particularity of combatants' strategic situations, I anticipate that my claims about the social and distributive nature of UN interventions will be broadly generalizable to other civil war peace processes, contingent on the goals, perceptions, and capabilities of the participants. The bulk of my analysis focuses on the 1990s, but as UN peace operations have expanded in scope and scale since the late 1990s, and as their mandates have become more similar, more predictable, and more embedded in a larger multilateral peacebuilding and post-conflict agenda, the prospective recipients of intervention have an even wider pool of examples to draw upon when they weigh the benefits of international participation in their peace processes. But peacekeepers are also now deployed to more difficult kinds of cases for more difficult kinds of tasks, which might produce greater uncertainty about outcomes for combatants. I anticipate that the dynamics I identify would be amplified in today's UN peace operations, where conflicts are often more complex, ongoing, and intractable, and where peacekeeping forces are often charged with protecting civilians. Peacekeeping is a less visibly successful enterprise in many of

these cases, and the UNSC today continues to extend mission mandates rather than close missions under duress. In some of these cases,
the very existence of any security for peacekeepers to guarantee might
be questionable – and so in fact, new developments in peace operations
still compel us to ask what, if *not* security, combatants might want
from the UN's involvement.

Accordingly, the arguments I make here contribute to an ongoing
debate about the future of peace operations. To say UN peacekeeping
is at a crossroads has become something of a cliché – but peacekeeping
*is*, in fact, perpetually at an impasse, as the UN is perennially asked to
manage more conflict with persistently insufficient means.[16] In its latest
incarnation, this impasse pits proponents who argue for peace operations to have more means to use force – which effectively turns peace
operations toward more military endeavors – against the UN
Secretariat's emphasis on the "primacy of politics," which stresses that
mediation, ceasefire monitoring, and helping implement peace accords
should headline the UN approach to conflict resolution.[17] What should
peacekeepers do to resolve this dilemma? Should they be soldiers,
meeting threats against the state with force, as the growing number
of UN-hatted counterterrorism missions do?[18] Or should they function
as lightly armed diplomats, acting only in accordance with the traditional principles the UN itself lays out: consent of the warring parties;
impartiality; and the nonuse of force, except in self-defense or in
defense of the mission's mandate?

Answering this question is crucial to the UN's future. UN peacekeepers are the largest deployed force in conflict zones worldwide; as of
mid-2020, there were thirteen missions staffed by over 81,000 personnel from 121 countries.[19] UN missions are also the most significant
area of UN action, with a separate budget of $6.5 billion, a figure that

---

[16] See, for example, Wassim Mir, "Financing UN Peacekeeping: Avoiding Another
Crisis," International Peace Institute, April 17, 2019, www.ipinst.org/wp-
content/uploads/2019/04/1904_Financing-UN-Peacekeeping.pdf.

[17] See, for example, dos Santos Cruz et al. 2017; S/RES/2378 (2017); António
Guterres, "Secretary-General's Remarks at Security Council High-Level Open
Debate on Peacekeeping Operations Regarding the Reform of UN Peacekeeping:
Implementation and Follow Up," September 17, 2017, www.un.org/sg/en/
content/sg/speeches/2017-09-20/sgs-reform-un-peacekeeping-remarks.

[18] John Karlsrud, "From Liberal Peacebuilding to Stabilization and
Counterterrorism," *International Peacekeeping* 26, no.1 (2019): 1–21.

[19] https://peacekeeping.un.org/en/data.

outstrips the UN Secretariat's entire budget by $3.5 billion.[20] Accordingly, the question of which direction peacekeeping should turn is central to contemporary debates about international security and global cooperation. With nearly all current UN missions tasked with protecting civilians under threat of violence, and large, complex, multidimensional UN operations in the Central African Republic, Mali, and the DRC increasingly resembling counterinsurgency and counterterrorism operations,[21] this dilemma is ultimately one that highlights the tension between mandates that protect civilians and models of peacekeeping that center the primacy and sovereignty of states.[22] This fissure runs through the entire UN system,[23] but is particularly acute when the organization sends its emissaries out into world with weapons.

Peacekeepers are essential in protecting civilians, and every complex mission authorized since 1999 has an explicit mandate to protect civilians under imminent threat of violence – but peacekeepers are far more successful at protecting civilians from rebels than government forces.[24] This last point should give us pause when we consider what direction future peacekeeping missions should take, particularly because offensive military action is a comparatively new dimension of peace operations.[25] Transforming peacekeeping into an offensive military endeavor threatens the entire enterprise, undermining its

[20] A/C.5/73/21, "Approved Resources for Peacekeeping Operations for the Period from 1 July 2019 to 30 June 2020," July 3, 2019, https://undocs.org/A/C.5/73/21; "General Assembly Approves $3 Billion UN Budget for 2020," December 27, 2019, https://news.un.org/en/story/2019/12/1054431.

[21] Lise Morjé Howard, *Power in Peacekeeping* (New York: Cambridge University Press, 2019).

[22] Patryk I. Labuda, "With or Against the State? Reconciling the Protection of Civilians and Host-State Support in UN Peacekeeping," International Peace Institute, May 2020; Howard 2019.

[23] Anjali Dayal, "Yogi Bear's Oddly Familiar Struggle for U.N. Recognition," Foreign Policy, December 25, 2019, https://foreignpolicy.com/2019/12/25/yogi-bears-oddly-familiar-struggle-for-u-n-recognition/.

[24] Lisa Hultman, Jacob Kathman, and Megan Shannon, "United Nations Peacekeeping and Civilian Protection in Civil War," *American Journal of Political Science* 57 (2013): 875–891, doi:10.1111/ajps.12036; Howard and Dayal 2018, 71–103; Hanne Fjelde, Hanne, Lisa Hultman, and Desirée Nilsson, "Protection Through Presence: UN Peacekeeping and the Costs of Targeting Civilians," *International Organization* 73, no. 1 (Winter 2019): 103–131.

[25] Denis M. Tull, "The Limits and Unintended Consequences of UN Peace Enforcement: The Force Intervention Brigade in the DR Congo," *International Peacekeeping* 25, no. 2 (2018): 167–190, doi:10.1080/13533312.2017.1360139.

legitimacy as a multilateral conflict resolution tool while potentially placing civilians – who already bear the brunt of civil war violence – in even more peril.

If peacekeeping is to serve *people* and not just states, then it must remain primarily a diplomatic and humanitarian tool – not a set of missions that resembles traditional military operations, or counterinsurgency and counterterrorism operations, as today's newer, complex missions do.[26] Indeed, if peacekeepers are increasingly undertaking counterinsurgency or counterterrorism work, and if they cannot meaningfully protect civilians from government forces, then peacekeepers are not doves among hawks; they are there primarily in service of the state, with troubling downstream consequences for people worldwide who live in fear of state violence, and with troubling implications for the UN's *other* tools for peacemaking.

Critically, force is not the only tool peacekeepers have. As originally envisioned, in fact, peace operations do not rely primarily on force at all. Instead, in language that still remains central to the *theory* of UN peace operations, three "inter-related and mutually reinforcing" principles underpin the practice of peacekeeping: consent of the parties to the conflict; impartiality; and the nonuse of force except in self-defense and defense of the mandate.[27] These principles clearly frame peace operations as a diplomatic endeavor, not a military one. Peacekeepers enact the international community's support of *peace,* not of one party or another to conflict. Peacekeeping in this style is in effect a conflict resolution tool, not a warfighting enterprise.

Both cases in this book illustrate this model of peacekeeping, which usually follows and accompanies a peace agreement: Parties to a conflict agree to the terms for peace, in which peacekeepers are an explicit part of the deal. Peacekeepers then help these parties uphold the terms of their agreement, alleviating the mistrust and fear that parties have about one another, overseeing the dangerous demobilization and disarmament phases of conflict termination, and preventing incidents from reigniting conflict.[28] The rationalist explanations we have tracked throughout this

---

[26] Howard 2019, Karlsrud 2019.
[27] https://peacekeeping.un.org/en/principles-of-peacekeeping.
[28] Virginia Page Fortna, *Does Peacekeeping Work? Shaping Belligerents' Choices after Civil War* (Princeton: Princeton University Press, 2008); Barbara Walter, *Committing to Peace: The Successful Settlement of Civil Wars* (Princeton: Princeton University Press, 2002).

book frame classic security dilemmas as the problem peacekeepers are trying to solve – with the implication for policy that a strong, neutral, and credible military force can help end wars, and that UN peacekeepers should strive to be this force.

In some sense, however, combatants must *already* be committed to the peace for this model to work[29] – it implies that they have decided to stop fighting, and then the UN and its peacekeepers help them achieve their goals. Where they are *not* necessarily strongly committed to this goal, the UN can attempt to persuade combatants to peace settlements – or they can deploy force: The UNSC can authorize peace enforcement operations, which strive to bring about a peace through military means.

Peace enforcement operations necessarily violate UN peacekeeping's principles on impartiality and the nonuse of force – and the genuine confusion between peace enforcement, civilian protection, and peacekeeping that suffuses recent UN missions reflects a fundamental transformation in the nature of peace operations. This is particularly true as peacekeepers increasingly arrive on the ground during active conflict, and before a peace agreement has been signed. Critically, even these missions have rarely *used* force, and can be more successful when they turn to other tools.[30] A stronger force posture from the UN raises complicated questions about the UN's neutrality and moral legitimacy – particularly since peace operations rest on the consent of the host country, and peacekeepers are reluctant to challenge the host country's authority, even when the host country victimizes civilians.[31]

The Security Council's decision to authorize every peace operation of the last twenty years to use force in defense of civilians reflects political dynamics between the Security Council's powerful permanent members – the United Kingdom, the United States, Russia, China, and France. It does not reflect a true belief that peacekeepers *ought* to use force to protect civilians.[32] Accordingly, even as the Security Council

---

[29] Suzanne Werner and Amy Yuen, "Making and Keeping Peace," *International Organization* 59 (Spring 2005): 261–292.
[30] Michael J. Gilligan and Ernesto J. Sergenti, "Do UN Interventions Cause Peace? Using Matching to Improve Causal Inference," *Quarterly Journal of Political Science* 3, no. 2 (2008): 89–122.
[31] Labuda 2020; Fjelde, Hultman, and Nilsson 2019, 103–131.
[32] Howard and Dayal 2018.

continues regularly authorizing these missions, there are abiding questions about the use of force for other member-states; for the UN Secretariat, charged with planning the missions; for the troop-contributing countries whose personnel staff peace operations; and for people on the ground in conflicts receiving peace operations.

The lure of peacekeeping forces backed by real military power comes from a clearly understandable position, in spite of these complicated questions: If peacekeepers are on the ground to protect civilians, then they should be given the means to do so; if they are there to force an end to hostilities, then they ought to be able to do that effectively, too. But this is not all that peacekeepers are currently being asked to do. Instead, in its largest, most complex recent operations, the UN has invoked the language of stabilization, counterterrorism, and counterinsurgency, and given discrete parts of UN missions the authorization to actively confront armed actors.[33]

Missions in the Central African Republic, Mali, and the DRC all employ one dimension or another of this model, engaging in offensive military action that is hard to reconcile with the traditional principles of peacekeeping. In *Power in Peacekeeping*, for example, Lise Morjé Howard outlines the struggle over whether and how peacekeepers should use the power of arrest, asking what, ultimately, peacekeepers in the Central African Republic are *there* for.[34] Are they present to persuade or compel? To help, or to punish? She argues that peacekeeping, in its most successful past iterations, has rarely worked by providing a security guarantee to combatants, and most often worked through other avenues, like persuasion – yet today, the drive toward ensuring security has become paramount. We could read her work, and John Karlsrud's work noting how even middle powers traditionally committed to liberal internationalism have invested heavily in the UN's counterterrorism work in Mali, and we could ask – what is the *point* of UN peacekeeping today?[35] It is not substitutive of the state in meaningful ways, as Howard's discussion of the UN's reluctance to catalog its arrests in Central African Republic highlights; it is decreasingly designed to credibly, efficiently, and neutrally uphold agreements; wielding offensive force contradicts one of its core purposes; it

---

[33] Alexander Gilder, "The Effect of 'Stabilization' in the Mandates and Practice of UN Peace Operations," *Netherlands International Law Review* 66 (2019): 47–73.
[34] Howard 2019.      [35] Karlsrud 2019.

does not wield that force effectively, when it wields it at all; and in a decreasingly liberal world where peacekeeping's authorizing body, the UNSC, is itself dominated by variably liberal states, it is less likely to be liberal. Are we entering an era when these missions are more closely going to approximate trusteeship situations? Are they exercises in maintaining international order and hierarchy? Are they becoming another tool in the totalizing drive toward reducing all questions of international peace and security to terrorism and insurgency?

In fact, we could look at the UN's missions in Mali, the Central African Republic, and the DRC and ask if they fundamentally transform the peacekeeping enterprise. Does the UN's turn toward counterterrorism in the Central African Republic and Mali make peacekeepers less effective using other, less coercive tools elsewhere? Does the UN's offensive military unit in the DRC, designed to apprehend a rebel group challenging the DRC's government, leave rebel groups elsewhere less willing to sit down with the UN in brokered peace talks?

If we have to ask those questions, then we have to ask: What is peacekeeping *for* in the twenty-first century? *Who* is peacekeeping for, if it does less of what it is good at and more of what the militaries of powerful states do? Is it in service of the conflict-stricken – the *peoples* of the UN, in whose name the United Nations Charter is issued, as Kofi Annan famously reminded the UN's member states?[36] Is it in service of a peace that allows for flourishing of these peoples? Or is it a tool primarily to uphold a particular idea of sovereignty – to keep reproducing the compact of states that constitute the UN, and that, in theory, are charged with protecting the rights of their people? We especially have to ask this question given the increasing challenges of transnational crises that states will face in the decades ahead – not the old horse of terrorism, but the new, pressing specters of climate change and mass displacement. The reaction we see from reluctant governments is to reassert the primacy of hard borders. Peacekeeping, as it is traditionally understood, is an international intervention into crisis that flourishes when it is all carrots and no sticks – but how can that kind of a tool survive and succeed in a world where restoring order may require enacting the work of increasingly illiberal states, and where alternative

[36] Kofi Annan, "Two Concepts of Sovereignty," *The Economist*, September 18, 1999.

mechanisms of resource distribution and order seem decreasingly possible?

Peacekeeping can work by turning further toward the use of force, or peacekeeping can work by reasserting the primacy of politics. My arguments have focused on the primacy of politics for elite actors – for, as Séverine Autesserre argues,

> The UN's strategy favors top-down deals struck with elites and fixates on elections. But that neglects what should be the other main component of their approach: embracing bottom-up strategies that draw on local knowledge and letting the people themselves determine how best to promote peace ... in many cases, calling on the blue helmets has become merely a convenient substitute for a serious grappling with what it would take to bring peace .... The good news is that there is a way to rethink the current strategy so that it has a better shot at establishing lasting peace: rely more on the very people it is ostensibly trying to protect.[37]

An approach that ties peace operations explicitly to the political dynamics of negotiation and that takes local conflict resolution seriously is a very different picture of contemporary peace operations than a more militarized set of Blue Helmets.

Peacekeeping as it was originally imagined, as it appears in this book, focused primarily on cases where combatants were already committed to the peace. This is a high bar that may be absent in many contemporary and future cases. Force is one way to compel combatants into a cessation of hostilities – but as this book argues, peacekeeping can also be desirable to combatants who are primarily interested in benefits beyond security and the cessation of hostilities. Thus, peacekeeping can be useful because it brings legitimacy to aspiring politicians, because it brings *things* to a conflict-scarred land, because it helps rebuild post-war states and helps manage the displaced as the dust from war dies down – not because it can try to force a military solution to a series of vexed political problems.

And the UN *does* many of these things on the ground in post-conflict situations. Its various agencies and diplomats manage displaced peoples, help build or rebuild both infrastructure and institutions, and provide humanitarian assistance; its presence also signals to other donors that they, too, can send further aid. This book has examined

---

[37] Séverine Autesserre, "The Crisis of Peacekeeping: Why the UN Can't End Wars," *Foreign Affairs* 98, no. 1 (January/February 2019): 101–116.

cases where parties to conflict have little faith in the UN's ability to enforce peace, or no expectation of being held to the terms of their peace agreement, or little actual interest in peace, and argued that *even* when parties to conflict are wary of the UN as a security guarantor, they still value these benefits the international community can bring to conflict-stricken places. If these cases are places where warring parties seek out the UN's peacemaking and peacekeeping assistance, then so, too, might parties to conflict in newer, equally complex cases – particularly if paired with local conflict resolution.

Of course, clear lessons from these earlier cases are not easy to draw; they cannot be simply imported into newer cases, and there exists no clear toolbox of intervention with time-invariant lessons just waiting to be applied to emerging crises.[38] But these cases affirm that the UN *has* other tools, that these tools are attractive even when actors are reluctant parties to peace, and that that these tools can be more desirable at times than yet another set of heavily armed actors in an already-suffering place. These tools might again be desirable – and the UN, along with the member-states who authorize, staff, and monitor these missions should retain their ability to use them.

Leaning heavily into the logic of greater force, counterterrorism, and counterinsurgency may make it harder for the UN to use the other levers it has at its disposal. The legitimating role the UN plays in negotiation processes in these stories is particularly tricky: A more military posture – particularly one that so favors the state – may undermine the UN's ability to bring rebels, insurgents, and secessionists to the table. Why, after all, accept negotiations under the auspices of an organization that might immediately partner with the state to fight you, instead of granting you legitimacy as an equal party to brokering peace? Emphasizing peacekeepers' role in post-conflict reconstruction, as opposed to their role in warfighting or counterinsurgency, offers an alternative path toward conflict resolution where the peace might otherwise seem out of reach.

In exploring the idea that the UN's involvement in peace processes might be desirable for political reasons that have little to do with protecting combatants and civilians with military force, however, this book suggests policy avenues that may mitigate suffering and loss of

---

[38] Anjali Kaushlesh Dayal and Paul Musgrave, "Teaching Counterfactuals from Hell," *Peace Review* 30, no. 1 (Spring 2018): 23–21.

life even when UN peacekeepers' abilities to force a cessation of hostilities seems out of reach. Peace operations may be well served by focusing on support for aid and humanitarian agencies in their imperative work – if, as this book demonstrates, parties to conflict can want peacekeepers on the ground *even when they do not think they can keep the peace*, then the international community can undertake important work to ameliorate the pain of war for many, even if it cannot force a peace.

Analysts have lamented the "Christmas Tree" style of peacekeeping mandate, which charges peacekeepers with everything from addressing the HIV/AIDS crisis to holding elections.[39] But the virtue of these mandates is that they may allow peacekeepers to do more of what people on the ground might presumably want – *particularly* if they are undertaken in consultation with the local community.[40] Divorced from meaningful local ownership and meaningful negotiation processes, this route is not without its own difficult ethical dilemmas – as the Syrian Civil War demonstrates, even without peacekeepers on the ground at all, the UN risks complicity in furthering citizen repression and death when its role in humanitarian aid and post-conflict reconstruction depends on the consent of a murderous regime.[41] But the UN is *already* doing that in some ways by being better able to protect civilians from rebels than the state, and difficulty navigating the complications of host–state interactions cannot be enough to abandon efforts at humanitarian relief where people need it most.

Accordingly, the UN's task in peacekeeping and peacemaking should be easing the suffering of civilians while attempting to arrive at a political solution for combatants. The UN is better served as executor and underwriter to those efforts than as another hand fueling the machinery of war. Granting peacekeepers the means to use force to protect civilians is important. How to make peacekeepers willing to *use* force in defense of civilians and in defense of their mandate – even

---

[39] Alex J. Bellamy and Charles T. Hunt, "Benefits of Paring Down Peacekeeping Mandates Also Come with Risks," *The Global Observatory*, March 15, 2019, https://theglobalobservatory.org/2019/03/benefits-paring-down-peacekeeping-mandates-come-with-risks/.

[40] von Billerbeck 2017; Autesserre 2010.

[41] Ben Parker and Annie Slemrod, "Outcry at UN Plans to Consolidate Syria Aid Operations in Damascus," *The New Humanitarian*, April 23, 2019, www.thenewhumanitarian.org/news/2019/04/23/outcry-un-plans-consolidate-syria-aid-operations-damascus.

when it is inconvenient for their host state – is a problem that rests with the UNSC, the UN Secretariat, and troop-contributing countries to solve.

But when the state decides who is and is not an insurgent, pushing peacekeeping to become just another way to enforce the will of insecure states through counterterrorism and counterinsurgency efforts is at best counterproductive and at worst a betrayal of the UN's commitment to civilians. Ralph Bunche Park, across the street from the United Nations' New York headquarters, has a wall facing First Avenue and inscribed with lines from Isaiah – "They shall beat their swords into plowshares, and their spears into pruning hooks; nation shall not lift up sword against nation, neither shall they learn war any more." The words apply to peacekeepers, as well – if peacekeeping is to embody the spirit of the UN, then peacekeepers cannot harden into simply soldiers alongside other soldiers, replacing plowshares with swords. People need fewer guards, while people's rights need more guardians.

Peacekeeping should not be understood solely as a solution to a state security problem – indeed, this book has demonstrated that it *cannot* be understood solely as a solution to a state security problem. Combatants sometimes do not want peace and prefer ineffective peacekeepers; they sometimes seek international involvement as a potential solution to a range of security, tactical, material, and legitimacy problems. International peacemakers and peacekeepers can and should center those goals in service of the people, as well.

# Bibliography

Abbott, Kenneth W. and Duncan Snidal. "Why States Act through Formal International Organizations." *Journal of Conflict Resolution* 42, no. 1 (February 1998): 3–32.

Adebajo, Adekeye. *UN Peacekeeping in Africa*. Boulder: Lynne Rienner, 2012.

Adelman, Howard and Astri Suhrke (eds.). *The Path of a Genocide: The Rwanda Crisis from Uganda to Zaire*. New York: Routledge, 2000.

Allen, Susan Hannah and Amy T. Yuen. "The Politics of Peacekeeping: UN Security Council Oversight across Peacekeeping Missions." *International Studies Quarterly* 58, no. 3 (September 2014): 621–632.

Allison, Michael. "The Guatemalan National Revolutionary Unit: The Long Collapse." *Democratization* 23, no. 6 (October 2016): 1042–1058.

Alt, James E., Randall L. Calvert, and Brian D. Humes. "Reputation and Hegemonic Stability: A Game-Theoretic Analysis." *American Political Science Review* 82, no. 1 (June 1988): 445–466.

Amoureux, Jack L. and Brent J. Steele (eds.). *Reflexivity and International Relations: Positionality, Critique, and Practice*. London: Routledge, 2015.

Andreas, Peter. *Blue Helmets and Black Markets: The Business of Survival in the Siege of Sarajevo*. Ithaca: Cornell University Press, 2008.

Anghie, Antony. *Imperialism, Sovereignty and the Making of International Law*. Cambridge: Cambridge University Press, 2007.

Annan, Kofi, "Two Concepts of Sovereignty," *The Economist*, September 18, 1999.

Annan, Kofi and Nader Mousavizadeh. *Interventions: A Life in War and Peace*. New York: The Penguin Press, 2012.

Anstee, Margaret J. *Orphan of the Cold War: The Inside Story of the Collapse of the Angolan Peace Process, 1992–1993*. Basingstoke: Macmillan, 1996.

Arnault, Jean. "Good Agreement? Bad Agreement? An Implementation Perspective." Princeton: Centre of International Studies, Princeton University, 2006. https://gsdrc.org/document-library/good-agreement-bad-agreement-an-implementation-perspective/.

Aronson, Jonathan D. "International Intellectual Property Rights in a Networked World." In Helen V. Milner and Andrew Moravcsik (eds.), *Power, Interdependence, and Nonstate Actors in World Politics.* Princeton: Princeton University Press, 2009, 185–203.

Autesserre, Séverine. "The Crisis of Peacekeeping: Why the UN Can't End Wars." *Foreign Affairs* 98, no. 1 (January/February 2019): 101–116.

"Dangerous Tales: Dominant Narratives on the Congo and Their Unintended Consequences." *African Affairs* 111, no. 443 (February 2012): 202–222.

"Hobbes and the Congo: Frames, Local Violence, and International Intervention." *International Organization* 63, no. 2 (April 2009): 249–280.

*Peaceland: Conflict Resolution and the Everyday Politics of International Intervention.* Cambridge: Cambridge University Press, 2014.

*The Trouble with the Congo: Local Violence and the Failure of International Peacebuilding.* Cambridge: Cambridge University Press, 2010.

Axelrod, Robert. *The Evolution of Cooperation.* New York: Basic Books, 1984.

Aydin, Aysegul and Patrick M. Regan. "Networks of Third-Party Interveners and Civil War Duration." *European Journal of International Relations* 18, no. 3 (September 2012): 573–597.

Ayoob, Mohammed, "Humanitarian Intervention and State Sovereignty." *The International Journal of Human Rights* 6, no. 1 (Spring 2002): 81–102.

Bandura, Albert. *Social Learning Theory.* Oxford: Prentice-Hall, 1977.

Bariagaber, Assefaw. "United Nations Peace Operations in Africa: A Cookie-Cutter Approach?." *Journal of Third World Studies* 23, no. 2 (Fall 2006): 11–29.

Barma, Naazneen H. *The Peacebuilding Puzzle: Political Order in Post-Conflict States.* Cambridge: Cambridge University Press, 2017.

Barnett, Michael. *Eyewitness to a Genocide: The United Nations and Rwanda.* Ithaca: Cornell University Press, 2003.

"The UN Security Council, Indifference, and Genocide in Rwanda." *Cultural Anthropology* 12, no. 4 (1997): 551–578.

Barnett, Michael and Martha Finnemore. "The Politics, Power, and Pathologies of International Organizations." *International Organization* 54, no. 4 (1999): 699–732.

*Rules for the World: International Organizations in Global Politics.* Ithaca: Cornell University Press, 2004.

Beardsley, Kyle. "Peacekeeping and the Contaigon of Armed Conflict." *The Journal of Politics* 73, no. 4 (October 2011): 1051–1064.

Beck, Nathaniel, Kristian Skrede Gleditsch, and Kyle Beardsley. "Space Is More Than Geography: Using Spatial Econometrics in the Study of Political Economy." *International Studies Quarterly* 50 (2006): 27–44.

Beck, Nathaniel, Jonathan N. Katz, and Richard Tucker. "Taking Time Seriously: Time-Series-Cross Section Analysis with a Binary Dependent Variable." *American Journal of Political Science* 42, no. 4 (1998): 1260–1288.

Bellamy, Alex J. and Charles T. Hunt. "Benefits of Paring Down Peacekeeping Mandates Also Come with Risks." *The Global Observatory*, March 15, 2019. https://theglobalobservatory.org/2019/03/benefits-paring-down-peacekeeping-mandates-come-with-risks/.

Bellamy, Alex J. and Paul D. Williams. *Understanding Peacekeeping*, 2nd ed. London: Polity, 2010.

Bennett, Andrew. *Condemned to Repetition? The Rise, Fall, and Reprise of Soviet-Russian Military Interventionism 1973–1996*. Cambridge, MA: The MIT Press, 1999.

"Disciplining Our Conjectures: Systematizing Process Tracing with Bayesian Analysis." In Andrew Bennett and Jeffrey Checkel (eds.), *Process Tracing: From Metaphor to Analytic Tool*. Cambridge: Cambridge University Press, 2014, 276–298.

"Process Tracing: A Bayesian Perspective." In Janet Box-Steffensmeier, Henry E. Brady, and David Collier (eds.), *The Oxford Handbook of Political Methodology*. Oxford: Oxford University Press, 2008, 217–270.

Benson, Michelle and Jacob Kathman. "United Nations Bias and Force Commitments in Civil Conflicts." *The Journal of Politics* 76, no. 2 (April 2014): 350–363.

Benton, Lauren and Lisa Ford. *Rage for Order: The British Empire and the Origins of International Law*. Cambridge, MA: Harvard University Press, 2018.

von Billerbeck, Sarah B. K. *Whose Peace? Local Ownership and United Nations Peacekeeping*. Oxford: Oxford University Press, 2017.

Böhmelt, Tobias. "The Spatial Contagion of International Mediation." *Conflict Management and Peace Science* 32, no. 1 (2015): 108–127.

Boot, Max. "Paving the Road to Hell: The Failure of UN Peacekeeping." *Foreign Affairs* 79, no. 2 (March/April 2000): 143–148.

Bosco, David. *Five to Rule Them All: The UN Security Council and the Making of the Modern World*. Oxford: Oxford University Press, 2009.

"The Price of Peace: How Much Is a UN Blue Helmet Actually Worth?." *Foreign Policy*, May 29, 2013. http://foreignpolicy.com/2013/05/30/thepriceofpeace/

Boutros-Ghali, Boutros. *Unvanquished: A U.S.-U.N. Saga*. New York: Random House, 1999.

Bowden, Mark. *Black Hawk Down: A Story of a Modern War*. New York: New American Press, 2001.

Braun, Dietmar and Fabrizio Gilardi. "Taking 'Galton's Problem' Seriously: Towards a Theory of Policy Diffusion." *Journal of Theoretical Politics* 18, no. 3 (2006): 298–322.

Buhaug, Halvard and Kristian Skrede Gleditsch. "Contagion or Confusion? Why Conflicts Cluster in Space." *International Studies Quarterly* 52, no. 2 (2008): 215–233.

Buhaug, Halvard, Lars-Erik Cederman, and Kristian Skrede Gleditsch. "Square Pegs in Round Holes: Inequalities, Grievances, and Civil War." *International Studies Quarterly* 58, no. 2 (June 2014): 418–431.

Call, Charles T. and Elizabeth M. Cousens. "Ending Wars and Building Peace: International Responses to War-Torn Societies." *International Studies Perspectives* 9, no. 1 (February 2008): 1–21.

Cameron, Maxwell A. "Self-Coups: Peru, Guatemala, and Russia." *Journal of Democracy* 9 no. 1 (1998): 125–139.

Campbell, Susanna P. *Global Governance and Local Peace: Accountability and Performance in International Peacebuilding*. Cambridge: Cambridge University Press, 2018.

Carnegie, Allison. "States Held Hostage: Political Hold-Up Problems and the Effects of International Institutions." *American Political Science Review* 108, no. 1 (February 2014): 54–70.

Carter, David B. and Curtis S. Signorino. "Back to the Future: Modeling Time Dependency in Binary Data." *Political Analysis* 18, no. 3 (2010): 271–292.

Chapman, Terrance L. and Dan Reiter. "The United Nations Security Council and the Rally 'Round the Flag Effect." *Journal of Conflict Resolution* 48, no. 6 (December 2004): 886–909.

Checkel, Jeffrey T. "Why Comply? Social Learning and European Identity Change." *International Organization* 55, no. 3 (2001): 553–588.

Chinchilla, Norma Stolz. "Of Straw Men and Stereotypes: Why Guatemalan Rocks Don't Talk." *Latin American Perspectives* 26, no. 109 (November 1999): 29–37.

Clarke, Walter and Jeffrey Herbst. "Somalia and the Future of Humanitarian Intervention." *Foreign Affairs* 75, no. 2. (March–April 1996): 70–85

Clapham, Christopher. "Being Peacekept." In Oliver Furley and Roy May (eds.), *Peacekeeping in Africa*. Aldershot: Ashgate, 1998, 303–319.

Claude, Inis L. "Collective Legitimation as a Political Function of the United Nations." *International Organization* 20, no. 3 (1966): 367–379.

Collier, David. "Understanding Process Tracing." *PS: Political Science and Politics* 44 (2011): 823–830.

Collier, David and Henry E. Brady. *Rethinking Social Inquiry: Diverse Tools, Shared Standards*. Lanham: Rowman and Littlefield, 2004.

Collier, David, Henry E. Brady, and Jason Seawright. "Outdated Views of Qualitative Methods: Time to Move On." *Political Analysis* 18, no. 4 (2010): 506–513.

Collier, Paul and Anke Hoeffler. "Greed and Grievance in Civil War." *Oxford Economic Papers* 56 (2004): 563–595.

Collier, Peter and Nicholas Sambanis. "Understanding Civil War: A New Agenda." *Journal of Conflict Resolution* 46, no. 1 (2002): 3–12.

Costalli, Stefano. "Does Peacekeeping Work? A Disaggregated Analysis of Deployment and Violence Reduction in the Bosnian War." *British Journal of Political Science* 44, no. 2 (January 2013): 357–380.

Dallaire, Roméo. *Shake Hands with the Devil: The Failure of Humanity in Rwanda*. New York: Carroll and Graf Publishers, 2003.

Davenport, Christian and Allan Stam. *Rwandan Political Violence in Space and Time*. Unpublished paper. http://bc.sas.upenn.edu/system/files/Stam_03.26.09.pdf.

Dayal, Anjali. "Beyond Do Something: Revisiting the International Community's Role in the Rwandan Genocide." *War on the Rocks*, October 5, 2018. https://warontherocks.com/2018/10/beyond-do-something-revisiting-the-international-communitys-role-in-the-rwandan-genocide/.

   "Yogi Bear's Oddly Familiar Struggle for U.N. Recognition." *Foreign Policy*, December 25, 2019. https://foreignpolicy.com/2019/12/25/yogi-bears-oddly-familiar-struggle-for-u-n-recognition/.

Dayal, Anjali and Lise Morjé Howard. "Peace Operations." In Jacob Cogan, Ian Hurd, and Ian Johnstone (eds.), *Oxford Handbook of International Organizations*. Oxford: Oxford University Press, 2016, 191–210, chapter 9.

Dayal, Anjali Kaushlesh and Paul Musgrave. "Teaching Counterfactuals from Hell." *Peace Review* 30, no. 1 (Spring 2018): 23–21.

de Waal, Alex. "US War Crimes in Somalia." *New Left Review* 1, no. 230 (July–August 1998).

Deitelhoff, Nicole and Müller, Harald. "Theoretical Paradise: Empirically Lost? Arguing with Habermas." *Review of International Studies* 31, no. 1 (January 2005): 167–179.

DeSombre, Elizabeth R. "Power, Interdependence, and Domestic Politics in International Environmental Cooperation." In Helen V. Milner and Andrew Moravcsik (eds.), *Power, Interdependence, and Nonstate Actors in World Politics*. Princeton: Princeton University Press, 2009, 147–163.

Diehl, Paul F. *International Peacekeeping*. Baltimore: Johns Hopkins Press, 1993.

*Peace Operations*. London: Polity, 2008.

Diehl, Paul F., Daniel Druckman, and James Wall. "International Peacekeeping and Conflict Resolution: A Taxonomic Analysis with Implications." *Journal of Conflict Resolution* 42, no. 1 (1998): 35–55.

Dobbin, Frank, Beth Simmons, and Geoffrey Garrett. "The Global Diffusion of Public Policies: Social Construction, Coercion, Competition, or Learning?" *Annual Review of Sociology* 33 (2007): 449–472.

Downs, George W. and Michael A. Jones. "Reputation, Compliance, and International Law." *The Journal of Legal Studies* 31, no. S1 (January 2002): S95–S114.

Doyle, Michael W. and Nicholas Sambanis. "International Peacebuilding: A Theoretical and Quantitative Analysis." *American Political Science Review* 94, no. 4 (December 2000): 779–801.

*Making War and Building Peace: United Nations Peace Operations*. Princeton: Princeton University Press, 2006.

Doyle, Kate. *The Pursuit of Justice in Guatemala: National Security Archive Electronic Briefing Book No. 373*. Washington, DC, 2012. www2.gwu.edu/~nsarchiv/NSAEBB/NSAEBB373/index.htm#note_02.

Durch, William (ed.). *UN Peacekeeping, American Policy, and the Uncivil Wars of the 1990s*. London: Palgrave Macmillan, 1996.

Edelstein, David M. "Occupational Hazards: Why Military Occupations Succeed or Fail." *International Security* 29, no. 1 (Summer 2004): 49–91.

Elkins, Zachary and Beth Simmons. "On Waves, Clusters, and Diffusion: A Conceptual Framework." *The ANNALS of the American Academy of Political and Social Science* 598, no. 1 (2005): 33–51.

Farrell, Henry and Martha Finnemore. "The End of Hypocrisy American Foreign Policy in the Age of Leaks." *Foreign Affairs* 92, no. 6 (November/December 2013): 22–26.

Faust, Drew Gilpin. *This Republic of Suffering: Death and the American Civil War*. New York: Vintage, 2009.

Fazal, Tanisha. *Wars of Law: Unintended Consequences in the Regulation of Armed Conflict*. Ithaca: Cornell University Press, 2018.

Fearon, James D. "Rationalist Explanations for War." *International Organization* 49, no. 3 (Summer 1995): 379–414.

"Why Do Some Civil Wars Last So Much Longer than Others?" *Journal of Peace Research* 41, no. 3 (2004): 275–301.

Fearon, James D. and David Laitin. "Ethnicity, Insurgency, and Civil War." *American Political Science Review* 97, no. 1 (February 2003): 75–90.

"Neotrusteeship and the Problem of Weak States." *International Security* 28, no. 4 (2004): 5–43.

Filson, Darren and Suzanne Werner. "A Bargaining Model of War and Peace: Anticipating the Onset, Duration, and Outcome of War." *American Journal of Political Science* 46, no. 4 (2002): 819–838.

Finnemore, Martha. "Legitimacy, Hypocrisy, and the Social Structure of Unipolarity: Why Being a Unipole Isn't All It's Cracked Up to Be." *World Politics* 61, no. 1 (2009): 58–85.

*National Interests in International Society.* Ithaca: Cornell University Press, 1996.

*The Purposes of Intervention.* Ithaca: Cornell University Press, 2003.

Finnemore, Martha and Kathryn Sikkink. "International Norm Dynamics and Political Change." *International Organization* 52, no. 4 (1998): 887–917.

Fjelde, Hanne, Lisa Hultman, and Desirée Nilsson. "Protection through Presence: UN Peacekeeping and the Costs of Targeting Civilians." *International Organization* 73, no. 1 (Winter 2019): 103–131.

Fortna, Virginia Page. *Does Peacekeeping Work? Shaping Belligerents' Choices after Civil War.* Princeton: Princeton University Press, 2008.

*Peacekeeping and the Peacekept: Data On Peacekeeping In Civil Wars 1989–2004.* Data notes, 2008. www.columbia.edu/~vpf4/.

"Where Have all the Victories Gone? Peacekeeping and War Outcomes." *Paper Presented at the Annual Meeting of the American Political Science Association*, September 2009.

Fortna, Virginia Page and Lise Morjé Howard. "Pitfalls and Prospects in the Peacekeeping Literature." *Annual Review of Political Science* 11 (2008): 283–301.

Fortna, Virginia Page and Lisa L. Martin. "Peacekeepers as Signals: The Demand for International Peacekeeping in Civil Wars." In Helen V. Milner and Andrew Moravcsik (eds.), *Power, Interdependence, and Nonstate Actors in World Politics.* Princeton: Princeton University Press, 2009, 87–107.

Fujii, Lee Ann. "Shades of Truth and Lies: Interpreting Testimonies of War and Violence." *Journal of Peace Research* 47, no. 2 (2010): 231–241.

*Killing Neighbors: Webs of Violence in Rwanda.* Ithaca: Cornell University Press, 2011.

Fukuyama, Francis. *State-Building: Governance and World Order in the Twenty-first Century.* Ithaca: Cornell University Press, 2004.

Gaibulloev, Khusrav, Todd Sandler, and Hirofumi Shimizu. "Demands for UN and Non-UN Peacekeeping: Nonvoluntary versus Voluntary Contributions to a Public Good." *Journal of Conflict Resolution* 53, no. 6 (December 2009): 827–853.

Garrard-Burnett, Virginia. *Terror in the Land of the Holy Spirit: Guatemala under General Efraín Rios Montt 1982–1983*. Oxford: Oxford University Press, 2011.

Gartzke, Erik. "War Is in the Error Term." *International Organization* 53, no. 3 (Summer 1999): 567–587.

Gasana, James K. *Rwanda: Du parti-état à l'état garnison*. Paris: L'Harmattan, 2002

George, Alexander L. and Andrew Bennett. *Case Studies and Theory Development in the Social Sciences*. Cambridge, MA: The MIT Press, 2005.

Gerring, John. "Is There a (Viable) Crucial-Case Method?" *Comparative Political Studies* 40, no. 3 (2007): 231–253.

Getachew, Adom. *Worldmaking after Empire: The Rise and Fall of Self-Determination*. Princeton: Princeton University Press, 2019.

Gilder, Alexander. "The Effect of 'Stabilization' in the Mandates and Practice of UN Peace Operations." *Netherlands International Law Review* 66 (2019): 47–73.

Gilligan, Michael. "Is Enforcement Necessary for Effectiveness? A Model of the International Criminal Regime." *International Organization* 60, no. 4 (October 2006): 935–967.

Gilligan, Michael J. and Ernest J. Sergenti. "Do UN Interventions Cause Peace? Using Matching to Improve Causal Inference." *Quarterly Journal of Political Science* 3, no. 2 (2008): 89–122.

Gilligan, Michael and Stephen John Stedman. "Where Do the Peacekeepers Go?" *International Studies Review* 5, no. 4 (December 2003): 37–54.

Girod, Desha M. "Effective Foreign Aid Following Civil War: The Nonstrategic-Desperation Hypothesis." *American Journal of Political Science* 56, no. 1 (January 2012): 188–201.

Gleditsch, Kristian Skrede. "Transnational Dimensions of Civil War." *Journal of Peace Research* 44, no. 3 (May 2007): 293–309.

Goldgeier, James and Philip Tetlock. "Psychology and International Relations Theory." *Annual Review of Political Science* 4 (2001): 67–92.

Goldsmith, Benjamin. "Imitation in International Relations: Analogies, Vicarious Learning, and Foreign Policy." *International Interactions* 29, no. 3 (2013): 237–267.

Gourevitch, Philip. *We Wish to Inform You that Tomorrow We Will Be Killed with Our Families*. New York: Picador, 1998.

*Granito: How to Nail a Dictator*. Directed by Pamela Yates, 2011.

Greif, Avner. "Reputations and Coalitions in Medieval Trade: Evidence on the Maghribi Traders." *Journal of Economic History* 49, no. 4 (December 1989): 857–882.

Hafner-Burton, Emilie M. and Alexander H. Montgomery. "Power Positions: International Organizations, Social Networks, and Conflict." *Journal of Conflict Resolution* 50, no. 1 (2006): 3–27.

Harbom, Lotta, Stina Högbladh, and Peter Wallensteen. "Armed Conflicts and Peace Agreements." *Journal of Peace Research* 43, no. 5 (2006).

Hassner, Ron E. *War on Sacred Grounds*. Ithaca: Cornell University Press, 2009.

Hayner, Priscilla B. *Unspeakable Truths: Confronting State Terror and Atrocity*. New York: Routledge, 2002.

Hegre, Håvard, Lisa Hultman, and Håvard Mokleiv Nygård. "Evaluating the Conflict-Reducing Effect of UN Peacekeeping Operations." *The Journal of Politics* 81, no. 1 (January 2019): 215–232.

Hilterman, Joost et al. *The War within the War: Sexual Violence against Women and Girls in Eastern Congo*. New York: Human Rights Watch, 2002.

Hoddie, Matthew and Caroline Hartzell. "Civil War Settlements and the Implementation of Military Power-Sharing Arrangements." *Journal of Peace Research* 40, no. 3 (May 2003): 303–332.

Holbrooke, Richard. *To End a War*. New York: The Modern Library, 1998.

Hopf, Ted. The Logic of Habit in International Relations. *European Journal of International Relations* 16, no. 4 (2010): 539–561.

Houzel, Renaud. *L'ONU et les operations de maintien de la paix: Rwanda 1993–1997*. Paris: Montchrestien, 1997.

Howard, Lise Morjé. *Power in Peacekeeping*. New York: Cambridge University Press, 2019.

    *UN Peacekeeping in Civil Wars*. New York: Cambridge University Press, 2008.

Howard, Lise Morjé and Anjali Kaushlesh Dayal. "The Use of Force in UN Peacekeeping." *International Organization* 72, no. 1 (Winter 2018): 71–103.

Howard, Lise Morjé and Alexandra Stark. "How Civil Wars End: The International System, Norms, and the Role of External Actors." *International Security* 42, no. 3 (Winter 2017/18): 127–171.

Huang, Reyko. "Rebel Diplomacy." *International Security* 40, no. 4 (Spring 2016): 89–126.

Hultman, Lisa. "UN Peace Operations and Protection of Civilians: Cheap Talk or Norm Implementation?" *Journal of Peace Research* 50, no. 1 (2013): 59–73.

Hultman, Lisa, Jacob Kathman, and Megan Shannon. "Beyond Keeping Peace: United Nations Effectiveness in the Midst of Fighting." *American Political Science Review* 108, no. 4 (2014): 737–753.

    "United Nations Peacekeeping and Civilian Protection in Civil War." *American Journal of Political Science* 57, no. 4, (October 2013): 875–891.

Hultman, Lisa, Jacob D. Kathman, Megan Shannon. "United Nations Peacekeeping Dynamics and the Duration of Post-Civil Conflict

Peace." *Conflict Management and Peace Science* 33, no. 3 (2016): 231–249.

Hurd, Ian. *After Anarchy: Legitimacy and Power in the United Nations Security Council*, Kindle ed. Princeton: Princeton University Press, 2008.

"Legitimacy, Power, and the Symbolic Life of the UN Security Council." *Global Governance* 35, no. 8 (2002): 35–51.

Jackson, Patrick T. and Daniel H. Nexon. "Constructivist Realism or Realist-Constructivism." *International Studies Review* 2, no. 6 (2006): 337–341.

"Paradigmatic Faults in International Relations." *International Studies Quarterly* 53, no. 4 (2009): 907–930.

Jervis, Robert. "Cooperation under the Security Dilemma." *World Politics* 30, no. 2 (January 1978): 167–214.

*The Logic of Images in International Relations.* Princeton: Princeton University Press, 1970.

Johnston, Alastair Iain. "Treating International Institutions as Social Environments." *International Studies Quarterly* 45, no. 4 (2001): 487–515.

Johnstone, Ian. "Legislation and Adjudication in the UN Security Council: Bringing Down the Deliberative Deficit." *American Journal of International Law* 102, no. 2 (2008): 275–308.

Jonas, Susanne. *The Battle for Guatemala: Rebels, Death Squads, and US Power.* Boulder: Westview Press, 1991.

*Of Centaurs and Doves: Guatemala's Peace Process.* Boulder: Westview Press, 2000.

Jones, Bruce D. "The Arusha Peace Process." In Howard Adelman and Astri Suhrke (eds.), *The Path of a Genocide: The Rwanda Crisis from Uganda to Zaire.* New Brunswick: Transaction Publishers, 1999, 131–156.

Jones, Bruce D. *The Best Laid Plans … Peace-Making in Rwanda and the Implications of Failure.* New York: Sage, 2001.

*Peacemaking in Rwanda: The Dynamics of Failure.* Boulder: Lynne Rienner, 2001.

Kalyvas, Stathis N. and Laia Balcells. "International System and Technologies of Rebellion: How the End of the Cold War Shaped Internal Conflict." *American Political Science Review* 104, no. 3 (2010): 415–429.

Karlsrud, John. "From Liberal Peacebuilding to Stabilization and Counterterrorism." *International Peacekeeping* 26, no. 1 (2019): 1–21.

Kentikelenis, Alexander E. and Leonard Seabrooke. "The Politics of World Polity: Script-writing in International Organizations." *American Sociological Review* 82, no. 5 (October 2017): 1065–1092.

Keohane, Robert and Lisa Martin. "The Promise of Institutionalist Theory." *International Security* 20, no. 1 (1995): 39–51.

Khong, Yuen Foong. *Analogies at War: Korea, Munich, Dien Bien Phu, and the Vietnam Decisions of 1965.* Princeton: Princeton University Press, 1992.

King, Charles. "The Benefits of Ethnic War: Understanding Eurasia's Unrecognized States." *World Politics* 53, no. 4 (July 2001): 524–552.

Kinne, Brandon J. "Network Dynamics and the Evolution of International Cooperation." *American Political Science Review* 107, no. 4 (2013): 766–785.

Kirshner, Jonathan D. "Rationalist Explanations for War?" *Security Studies* 10, no. 1 (Autumn 2000): 143–150.

Krasner, Stephen D. *Sovereignty: Organized Hypocrisy.* Princeton: Princeton University Press, 1999.

Kratochwil, Friedrich and John Gerard Ruggie. "International Organization: A State of the Art on an Art of the State." *International Organization* 40, no. 4 (1986): 753–775.

Kroc Institute for International Peace Studies, University of Notre Dame. "UN Internal Verification." *Peace Accords Matrix.* https://peaceaccords .nd.edu/matrix/status/43/un_internal_verification (accessed August 15, 2012).

"UN Peacekeeping Force." *Peace Accords Matrix.* https://peaceaccords.nd .edu/matrix/status/43/un_peacekeeping_force (accessed August 15, 2012).

Kroezen, Jessica M. "All Interventions Are Not Created Equal: Conceptualizing and Assessing the Credibility of UN-Authorized Interventions since 1948." Paper presented at the MPSA Annual National Conference, Chicago, Illinois, March–April 2011.

Krznaric, Roman. "Guatemalan Returnees and the Dilemma of Political Mobilization." *Journal of Refugee Studies* 10, no. 1 (1997): 61–78.

Kuperman, Alan J. *The Limits of Humanitarian Intervention: Genocide in Rwanda.* Washington, DC: Brookings, 2001.

"The Moral Hazard of Humanitarian Intervention: Lessons from the Balkans." *International Studies Quarterly* 52, no. 1 (2008): 49–80.

"Provoking Genocide: A Revised History of the Rwandan Patriotic Front." *Journal of Genocide Research* 6, no. 1 (2004): 61–84.

Kydd, Andrew. *Trust and Mistrust in International Relations.* Princeton: Princeton University Press, 2005.

Lacina, Bethany and Nils Petter Gleditsch. "Monitoring Trends in Global Combat: A New Dataset of Battle Deaths." *European Journal of Population* 21, no. 2–3 (2005): 145–166.

Lawson, Letitia. "US Africa Policy since the Cold War." *Strategic Insights* VI, no. 1 (January 2007).

Lebovic, James H. and Erik Voeten. "The Politics of Shame: The Condemnation of Country Human Rights Practices in the UNCHR." *International Studies Quarterly* 50, no. 4 (2006): 861–888.

Lewis, David. *Convention*. London: Blackwell, 1969 [2002].

Lim, Daniel Yew Mao and James Raymond Vreeland. "Regional Organizations and International Politics: Japanese Influence over the Asian Development Bank and the UN Security Council." *World Politics* 65, no. 1 (2013): 34–72.

Lipson, Michael. "Peacekeeping: Organized Hypocrisy?" *European Journal of International Relations* 13, no. 5 (2007): 5–34.

MacQueen, Norrie. *Peacekeeping and the International System*. London: Routledge, 2006.

Mahoney, James. "After KKV: The New Methodology of Qualitative Research." *World Politics* 62, no. 1 (2010): 120–147.

Malone, David M. *Decision-Making in the UN Security Council: The Case of Haiti, 1990–1997*. New York: Oxford University Press, 1998.

"Security Council." In Thomas G. Weiss and Sam Daws (eds.), *The Oxford Handbook on the United Nations*. New York: Oxford University Press, 2007, 117–135.

Mamdani, Mahmood. *When Victims Become Killers: Colonialism, Nativism, and Genocide in Rwanda*. Princeton: Princeton University Press, 2001.

Marten, Kimberly Zisk. *Enforcing the Peace: Learning from the Imperial Past*. New York: Columbia University Press, 2004.

Martin, Lisa. "Interests, Powers, and Multilateralism." *International Organization* 46, no. 3 (1992): 765–792.

Martin, Lisa and Beth Simmons. "Theories and Empirical Studies of International Institutions." *International Organization* 52, no. 3 (1998): 729–757.

Mastanduno, Michael. "System Maker and Privilege Taker: U.S. Power and the International Political Economy." *World Politics* 61, no. 1 (2009) : 121–154.

Mazower, Mark. *No Enchanted Palace: The End of Empire and the Ideological Origins of the United Nations*. Princeton: Princeton University Press, 2013.

McAdams, Richard H. "A Focal Point Theory of Expressive Law." *Virginia Law Review* 86 (2000): 1689–1729.

McCarty, Nolan and Adam Meirowitz. *Political Game Theory: An Introduction*. Cambridge: Cambridge University Press, 2007.

McDermott, Rose. *Risk-Taking in International Politics*. Ann Arbor: University of Michigan Press, 2001.

Melander, Erik. "Selected to Go Where Murderers Lurk? The Preventive Effect of Peacekeeping on Mass Killings of Civilians." *Conflict Management and Peace Science* 26, no. 4 (2009): 389–406.

Mercer, Jonathan. *Reputation and International Politics*. Ithaca: Cornell Studies in International Affairs, 1996.

Meseguer, Covadonga. *Learning, Policy Making, and Market Reforms*. Cambridge: Cambridge University Press, 2009.

Meyer, John W., John Boli, George M. Thomas, and Francisco O. Ramirez. "World Society and the Nation-State." *American Journal of Sociology* 103, no. 1 (July 1997): 144–181.

Mosley, Layna (ed.). *Interview Research in Political Science*. Ithaca: Cornell University Press, 2013.

Mpungwe, Ami R. "Crisis and Response in Rwanda: Reflections on the Arusha Peace Process." In Michael Malan (ed.), *Whither Peacekeeping in Africa?*. Stockholm: Norwegian Institute for International Affairs (NUPI) and the African Centre for the Constructive Resolution of Disputes (ACCORD), 1999.

Müller, Harald. "Arguing, Bargaining, and All That: Communicative Action, Rationalist Theory and the Logic of Appropriateness in International Relations." *European Journal of International Relations* 10, no. 3 (2004): 395–435.

Newbury, Catharine. *The Cohesion of Oppression*. New York: Columbia University Press, 1993.

North, Douglass. *Structure and Change in Economic History*. New York: Norton, 1981.

Olonisakin, Funmi. *Peacekeeping in Sierra Leone: The Story of UNAMSIL*. Boulder: Lynne Rienner, 2008.

Orford, Anne. *International Authority and the Responsibility to Protect*. Cambridge: Cambridge University Press, 2011.

Ostrom, Elinor. "Collective Action and the Evolution of Social Norms." *Journal of Economic Perspective* 14, no. 33 (Summer 2000): 137–158.

Pareles, Iosu. *Guatemala insurrecta: entrevista con el comandante en jefe del Ejército Guerrillero de los Pobres*. Madrid: Editorial Revolución, 1990.

Park, Susan. "Theorizing Norm Diffusion within International Organizations." *International Politics* 43 (2006): 342–361.

*PBS Frontline: Ghosts of Rwanda*. 2004.

Pelc, Krzyzstof J. "The Politics of Precedent in International Law: A Social Network Application." *American Political Science Review* 108, no. 3 (2014): 547–564.

Pitts, Jennifer. *Boundaries of the International: Law and Empire.* Cambridge, MA: Harvard University Press, 2018.

Pouligny, Béatrice. "Les casques bleus sont là, mais on ne voit pas ce qu'il font." In Jocelyn Coulon (ed.), *Guide de maintien de la paix.* Québec: Centre d'Études de Politiques Étrangères et de Sécurité, 2006, 171–186.

*Peace Operations Seen from Below: UN Missions and Local People.* Bloomfield: Kumarian Press, 2006.

Pouliot, Vincent. "The Logic of Practicality: A Theory of Practice of Security Communities." *International Organization* 62, no. 2 (2008): 257–288.

Powell, Robert. "Bargaining and Learning While Fighting." *American Journal of Political Science* 48, no. 20 (2004): 344–361.

"War as a Commitment Problem." *International Organization* 60, no. 1 (Winter 2006): 169–203.

Power, Samantha. *Chasing the Flame: One Man's Fight to Save the World.* New York: Penguin Books, 2008.

*A Problem from Hell: America in the Age of Genocide.* New York: Basic Books, 2002.

Press, Daryl G. "The Credibility of Power: Assessing Threats during the Appeasement Crises of the 1930s." *International Security* 29, no. 3 (2004): 136–169.

Prunier, Gérard. *Africa's World War: Congo, the Rwandan Genocide, and the Making of a Continental Catastrophe.* Oxford: Oxford University Press, 2011.

"Opération Turquoise: A Humanitarian Escape from a Political Dead End." In Howard Adelman and Astri Suhrke (eds.), *The Path of a Genocide: The Rwanda Crisis from Uganda to Zaire.* New Brunswick: Transaction Publishers, 2000, 281–306.

*The Rwanda Crisis: History of a Genocide.* New York: Columbia University Press, 1995.

Regan, Patrick M. "Third-Party Intervention and the Duration of Interstate Conflicts." *Journal of Conflict Resolution* 46, no. 1 (February 2002): 55–73.

Reiter, Dan. "Exploring the Bargaining Model of War." *Perspectives on Politics* 1, no. 1 (March 2003): 27–43.

Reyntjens, Filip. *Afrique des Grands Lacs en Crise: Rwanda, Burundi: 1988–1994.* Paris: Karthala, 1994.

"Rwanda, Ten Years On: From Genocide to Dictatorship." *African Affairs* 103 (2004): 177–210.

Rovner, Joshua. "Delusion of Defeat: The United States and Iraq, 1990–1998." *Journal of Strategic Studies* 37, no. 4 (2014): 482–507

Ruggeri, Andrea, Han Dorussen, and Theodora-Ismene Gizelis. "Winning the Peace Locally: UN Peacekeeping and Local Conflict." *International Organization* 71, no. 1 (Winter 2017): 163–185.

Ruggeri, Andrea, Theodora-Ismene Gizelis, and Han Dorussen. "Managing Mistrust: An Analysis of Cooperation with UN Peacekeeping in Africa." *Journal of Conflict Resolution* 57, no. 3 (June 2013): 387–409.

Salehyan, Idean. *Rebels without Borders: Transnational Insurgencies and World Politics*. Ithaca: Cornell University Press, 2009.

Salehyan, Idean and Kristian Skrede Gleditsch. "Refugee Flows and the Spread of Civil War." *International Organization* 60, no. 2 (2006): 335–366.

Salverda, Nynke. "Blue Helmets as Targets: A Quantitative Analysis of Rebel Violence against Peacekeepers, 1989–2003." *Journal of Peace Research* 50, no. 6 (2013): 707–720.

Sanford, Victoria. *Buried Secrets: Truth and Human Rights in Guatemala*. New York: Palgrave Macmillan, 2003.

Schelling, Thomas C. *Arms and Influence*. New Haven: Yale University Press, 1966.

*Micromotives and Macrobehavior*. New York: W.W. Norton, 1978.

*The Strategy of Conflict*. Cambridge, MA: Harvard University Press, 1960.

Schiemann, John W. "Meeting Halfway between Rochester and Frankfurt: Generative Salience, Focal Points, and Strategic Interaction." *American Journal of Political Science* 44, no. 1 (2000): 1–16.

Schimmelfennig, Frank. "The Community Trap: Liberal Norms, Rhetorical Action, and the Eastern Enlargement of the European Union." *International Organization* 55, no. 1 (2001): 47–80.

"Strategic Calculation and International Socialization: Membership Incentives, Party Constellations, and Sustained Complained in Central and Eastern Europe." *International Organization* 59, no. 4 (2005): 827–860.

Schirmer, Jennifer. *The Guatemalan Military Project: A Violence Called Democracy*. Philadelphia: University of Pennsylvania Press, 1999.

Schlicte, Klaus and Ulrich Schneckener. "Armed Groups and the Politics of Legitimacy." *Civil Wars* 17, no. 4 (2015): 409–424.

Seymour, Lee J. M. "Legitimacy and the Politics of Recognition in Kosovo." *Small Wars & Insurgencies* 28, no. 4–5 (2017): 817–838.

Short, Nicola. *The International Politics of Post-Conflict Reconstruction in Guatemala*. New York: Palgrave, 2007.

Simmons, Beth A. and Allison Danner. "Credible Commitments and the International Criminal Court." *International Organization* 64, no. 2 (2010): 225–256.

Simmons, Beth A. and Zachary Elkins. "The Globalization of Liberalization: Policy Diffusion in the International Political Economy." *American Political Science Review* 98, no. 1 (February 2004): 1710189.

Skidmore, Thomas E. and Peter H. Smith. *Modern Latin America*. Oxford: Oxford University Press, 2001.

Slantchev, Branislav. "The Principle of Convergence in Wartime Negotiations." *American Political Science Review* 97, no. 4 (November 2003): 621–632.

Smith, Alastair and Allan C. Stam. "Bargaining and the Nature of War." *Journal of Conflict Resolution* 48, no. 6 (2004): 783–813.

Stanley, William. *Enabling Peace in Guatemala: The Story of MINUGUA*. Boulder: Lynne Rienner, 2013.

Stedman, Stephen. "Spoiler Problems in Peace Processes." *International Security* 22, no. 2 (1997): 5–53.

Stedman, Stephen, Donald Rothchild, and Elizabeth M. Cousens, *Ending Civil Wars: The Implementation of Peace Agreements*. Boulder: Lynne Rienner, 2002.

Stoll, David. *Between Two Armies in the Ixil Towns of Guatemala*. New York: Columbia University Press, 1993.

Storey, Andy. "Structural Violence and the Struggle for State Power in Rwanda: What Arusha Got Wrong." *African Journal of Conflict Resolution* 12, no. 3 (2012): 7–32.

Straus, Scott. *The Order of Genocide: Race, Power, and War in Rwanda*. Ithaca and London: Cornell University Press, 2006.

Straus, Scott and Lars Waldorf. *Remaking Rwanda: State Building and Human Rights after Mass Violence*. Madison: University of Wisconsin Press, 2011.

Sugden, Robert. "Salience, Inductive Reasoning, and the Emergence of Conventions." *Journal of Economic Behavior and Organization* 79, no. 1–2 (2011): 35–47.

Svensson, Isak. "Who Brings Which Peace: Biased versus Neutral Mediation and Institutional Peace Arrangements in Civil Wars." *Journal of Conflict Resolution* 53, no. 3 (2009): 446–469.

Taliaferro, Jeffrey W. "Security Seeking under Anarchy: Defensive Realism Revisited." *International Security* 25, no. 3 (Winter 2000/01): 128–161.

Thompson, Alexander. *Channels of Power: The UN Security Council and U.S. Statecraft in Iraq*. Ithaca: Cornell University Press, 2009.

Tiernay, Michael. "Which Comes First? Unpacking the Relationship between Peace Agreements and Peacekeeping Missions." *Conflict Management and Peace Science* 32 no. 2 (April 2015): 135–152.

Toft, Monica Duffy. *The Geography of Ethnic Violence: Identity, Interests, and the Indivisibility of Territory*. Princeton: Princeton University Press, 2005.

*Securing the Peace: The Durable Settlement of Civil Wars*. Princeton: Princeton University Press, 2010.

Tomuschat, Christian. "Clarification Commission in Guatemala." *Human Rights Quarterly* 23, no. 2 (2001): 233–258.

Tomz, Michael. *Reputation and International Cooperation: Sovereign Debt across Three Centuries.* Princeton: Princeton University Press, 2007.

Traub, James. *The Best Intentions: Kofi Annan and the UN in the Era of American World Power.* New York: Farrar, Straus and Giroux, 2006.

Tull, Denis M. "The Limits and Unintended Consequences of UN Peace Enforcement: The Force Intervention Brigade in the DR Congo." *International Peacekeeping* 25, no. 2 (2018): 167–190.

*UN Department of Peacekeeping Operations.* www.un.org/en/peacekeeping/.

United Nations. "What Is Peacekeeping?" www.un.org/en/peacekeeping/operations/peacekeeping.shtml (accessed September 2014).

United Nations Department of Peacekeeping Operations. "LIST OF PEACEKEEPING OPERATIONS 1948 – 2012." www.un.org/en/peacekeeping/operations/history.shtml.

United Nations Department of Peacekeeping Operations. "Peacekeeping Fact Sheet." *United Nations Department of Peacekeeping Operations,* 2013. www.un.org/en/peacekeeping/resources/statistics/factsheet.shtml.

Uvin, Peter. *Aiding Violence: The Development Enterprise in Rwanda.* West Hartford: Kumarian Press, 1998.

Van Evera, Stephen. *Guide to Methods for Students of Political Science.* Ithaca: Cornell University Press, 1997.

Verwimp, Philip. "Testing the Double-Genocide Thesis for Central and Southern Rwanda." *Journal of Conflict Resolution* 47, no. 4 (August 2003): 423–442.

Voeten, Erik. "Outside Options and the Logic of Security Council Action." *American Political Science Review* 95, no. 4 (2001): 845–858.

"The Political Origins of the UN Security Council's Ability to Legitimize the Use of Force." *International Organization* 59, no. 3 (2005): 527–557.

"Why No UN Security Council Reform? Lessons for and from Institutionalist Theory." In Dimitris Bourantonis, Kostas Ifantis, and Panayotis Tsakonas (eds.), *Multilateralism and Security Institutions in the Era of Globalization.* London: Routledge, 2008, 388–205.

Wagner, R. Harrison. "Bargaining and War." *American Journal of Political Science* 44, no. 3 (2000): 469–484.

Wallensteen, Peter. *Understanding Conflict Resolution,* 3rd ed. London: Sage, 2012.

Walter, Barbara F. "Building Reputation: Why Governments Fight Some Separatists but Not Others." *American Journal of Political Science* 50, no. 2 (April 2006): 313–330.

*Committing to Peace: The Successful Settlement of Civil Wars.* Princeton: Princeton University Press, 2002.

"The Critical Barrier to Civil War Settlement." *International Organization* 51, no. 3 (1997): 335–364.

*Reputation and Civil War: Why Separatist Conflicts Are So Violent.* Cambridge: Cambridge University Press, 2009.

Waltz, Kenneth. *Theory of International Politics.* New York: McGraw-Hill, 1979.

Weaver, Catherine. *The World Bank and the Poverty of Reform.* Princeton: Princeton University Press, 2008.

Werner, Suzanne and Amy Yuen. "Making and Keeping Peace." *International Organization* 59, no. 2 (Spring 2005): 261–292.

Western, Jon. "Sources of Humanitarian Intervention." *International Security* 26, no. 4 (Spring 2002): 112–142.

Weyland, Kurt. "The Diffusion of Revolution: '1848' in Europe and Latin America." *International Organization* 63, no. 3 (2009): 391–423.

Widmaier, Wesley W., Mark Blyth, and Leonard Seabrooke. "Exogenous Shocks or Endogenous Constructions? The Meanings of Wars and Crises." *International Studies Quarterly* 51, no. 4 (December 2007): 747–759.

Wolford, Scott, Dan Reiter, and Clifford J. Carrubba. "Information, Commitment, and War." *Journal of Conflict Resolution* 55, no. 4 (August 2011): 556–579.

Zhang, Jun and Kai F. Yu. "What's the Relative Risk? A Method of Correcting the Odds Ratio in Cohort Studies of Common Outcomes." *Journal of the American Medical Association* 280 (1998): 1690–1691.

## Selected List of United Nations Documents Cited

*Letters, Statements, and Resolutions*

A/C.5/73/21
A/RES/48/267
S/26004
S/24699
S/23850
S/1996/1045
S/1998/285
S/1998/287
S/1998/827
S/RES/686

S/RES/776
S/RES/1270
S/RES/1299
S/RES/1313
S/RES/1356
S/RES/2098
S/RES/2378


## Provisional Verbatim Records of UNSC Meetings

S/PV.2896
S/PV.2928
S/PV.2933
S/PV.2937
S/PV.2938
S/PV.2939
S/PV.2981
S/PV.2974
S/PV.2977
S/PV.2981
S/PV.2304
S/PV.2932
S/PV.2951
S/PV.2933
S/PV.2934
S/PV.2951
S/PV.2946
S/PV.2949
S/PV.2856
S/PV.2951
S/PV.2953
S/PV.2080
S/PV.3004
S/PV.3009
S/PV.3136
S/PV.3137
S/PV.3138
S/PV.3203
S/PV.3229
S/PV.3277
S/PV.3293

S/PV.3293
S/PV.3336
S/PV.3336, Resumption No. 1
S/PV.3517
S/PV.3549
S/PV.3868
S/PV.4011
S/PV.4035
S/PV.4054
S/PV.4072
S/PV.4437
S/PV.4709
S/PV.5082
S/PV.3549
S/PV.4054
S/PV.4139
S/PV.5082

## Archival Documents Cited

Acuerdo sobre el Establecimiento de la Comisión para el Esclarecimiento Histórico de las Violaciones de los Derechos Humanos y los Hechos de Violencia que Han Causado Sufrimientos a la Población Guatemalteca, Oslo, Norway, June 23, 1994.

Agreement on the Social and Economic Aspects and Agrarian Situation, Guatemala, 1995.

Albright, Madeleine for the US Mission to the UN to the US Secretary of State. "Subj: Possible Peacekeeping Operation in the Rwanda." *Department of State Document Accessed through the National Security Archive*. New York, July 14, 1993. www2.gwu.edu/~nsarchiv/NSAEBB/NSAEBB469/docs/DOCUMENT 15.PDF.

Ambassador David Rawson for US Embassy Kigali to US Secretary of State. "Subject: The Military and the Transition to Peace." *US Department of State Declassified Document Accessed through the National Security Archive*. Kigali, Feburary 17, 1994. www2.gwu.edu/~nsarchiv/NSAEBB/NSAEBB458/docs/DOCUMENT%205.pdf.

Ambassador Robert Flaten for US Embassy in Kigali to US Secretary of State. "Subj: GOR Outlines Strategy to Negotiations to End War." *Department of State Document Accessed through National Security Archive*. May 13, 1992. www2.gwu.edu/~nsarchiv/NSAEBB/NSAEBB469/docs/DOCUMENT 1.pdf.

Ambassador Robert Flaten for US Embassy Kigali to US Secretary of State. "Subj: Tensions in Rwanda." *Department of State Document Accessed through the National Security Archive.* Kigali, June 1, 1992. www2 .gwu.edu/~nsarchiv/NSAEBB/NSAEBB469/docs/DOCUMENT%202 .pdf.

Ambassador Robert Flaten, US Embassy Kigali, to US Secretary of State. "Subj: Integration of the Armies and Demobilization." *Department of State Document Accessed through National Security Archive.* Kigali, November 20, 1992. www2.gwu.edu/~nsarchiv/NSAEBB/NSAEBB469/ docs/DOCUMENT%207.pdf.

Ambassador Thomas Stroock to US Secretary of State. "Secret Cable: Selective Violence Paralyzes the Left." *US Department of State Document Accessed through National Security Archive.* Guatemala City, May 10, 1991. www2.gwu.edu/~nsarchiv/NSAEBB/NSAEBB11/docs/doc26.pdf.

Booh-Booh, J.-R., Kigali, to Annan, UNations. "SUBJ: Daily Sitrep 080600B Jan to 090600B Jan 94 No: MIR 053." *United Nations Document Accessed through National Security Archive.* Kigali, January 9, 1994. www2.gwu .edu/~nsarchiv/NSAEBB/NSAEBB455/documents/DOCUMENT05.pdf.

Kigali, to Annan, UNations. "SUBJ: Daily Sitrep 140600B Jan to 150600B Jan 94." *United Nations Document Accessed through National Security Archive.* Kigali, January 15, 1994. www2.gwu.edu/~nsarchiv/NSAEBB/ NSAEBB455/documents/DOCUMENT10.pdf.

Kigali, to Annan, UNations. "SUBJ: Daily Sitrep 300600B Jan to 310600B Jan 94 No: MIR 220." *United Nations Document Accessed through National Security Archive.* Kigali, January 31, 1994. www2.gwu.edu/ ~nsarchiv/NSAEBB/NSAEBB455/documents/DOCUMENT17.pdf.

Colonel BEMS Bagosora, et al., to Juvénal Habyarimana. "Subj: Negotiations in Arusha from 22 November 1992 to 9 January 1993." *International Criminal Tribunal for Rwanda (ICTR) Evidence accessed through the National Security Archive.* January 15, 1993. www2.gwu .edu/~nsarchiv/NSAEBB/NSAEBB469/docs/DOCUMENT%208.pdf.

Colonel Théoneste Bagosora To: Rwandan Minister of Foreign Affairs. "Subj: Negotiation Strategy." *Evidence from the International Criminal Tribunal for Rwanda, accessed through the US National Security Archive.* June 1, 1993. www2.gwu.edu/~nsarchiv/NSAEBB/ NSAEBB469/docs/DOCUMENT%2013.pdf.

Dallaire/UNAMIR/Kigali to Annan/DPKO/UNations. "Subj: Interaction Force HQ/UNDP For Demobilization and Integration Process." *United Nations Internal Document Accessed through International Criminal for Rwanda Database (ICTR).* January 26, 1993. www2 .gwu.edu/~nsarchiv/NSAEBB/NSAEBB469/docs/DOCUMENT%2019 .pdf.

Deschamps, Marie, Hassan B. Jallow, and Yasmin Sooka. "Taking Action on Sexual Exploitation and Abuse by Peacekeepers: Report of an Independent Review on Sexual Exploitation and Abuse by International Peacekeeping Forces in the Central African Republic." December 17, 2015. www.un.org/News/dh/infocus/centafricrepub/Independent-Review-Report.pdf.

Eagleburger, Lawrence. "Subject: Rwandan Minister of Defense on Integration of Forces, from US Secretary of State to US Embassy in Kigali." *State Department Electronic Reading Room, Accessed through National Security Archive.* Washington, DC, November 16, 1992. www2.gwu.edu/~nsarchiv/NSAEBB/NSAEBB469/docs/DOCUMENT%205.pdf.

ECOSOC Commission on Human Rights Report. "Extrajudicial, Summary, or Arbitrary Executions [in Rwanda]." August 11, 1993. Rapporteur: Bacre W. Ndiaye.

Ehrenreich, Rick. "INR/AA's African Trends-9/18/92 (No. 19)." *Declassified Department of State Document Accessed through the National Security Archive.* Washington, DC: U.S. Department of State, September 18, 1992. Declassified, www2.gwu.edu/~nsarchiv/NSAEBB/NSAEBB458/docs/DOCUMENT%202.pdf.

Framework Agreement for the Resumption of the Negotiating Process between the Government of Guatemala.

Guterres, António. "Secretary-General's Remarks at Security Council High-Level Open Debate on Peacekeeping Operations Regarding the Reform of UN Peacekeeping: Implementation and Follow Up." September 17, 2017. www.un.org/sg/en/content/sg/speeches/2017-09-20/sgs-reform-un-peacekeeping-remarks.

Leader, Joyce for US Embassy Kigali to US Secretary of State. "Subj: Internal Insecurity: An Ongoing Problem." *Department of State Document Accessed through National Security Archive.* Kigali, August 21, 1992. www2.gwu.edu/~nsarchiv/NSAEBB/NSAEBB469/docs/DOCUMENT%204.pdf.

Leader, Joyce for US Embassy Kigali to US Secretary of State. "Subj: RPF Perspective on the Peace Process." *Department of State Document Accessed through National Security Archive.* Kigali, December 10, 1993. www2.gwu.edu/~nsarchiv/NSAEBB/NSAEBB469/docs/DOCUMENT%202034.pdf.

Leader, Joyce for US Embassy Kigali to US Secretary of State. "Subj: The Rwandan Peace Process: Problems and Prospects for Implementing the Peace." *Department of State Document Accessed through the National Secrity Archive.* August 19, 1993. https://nsarchive2.gwu.edu/NSAEBB/NSAEBB469/docs/DOCUMENT%2018.pdf.

Lt. Col. Nsengiyumva Anatole to Army Chief of Staff, Rwanda Defense Ministry. "Subject: Mood of the Military and Civilians." *International Criminal Tribunal for Rwanda Evidence Accessed through the National Security Archive.* Kigali, July 27, 1992. www2.gwu.edu/~nsarchiv/ NSAEBB/NSAEBB469/docs/DOCUMENT%203.pdf.

"Members of the Government Peace Commission Talk About the Peace Process." Memo from Department of Defense Joint Staff Washington DC to RUEKJCS/DIA WASHDC, RHLBAAA/USCINCSO Quarry Heights PM//SCJ2//info RUEHME/USDAO Mexico City MX RUESHSN/USDAO San Salvador ES, December 1991. In National Security Archive Guatemala Documentation Project, Offsite Box 28, 1991 Folder.

Panel on United Nations Peace Operations. "Report of the Panel on UN Peacekeeping Operations [Brahimi Report]." United Nations, New York, 2000.

Peace Agreement between the Government of the Republic of Rwanda and the Rwandese Patriotic Front (the Arusha Accords), 1994.

Peacekeeping Best Practices Unit, Department of Peacekeeping Operations. *Handbook on UN Multidimensional Peacekeeping Operations.* New York: United Nations, 2003.

Private Letter from UN Secretary General Kofi Annan to His Excellency Mr. Njuguna Moses Mahugu, O.G.W., President of the Security Council, February 5, 1997. http://ccnydigitalscholarship.org/kofiannan/items/ show/4396.

"Statement by Richard Boucher on Guatemala: Stopping Deliveries of Military Assistance." Office of the Assistant Secretary/Spokesman, US Department of State, December 21, 1990, Guatemala Documentation Project, National Security Archive, Washington, DC, Offsite Box No. 21, Folder "Arms Sales to Guatemala after 1990, 1989–1994"

United Nations. "A More Secure World: Our Shared Responsibility." Report of the High-level Panel on Threats, Challenges and Change, New York, 2004.

US Department of Defense. "IIR [Censored] Report on Breakfast for Attaches Hosted by Army Chief of Staff." July 1992, National Security Archive, Guatemala Documentation Project, Documents Not Included, Offsite Box 28, Folder 1992.

US Department of State. "Confidential Cable: GOG Meets Most FMF Human Rights Benchmarks: Time for "Small Steps" in Response to Big Ones." *US Department of State Document Accessed Through National Security Archive.* Washington, DC, November 22, 1991. www2.gwu.edu/~nsarchiv/NSAEBB/NSAEBB11/docs/doc27.pdf.

US Department of State Briefing Paper. "The Vice-President's Meeting with Guatemalan President Vinicio Cerezo." *Declassified State Department Document Accessed through the National Security Archive*, January 19, 1990. www2.gwu.edu/~nsarchiv/NSAEBB/NSAEBB11/docs/doc24.pdf.

US Embassy Brussels to US Secretary of State. "Subject: FONMIN Claes' Interview on His Trip to Rwanda and Burundi and on Situation in Zaire." *Department of State Document Accessed through National Security Archive*. Brussels, March 11, 1994. www2.gwu.edu/~nsarchiv/NSAEBB/NSAEBB458/docs/DOCUMENT 10.pdf.

US Embassy Dar-es-Salaam to US Secretary of State. "Subj: Rwanda Negotiations: Texts from Arusha." *Department of State Document Accessed through the National Security Archive*. Dar-es-Salaam, Document 12 Date: May 14, 1993. www2.gwu.edu/~nsarchiv/NSAEBB/NSAEBB469/docs/DOCUMENT%2012.pdf

US Embassy in Dar-es-Salaam to US Secretary of State. "Subj: Arusha V: Going Ahead on Nov. 23, Military Integration to Top Agenda." *Department of State Document Accessed through National Security Archive*, November 20, 1992. https://nsarchive2.gwu.edu/NSAEBB/NSAEBB469/docs/DOCUMENT%206.pdf.

US Embassy Nairobi to US Secretary of State. "Subj: Arusha Talks: Status Report." *Department of State Document Accessed through the National Security Archive*. Nairobi, May 3, 1993. www2.gwu.edu/~nsarchiv/NSAEBB/NSAEBB469/docs/DOCUMENT%2010.pdf.

US Mission to the United Nations to US Secretary of State. "Subj: Possible Peacekeeping Operation in Rwanda." *Department of State Document Accessed through National Security Archive*, July 14, 1993. www2.gwu.edu/~nsarchiv/NSAEBB/NSAEBB469/docs/DOCUMENT 15.PDF.

US Secretary of State to US Embassy in Kigali. "Subj: Rwandan Minister of Defense on Integration of Forces." *Department of State Document Accessed through National Security Archive*, November 16, 1992. www2.gwu.edu/~nsarchiv/NSAEBB/NSAEBB469/docs/DOCUMENT%205.pdf.

## Interviews and Oral Histories Cited

Arria, Diego, interview by Jean Krasno. *Yale-UN Oral History Project*. New York, September 5, 1997.

Beardsley, Brent, interview by Michael Dobbs. "Disarmament, Demobilization and Reintegration (Extended)." *National Security Archive Oral History Interview*, Washington, DC, April 30, 2013. www.youtube.com/watch?v=xsV3qUIpOXg.

Cammaert, Patrick, interview by Anjali Dayal. New York, April 15, 2013.

Gasamagera, Wellars, interview by Anjali Dayal. Kigali, July 30, 2013.

Goulding, Marrack, interview by James S. Sutterlin. *Yale-UN Oral History Project*. Oxford, June 20, 1998.

Leader, Joyce, interview by Michael Dobbs. "Impact of Democratization and Peace." *National Security Archive Oral History*. Washington, DC, October 29, 2013. www.youtube.com/watch?v=YRQ-UWnbAAI.

  interview by Michael Dobbs. "Military Power Sharing Negotiations." *National Security Archive Oral History Interview*. Washington, DC, Otober 29, 2013. www.youtube.com/watch?v=bayUJPxfHFg#t=27.

Mazimhaka, Patrick, interview by Anjali Dayal. Kigali, July 30, 2013.

Montaño, Jorge, interview by Jean Krasno. *Yale-UN Oral History Project*. Mexico City, October 1, 1999.

Rangel, Beatrice, interview by Jean Krasno. *Yale-UN Oral History Project*. New York, September 16, 1997.

Rutaremara, Tito, interview by Anjali Dayal. Kigali, July 31, 2013.

Vendrell, Francesc, interview by Jean Krasno. *Yale-UN Oral History Project*. New York, April 16, 1996.

Vieira de Mello, Sergio. Interview by James S. Sutterlin. *Yale-UN Oral History Project*. New York, May 5, 1998.

## NGO and International Organization Reports Cited

Accord: An International Review of Peace Initiatives in Association with the Latin American Faculty of Social Sciences, Guatemala City. *Negotiating Rights: The Guatemalan Peace Process*. London: Conciliation Resources, 1997.

Council on Foreign Relations. "More than Humanitarianism." Task Force Report No. 56, Washington, DC, January 2006.

Des Forges, Alison L. *Leave None to Tell the Story*. New York: Human Rights Watch, 1999.

Deschamps, Marie, Hassan B. Jallow, and Yasmin Sooka. "Taking Action on Sexual Exploitation and Abuse by Peacekeepers: Report of an Independent Review on Sexual Exploitation and Abuse by International Peacekeeping Forces in the Central African Republic." December 17, 2015, www.un.org/News/dh/infocus/centafricrepub/Independent-Review-Report.pdf.

ECOSOC Commission on Human Rights Report, "Extrajudicial, summary, or arbitrary executions [in Rwanda]," August 11, 1993. Rapporteur: Bacre W. Ndiaye. E/CN.4/1994/7/Add.1.

Hilterman, Joost et al. *The War within the War: Sexual Violence against Women and Girls in Eastern Congo*. New York: Human Rights Watch, 2002

Holt, Victoria K. and Tobias C. Berkman. *The Impossible Mandate? Military Preparedness, The Responsibility to Protect, and Modern Peace Operations.* Washington, DC: The Henry L. Stimson Center, 2006.

International Human Rights Clinic. *No Place to Hide: Gang, State, and Clandestine Violence in El Salvador.* Cambridge, MA: Human Rights Program, Harvard Law School, 1997.

Jones, Bruce and Rahul Chandran. *From Fragility to Resilience: Concepts and Dilemmas of State Building in Fragile Situations.* Organization for Economic Co-operation and Development, 2008.

Labuda, Patryk I. "With or Against the State? Reconciling the Protection of Civilians and Host-State Support in UN Peacekeeping." International Peace Institute, May 2020.

Mir, Wassim. "Financing UN Peacekeeping: Avoiding Another Crisis." International Peace Institute, April 17, 2019, www.ipinst.org/wp-content/uploads/2019/04/1904_Financing-UN-Peacekeeping.pdf.

dos Santos Cruz, Carlos Alberto, et. al. "Improving Security of United Nations Peacekeepers: We Need to Change the Way We Are Doing Business." December 19, 2017. https://peacekeeping.un.org/sites/default/files/improving_security_of_united_nations_peacekeepers_report.pdf.

## News Articles Cited

Abdelaziz, Khalid. "Heavy Fighting Rages in Sudan's Darfur Region." *Reuters*, January 9, 2013. http://news.yahoo.com/heavy-fighting-rages-sudans-darfur-region-220204026.html.

Abdelaziz, Khalid and Louis Charbonneau. "Question Marks Hang Over Flawed Darfur Peacekeeping Force." *Reuters*, March 11, 2015, www.reuters.com/article/us-sudan-unitednations-darfur-insight/question-marks-hang-over-flawed-darfur-peacekeeping-force-idUSKBN0M70ZV20150311.

Ashbrook, Tom. "UN Effects Everywhere Turn to Dust – Downed Helicopter in Somalia Doomed a 'New World Order.'" *Boston Globe*, April 30, 1995.

"France Grants Researcher Access to Mitterrand's Archive on Rwandan Genocide." *France24*, June 12, 2020, www.france24.com/en/20200612-france-grants-researcher-access-to-mitterrand-s-archive-on-rwandan-genocide.

"General Assembly Approves $3 Billion UN Budget for 2020." December 27, 2019, https://news.un.org/en/story/2019/12/1054431.

Hatcher, Jessica and Alex Perry. "Defining Peacekeeping Downward: The U.N. Debacle in Eastern Congo." *New Times (Rwanda)*, November 28, 2012.

Ignatius, David. "The Failure of a Noble Idea." *The Washington Post*, August 31, 2012.

Katz, Jonathan. "In the Time of Cholera: How the U.N Created an Epidemic – Then Covered It Up." *Foreign Policy*, January 10, 2013. www.foreignpolicy.com/articles/2013/01/10/in_the_time_of_cholera.

Lynch, Colum. "Scientists Now Say U.N. Peacekeepers Likely Culprit in Cholera Outbreak That Killed Thousands." *Foreign Policy*, 2013. http://turtlebay.foreignpolicy.com/posts/2013/07/25/scientists_now_say_un_peacekeepers_likely_culprit_in_cholera_outbreak_that_killed_t.

MacFarquhar, Neil. "In Peacekeeping, a Muddling of the Mission." *The New York Times*, February 10, 2009.

Parker, Ben and Annie Slemrod. "Outcry at UN Plans to Consolidate Syria Aid Operations in Damascus." *The New Humanitarian*, April 23, 2019. www.thenewhumanitarian.org/news/2019/04/23/outcry-un-plans-con solidate-syria-aid-operations-damascus.

Rever, Judi and Benedict Moran. "Exclusive: Top-Secret Testimonies Implicate Rwanda's President in War Crimes." *Mail & Guardian*, November 29, 2020. https://mg.co.za/africa/2020-11-29-exclusive-top-secret-testimonies-implicate-rwandas-president-in-war-crimes/.

Silver, Nate. "The Media Has a Probability Problem: The Media's Demand for Certainty – and Its Lack of Statistical Rigor — Is a Bad Match for Our Complex World." *FiveThirtyEight*, September 21, 2017. https://fivethirtyeight.com/features/the-media-has-a-probability-problem/

# Index